Econometric applications of Maximum Likelihood methods

Econometric applications of Maximum Likelihood methods

J. S. CRAMER
University of Amsterdam

The right of the University of Cambridge to print and sell all manner of books was granted by Henry VIII in 1534. The University has printed and published continuously since 1584.

CAMBRIDGE UNIVERSITY PRESS
Cambridge
London New York New Rochelle
Melbourne Sydney

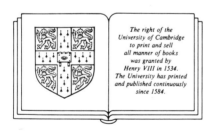

Published by the Press Syndicate of the University of Cambridge
The Pitt Building, Trumpington Street, Cambridge CB2 1RP
32 East 57th Street, New York, NY 10022, USA
10 Stamford Road, Oakleigh, Melbourne 3166, Australia

First published 1986

Printed in the United States of America

Library of Congress Cataloging in Publication Data

Cramer, J. S. (Jan Salomon), 1928–

Econometric applications of maximum likelihood methods.

Bibliography: p.
1. Econometrics. 2. Estimation theory. I. Title.
HB139.C72 1986 330′.028 85-16636

British Library Cataloguing in Publication Data

Cramer, J. S.

Econometric applications of Maximum Likelihood methods.

1. Econometric models 2. Estimation theory
3. Maximum principles (Mathematics)
I. Title
330′.0724 HB141

ISBN 0 521 25317 9

Contents

Preface

Over the past decades, the advent of high-speed electronic computing has drastically altered the practice of applied econometrics by permitting the adoption of specific models of much greater intricacy and of a higher theoretical content than before. The estimation and testing of these models draw heavily on Maximum Likelihood methodology, and practitioners in the field freely use the theorems of this statistical theory along with dispersed results from linear algebra and the canons of numerical maximization. The aim of this book is to set out the main elements of this common basis of so many current empirical studies. To this end I have collected the various parts, adapted them to the particular conditions of econometric analysis, and put them all together in the form of a separate paradigm.

There is a growing realization that some of the basic theorems have not yet been proved with sufficient generality to cover all the cases that arise in econometrics, and much fundamental work is being undertaken to remedy this defect. At the same time, progress is being made in the design of robust methods that may well, in due course, replace Maximum Likelihood as a general method of inference. The present book does not deal with these new developments. It contains nothing new, but some old things that may surprise. While there *is* progress in econometrics, some of the fashionable novelties have quite old roots, which are generally ignored. Whenever I happened to know this, I have mentioned it, in the interest of a proper historical perspective.

As a text, the book is a complement of, rather than a substitute for, the existing textbooks of econometric methods. The reader is expected to have a fair knowledge of statistics and the theory of inference, of linear algebra, and of the standard linear regression model: This is often used as an example, and occasionally as a counterexample. The treatment is at an intermediate level. I do not give proper mathematical proofs, even where they exist, but I do sketch the theoretical argument insofar as it provides a unifying frame of reference. This holds in particular for the first part of the book, which contains a quite elementary introduction to the general theory of Maximum Likelihood estimation and testing. In the second part this theory is put to work on models with additive Normal disturbances, and we come across a number of familiar regression models, now approached from a different angle than in traditional econometric theory. The third and last part of the book is devoted to discrete choice models and other probability models. In these two later parts where we review various applications, the treatment is again illustrative rather than exhaustive: A wide range of models is covered, but it is covered lightly. Chapters 7, 8, and 9, and Chapters 11 and 12, consequently, resemble an extended catalogue of the many cases that can arise. If this is tiresome to read from end to end, the solution is to concentrate on a few models of immediate interest, and to leave the others for future reference. Throughout the book I have been led by the expectation that readers will wish to try their hands at applications of their own, and by the firm hope that they will acquire the knowledge and taste to continue their reading with more advanced sources and with original research papers.

Many people have enlightened me by their replies to my pressing questions, by chance remarks, and by spontaneous accounts of their way of thinking. I wish to acknowledge the help I have thus received from Herman Bierens, Angus Deaton, Erwin Diewert, Chris Elbers, Risto Heijmans, Jan Kiviet, Heinz Neudecker, and Geert Ridder. Mrs. J. H. van Wijk faithfully typed my smeared notes, and Jaap Verhees checked the final draft with quiet zeal. At the last moment an anonymous reader permitted me to correct a number of inaccuracies. I take the full blame for the errors and imperfections that remain.

J. S. Cramer

List of illustrations

Notation

I have aimed at a distinctive and consistent use of symbols while respecting established usage. Because these aims are incompatible, the resulting notation is not completely uniform. I hope that its ambiguities will be resolved by the context.

The first broad distinction is that, as a rule, the Greek alphabet is used for unknown parameters and other unobservables, such as disturbances, and Latin letters for everything else. But Greek letters are also occasionally employed for functions, and we follow tradition in using them for Lagrange multipliers.

In either alphabet, most scalars and all (column) vectors are denoted by lowercase letters, a few scalars and all matrices by capitals. As a rule, therefore, scalars and vectors cannot be distinguished by their notation. This also holds for functions, so that in

$$y = f(x)$$

y may be scalar or vector, f accordingly a scalar or vector function, and x a scalar or vector argument. Differentiation may thus yield various arrays. If both y and x are scalar, f' is of course scalar, too. If y is scalar and x a vector, f' is by convention a *row* vector of partial derivatives, and it is a *column* vector of ordinary derivatives in the reverse case, with y a column vector and x a scalar. Finally, if y is an $r \times 1$ vector and x an $s \times 1$ vector, f' is an $r \times s$ matrix of partial derivatives, and if we name it we should use a capital letter. Unless we write the derivative in full, differentiation is indicated by a prime (as in f'), which is exclusively reserved for this purpose; the transposition of vectors and matrices is therefore indicated by a superscript T.

A second major typographical distinction is made between random variables, or variates, which are set in boldface, and all other variables, which are not. Random variables and their realizations are thus denoted by the same letter in a different font; $\boldsymbol{y}$ is a variate, and y is its realization. Similarly θ is a parameter, $\hat{\boldsymbol{\theta}}$ is its estimator, and $\hat{\theta}$ its estimate. All can be scalars or vectors. Functions of random variables of course take random values, too, so that we write

$$\boldsymbol{y} = f(\boldsymbol{x})$$

The function operator f itself is, however, not stochastic, and hence not in bold type.

The only specific probability distribution that occurs at all frequently is the Normal, and we write

$$\boldsymbol{x} \sim N(\mu, \Omega)$$

to indicate that the stochastic vector $\boldsymbol{x}$ has a multidimensional Normal distribution with mean μ and covariance matrix Ω; the reader should be familiar with this distribution and its density function. At times we come across disturbance vectors that are independent and identically $N(0, \Omega)$ distributed, and we reserve the letter $\boldsymbol{\epsilon}$ for these variates.

In general we write $E\boldsymbol{y}$ or $Ef(\boldsymbol{x})$ for the mathematical expectation of random variables, and $V\boldsymbol{y}$ or $Vf(\boldsymbol{x})$ for their variance or for their covariance matrix, as the case may be. In these expressions parentheses are reserved as much as possible for enclosing the argument of the function as opposed to the random variable to which the expectation operator applies. If the variance of $\boldsymbol{y}$ depends on a parameter ψ we would write

$$V\boldsymbol{y} = V(\psi)$$

An estimate of this variance would in turn be denoted as $\hat{V}$, and if this is evaluated at a particular estimate $\hat{\psi}$ of ψ we write $V(\hat{\psi})$. The corresponding estimators are $\hat{\boldsymbol{V}}$ and $V(\hat{\boldsymbol{\psi}})$, respectively.

Over and above these intricacies in the representation of stochastic variables and their realizations, expressions and variables may quickly acquire strings of arguments and qualifying variables as well as subscripts and superscripts, carets, tildes, and dots. Many distinctions are, however, only locally relevant: As the argument proceeds, qualifications that were once essential become commonplace, and many embellishments can be omitted without risking confusion. We shall often make use of this freedom.

References to sections are always given in full; we refer to equations within the same chapter by a single serial number, and to equations in other chapters by double numbers.

CHAPTER 1

The technology of estimation

Many statistical techniques were invented in the nineteenth century by experimental scientists who personally applied their methods to authentic data sets. In these conditions the limits of what is computationally feasible are spontaneously observed. Until quite recently these limits were set by the capacity of the human calculator, equipped with pencil and paper and with such aids as the slide rule, tables of logarithms, and other convenient tables, which have been in constant use from the seventeenth century until well into the twentieth. Thus Fisher and Yates's *Statistical Tables*, which were first published in 1938, still contain tabulations of squares, square roots, and reciprocals, which are of great help in performing routine computations by hand. Yet by that time mechanical multiplicators, which came into fashion in the 1920s, were already quite common, as were mechanical adding machines. By 1950 addition and multiplication were combined in noisy and unwieldy desk machines driven by a small electric motor; some were capable of long division, or even of taking square roots. These improvements may have doubled or trebled the speed of computing, but they did not materially alter its scope: Until the advent of the electronic computer, the powers of the human operator set the standard. This restriction has left its mark on statistical technique, and many new developments have taken place since it was lifted. This is the theme of this introductory chapter.

1.1 Least Squares

We have a set of n observations on $(k+1)$ scalar variables $(y_i, x_{1i}, \ldots, x_{ki})$ for $i = 1, 2, \ldots, n$, we assume that

$$y_i = \beta_0 + \beta_1 x_{1i} + \cdots + \beta_k x_{ki} + v_i \qquad (1)$$

with the v_i independent random disturbances with zero mean, and we estimate the β_j by Ordinary Least Squares (OLS). Linearity abounds. First, the systematic variation of the y_i is described by a linear function of the regressor variables x_{ji}. This *linear functional form* can be regarded as a first-order approximation of the unknown true relation. Coupled with additive disturbances it leads naturally to *linear estimators* of the β_j, estimators that are linear in the random $\mathbf{y}_i$ of which we have observed the realizations y_i. This in turn implies *linear computation* in the sense that the estimates are obtained by solving a set of linear equations, the renowned *normal equations* in the sample moments,

$$\begin{aligned}
\hat{\beta}_0 n + \hat{\beta}_1 \sum_i x_{1i} \quad &+ \cdots + \hat{\beta}_k \sum_i x_{ki} &&= \sum_i y_i \\
\hat{\beta}_0 \sum_i x_{1i} + \hat{\beta}_1 \sum_i x_{1i}^2 \quad &+ \cdots + \hat{\beta}_k \sum_i x_{1i}x_{ki} &&= \sum_i x_{1i}y_i \\
\cdots \qquad &\qquad \cdots && \cdots \\
\hat{\beta}_0 \sum_i x_{ki} + \hat{\beta}_1 \sum_i x_{1i}x_{ki} &+ \cdots + \hat{\beta}_k \sum_i x_{ki}^2 &&= \sum_i x_{ki}y_i
\end{aligned} \tag{2}$$

To stress the computational simplicity of OLS is as old-fashioned as our notation of the normal equations. But no doubt the convenience of the adjustment contributed to its adoption as a means of establishing planetary orbits from deficient observations. History has it that is how the method originated, a few years after 1800, with Gauss, Legendre, and Laplace. To this day the computational simplicity of the method is as attractive as the statistical properties of the result, which were explored equally early (Seal 1967; van der Waerden 1957: Chapter 7).

From its origin in the calculus of errors in astronomy, least squares regression has spread to engineering and to anthropology, biology, experimental agriculture, and psychology, accumulating a wealth of statistical interpretation on the way. Historically it is by no means an exclusively econometric technique; but it was so greedily adopted when econometrics first took shape around 1930 that for several decades it remained the standard tool and common basis of all econometric analyses. Most textbooks of econometrics present OLS in this light, and few point out that its origins and its major development lie elsewhere. Traditionally the supreme art of the skillful econometrician was to twist the model and to manipulate the data until the estimation problem would fit the linear regression mold. And in such an advanced problem as the estimation of an overidentified equation from a simultaneous system, Two-Stage Least Squares took precedence over other methods principally because its computations (and its theory) could be made to follow the linear regression format.

The econometric applications of linear regression and of its later extensions have traditionally been restricted to a limited number of between, say, 20 and 50 observations. This does not only hold for studies of macroeconomic aggregates – national time series and cross-sections across countries alike – where the sample is necessarily small, but also for the analysis of census and survey data; this was invariably based on cell means, even when the individual data were available. The reason for this is that the punched-card technology for handling large data sets readily permits tabulation and summation, and hence the determination of cell means, but is much less suited to the multiplications needed for the calculation of sample moments of individual observations.

1.2 Modern computing

The advent of high-speed electronic computing and of programming languages has changed conditions beyond recognition by removing almost all size restrictions on calculations. Electronic computing was probably first adopted in econometrics at the Department of Applied Economics at Cambridge, England, where it was already in use for the analysis of family budgets in the early 1950s (Brown, Houthakker, and Prais 1953; Prais and Houthakker, 1955). The machine involved was known as EDSAC, for Electronic Delay Storage Automatic Calculator; like all computers of that era this was a custom-built, experimental laboratory machine, and it was the first to permit the use of stored programs.[1] The authors we have just named devote some touching paragraphs to it. Since then the use of these rapid and powerful machines has become commonplace. It has changed and is still changing the nature of econometric research. The full effects of this technological revolution will only be realized after the teaching of econometrics has been fully taken over by a generation that has first-hand experience of programming and operating computers.

The first result of this revolution is that estimates defined by nonlinear equations can be established as a matter of routine by the appropriate iterative algorithms. This permits the use of nonlinear functional forms. In some cases this is a definite advantage since a linear specification is unacceptable on theoretical grounds, as in certain money demand functions and production function models, and in models of discrete choice and probability models generally. But in most applications the substitution of a more elaborate function for the linear approximation, possibly applied to transformations of the original observations, is a superfluous embellishment.

Nonlinear determination of the estimates may, however, also arise with linear specification of the systematic relationships, coupled with restrictions on the coefficients or with special properties of the distur-

[1] The Cambridge applied economists were quick off the mark: EDSAC, completed in 1949, was the second operational electronic computer in the world, after ENIAC, built in the United States in 1944–5.

bance terms. Overidentified structural equations in a simultaneous setting, Seemingly Unrelated Regression Equation (SURE) sets, and the Generalized Least Squares (GLS) model with an unknown covariance matrix are three major cases in point. The first of these, the overidentified simultaneous equation, can be regarded as a particular case of a set of linear equations with coefficient restrictions across equations, whether these are part of a reduced form or not. All these extensions of the traditional linear regression model have arisen from its adaptation to statistical inference from nonexperimental observations, and to a large extent they represent original contributions of econometrics to statistical theory.

Most of these estimation problems had of course already been recognized and dealt with by the proper iterative procedures long before the electronic computer became a commonplace tool; but these were isolated instances of laborious exercises, which would take weeks or months of intensive human effort. By now it may take only a few seconds to complete such an analysis, once the program has been set up. The principles of estimation involved are derived from Maximum Likelihood methodology, and they are treated in this book.

The other new option provided by electronics is the analysis of large data sets such as the individual records from censuses, surveys, and panels. So far, this has not seriously been taken up in econometrics. Prais and Houthakker's pioneer application of a computer to household budgets served to fit intricate models of family size to cell means, not to estimate simple Engel curves from massed individual data. To my knowledge the latter project was shortly afterward taken up independently by two other analysts, who were so horrified by the unfamiliar combination of highly significant coefficients and very low values of R^2 that they abandoned their attempts. If they had had any experience of analyzing individual behavior they would have persisted, for with individual observations such results are to be expected.

It is a pity that econometricians have for so long neglected individual, microeconomic behavior as a fruitful field of study on the grounds that data are hard to obtain and laborious to handle. The second argument has been superseded by the advent of electronic processing, and the first has never been valid. As a profession, econometric has been much too shy in the field of data collection. It is of course true that economic behavior does not permit of controlled experiments, but this means only that we cannot manipulate economic conditions, and must leave the experimental design to society, to the government of the day, and to other chance events; it does not mean that we cannot extend the field of our observations, if necessary in a selective manner. There are some welcome signs of a growing realization that it is perfectly proper and feasible to go out and collect the data needed to answer a particular question.

1.3 An example: money demand

We illustrate recent developments in estimation technique and expertise by the treatment of the same nonlinear equation in a sequence of three learned papers. The equation is an aggregate demand function for money in the presence of the "liquidity trap," or an asymptote for the quantity of money demanded M at a low but nonzero value α of the rate of interest R. Allowing for shifts of the demand schedule with national income Y, Konstas and Khouja specify the nonlinear relation

$$M = \gamma Y + \frac{\beta}{R - \alpha} \tag{3}$$

(Konstas and Khouja 1969). Faced with the problem of fitting this equation to United States time series data, the authors propose three alternative solutions, all of which end up in an application of OLS. The first two solutions are to multiply both sides of (3) by $(R - \alpha)$ and to rearrange the terms as either

$$MR = \alpha M + \gamma RY - \lambda Y + \beta \tag{4}$$

or

$$M = \alpha \frac{M}{R} + \gamma Y - \lambda \frac{Y}{R} + \beta \frac{1}{R} \tag{5}$$

where λ stands for the product $\alpha\gamma$. Both equations are then estimated by OLS, ignoring the implied restriction on the parameters as well as the transformation imposed on the disturbances of (3) in the passage to (4) and (5); the statistical specification of the model is not discussed at all. The third method of fitting (3) is to let α vary by fixed intervals, and to regard each value in turn as if it were a known constant. This can then be used to generate observations on $(R - \alpha)^{-1}$, which permit direct OLS estimation of (3). The "best" of these conditional regressions is then selected by the Least Squares criterion. In the interpretation of the ensuing estimates of β and γ, and of their standard errors, no allowance is made for the fact that the "optimal" value of α is itself an estimate, and hence the realisation of a random variable. From the vantage point we have reached over 15 years later it is easy to criticize the paper for the absence of a proper statistical specification and for highly inefficient estimation; but the point is not that we can find fault with these methods, but that they are so obviously geared to the use of the OLS algorithm.

Four years later the same model and the same data were taken up by Kliman and Oksanen (1973). These authors have an iterative algorithm for nonlinear estimation at their disposal, and they use it to improve on Konstas and Khouja's work by re-estimating the same three equations. As for equations (4) and (5), Kliman and Oksanen argue that the constraint $\lambda = \alpha\gamma$ should have been observed in the estimation, and they proceed to do so in a *constrained Least Squares* estimation of the parameters of these equations. Equation (3) is also fitted once more to the same data, but this time by a direct nonlinear Least Squares algorithm that determines all three parameter estimates simultaneously by minimizing the sum of squared residuals. No theoretical basis for this criterion is provided, and it is indiscriminately applied to all three equations, even though these have been obtained by various transformations of the same initial model, and differ in the implied transformation of the disturbance term. This is indeed the only reason why the estimates differ from one equation to another. As it turns out, the estimates are also quite different from those of the previous authors. In the case of (3) this is difficult to understand, as the estimation method varies in technique but not in principle, but no explanation is put forward.

From our point of view the main interest of this paper is that, while Kliman and Oksanen employ a nonlinear, iterative method of estimation, they clearly regard this as a mysterious novelty. There is an abundance of explanatory footnotes with references to an unpublished paper for such questions as how to calculate confidence intervals for a nonlinear estimate; significant differences from zero are indicated, but standard errors are not given.

The third author to deal with this example is Spitzer, who once more fits the same models to the same data by the same Least Squares criterion, which is here, however, derived in a brief paragraph from Maximum Likelihood principles (Spitzer 1976). Spitzer turns at once to equation (3), spurning the curious constructs of (4) and (5), but he is unable to reproduce the results reported by Kliman and Oksanen and suggests that their iterations have converged to a local but not to a global extremum of the criterion function. This leads once more to substantial changes in the empirical results, as does Spitzer's discovery that both previous articles have in part been based on incorrect data series, the wrong column having been copied from the statistical source book – Konstas and Khouja obligingly reproduced their data in an appendix. Spitzer concentrates on these technical points, and is rather sceptical about the importance of the empirical results and about their relevance to policy issues, pointing out that the major question of the existence of a liquidity trap is settled by the functional form adopted in equation (3), regardless of observational evidence.

Since Spitzer's paper the same readily accessible data set has continued to serve as a methodological testing ground with a corresponding decline of interest in the substantive issues that prompted the original research.[2] The three papers we have summarized are, however, sufficient to illustrate the joint development of improved techniques of computation and of their understanding in the light of statistical theory. Over the last three decades this has occurred in all applications of econometrics, and the moving force has been the spread of easy access to high-speed computing, brought about by rapid technological advances in both hardware and software. One may expect that as these possibilities are exploited to the limits of their useful application and beyond, they will largely replace linear regression as the major tool of applied econometrics.

The new computational techniques permit more flexible models and more thorough statistical analyses, a wider exploration of alternative specifications, and a much more conscientious and sophisticated modeling of the stochastic structure of the data-generating process. In view of the much wider choices open to the investigator it is no accident that hypothesis testing is taken more seriously in econometrics than it was before. These developments constitute progress, although at times models are made to carry a larger intellectual investment than the data can bear.

1.4 Maximum Likelihood methodology

Although the progress of computing technology made nonlinear estimation possible, the statistical theory of Maximum Likelihood provided techniques and respectability. Its principle was first put forward as a novel and original method of deriving estimators by R.A. Fisher in the early 1920s (1921, 1925). It very soon proved to be a fertile approach to statistical inference in general, and was widely adopted; but the exact properties of the ensuing estimators and test procedures were only gradually discovered in the decades that followed. This task is not completed, and the process continues to this day. Several classical cases were proved by Wald in the 1940s, and Mann and Wald contributed the first rigorous application of the theory to a class of econometric equa-

[2] The reader should not follow this example. Even with the correct data set, the estimation of Konstas and Khouja's model is beset by numerical difficulties. See Exercise 6.5.

tions (1943). The first major breakthrough occurred however only after Haavelmo placed econometric models generally firmly in the context of statistical inference (1943, 1944), and Maximum Likelihood pervades the work on the estimation of econometric models subsequently developed at the Cowles Commission for Research in Economics (Hood and Koopmans 1953; Koopmans 1950). At that time, however, the computations involved were hardly practicable, and this prevented a widespread adoption of these methods. As far as econometrics are conerned, Maximum Likelihood (ML) methodology lay dormant until the new computer technology had become generally accessible.

It is a constant theme of the history of the method that the use of ML techniques is not always accompanied by a clear appreciation of their limitations. Thirty years after the method's inception Le Cam complains that

> . . . although all efforts at a proof of the general existence of [asymptotically] efficient estimates . . . as well as at a proof of the efficiency of ML estimates were obviously inaccurate and although accurate proofs of similar statements always referred not to the general case but to particular classes of estimates . . . a general belief became established that the above statements are true in the most general sense (1953: 280).

Still another 30 years onward most practitioners of econometrics hold likewise that all ML estimators are consistent and asymptotically efficient, and this belief is equally unfounded. In spite of considerable progress in extending the validity of these claims to ever-widening classes of estimates, it is always qualified by certain conditions. One complicating factor is that the classical theory is concerned with inference about the parameters of a distribution from a sample of independent drawings from that distribution, while econometrics deals with parameters that govern a particular relation. This raises a number of technical and conceptual problems. Even when these are resolved, most results of ML theory hold only asymptotically, and in the usual conditions of econometric research these are fairly abstract virtues; they merely show that the estimates and tests meet certain minimal standards.

Part of the attraction of ML theory is of course that it does offer estimators and test procedures that are technically almost universally applicable, provided one has a reasonably precise model. But, as the attractive properties of the resulting statistics hold only asymptotically, if they hold at all, this is insufficient justification for their indiscriminate use in econometrics. There is a much better reason for using likelihood theory, however, in that it provides a coherent framework for statistical inference in general. In econometrics it has, for instance, contributed substantially to such seemingly specific issues as identification, the definition of exogeneity, and the selection bias in certain sampling schemes. Its usefulness as an aid to understanding such typical problems of empirical inference has certainly not yet been exploited to the full.

1.5 Computing and clerical errors

The story of Konstas and Khouja's money demand equation includes the erroneous solution of a minimum problem and the discovery of a clerical error. This is nothing exceptional, for it must be feared that the published results of statistical analyses at all times have contained a fair proportion of errors. I am certainly aware of a number of errors in my own earlier work, and there must be others I have not yet discovered. Even the publications of famous scholars are occasionally found wanting. Certain sums of squares of potato yields reported by Sir Ronald Fisher could not be reproduced from the data (Seal 1967: 18), Finney inadvertently displaced a decimal point (Pregibon 1981: 723), Solow committed a clerical error (Hogan 1958), and certain estimates of Malinvaud could not be reconstructed by Wallis (Wallis 1973: 4). None of these anomalies was serious, as they did not affect the conclusions of the original analyses. But the four examples were gleaned without effort from published papers, and there is no doubt that only a small fraction of the actual mistakes and errors is ever reported. The point is not that these scholars were careless, or that the profession is negligent, but that errors are inevitable, and will always occur even in the published results of painstaking statistical and econometric research. If readers doubt this, they should try their hands at repeating some published analysis; this will probably give them the salutary experience of committing and discovering some errors of their own before discovering the errors of others.

It must be feared that the adoption of iterative methods of estimation, carried out on high-speed computers, increases the incidence of serious errors. The vast change in the relative cost of reflection and of calculation leads to computations being undertaken nonchalantly, even frivolously. Models are less transparent and the outcome is less easily checked than before. Together with the tedium of the old hand calculations we have also abandoned the craftsmanship, the written worksheets which provided a record, and the intermediate checks human calculators include for fear of having to repeat the entire computation. Advanced estimation methods seldom permit an intuitive plausibility check of the result, as, for example, when a regression line is fitted to a scatter diagram that has been previously inspected. The only proper check is the independent replication of the work by an outsider, but this may well constitute a major operation.

As the purpose of this book is to put the new methods at the disposal of the reader, we feel you should be warned to check and check again at each stage of the analysis. Check the data, check their transfer into the computer, check the actual computations (preferably by repeating at least a sample by a rival program), and always remain suspicious of the results, regardless of their appeal.

CHAPTER 2

Likelihood

The next four chapters contain a quite general introduction to the statistical theory of Maximum Likelihood estimation and testing, and to the numerical determination of the estimates and of other statistics. We review the main theorems and techniques that are used in current econometric studies, and we sketch the underlying theory, which unifies seemingly unrelated results. Mathematical rigor is beyond our scope; we try to convey the drift of the argument, not to give proofs. A more thorough treatment of the mathematical theory involved can be found in statistical textbooks (Cox and Hinkley 1974; Silvey 1970). But while statistical theory deals with inference about a *distribution*, econometrics is usually concerned with a *relation*. We therefore allow from the very start for regressor variables. Apart from this, the discussion is quite general, in the sense that it is not restricted to a particular class of econometric models. Up to Chapter 6 the model formulation is indeed so general that the basic asymptotic properties of Maximum Likelihood estimates, which we quote below and use in Chapter 3, have not in fact been established. These properties have, however, been proved for several variants of the two main classes of econometric models that we shall consider, if only under particular qualifying conditions; moreover, considerable progress has been made in weakening the relevant restrictions. But we shall not take up this matter.

2.1 Simple linear regression

Although Section 7.1 is the proper place for this point, we wish to mention here already that the application of Maximum Likelihood theory to a simple linear regression equation with Normal disturbances will lead to OLS estimation of the regression coefficients. This illustration may help the reader in understanding the general argument, which is fairly abstract; at any rate, we shall be using it in exercises to this end.

We briefly review the model and its estimation to establish its notation for future reference. We have observed values of an $(n \times 1)$ vector y and of an $(n \times k)$ matrix X of full column rank k. We regard y as the realization of a random vector y that is generated by

$$y = X\beta + \epsilon$$

with β a $(k \times 1)$ vector of unknown coefficients, and ϵ an $(n \times 1)$ vector of independent Normal variates with zero mean and unknown variance σ^2. At times it may be advantageous to revert to the simpler formulation that for all scalar y_i with $1 = 1, 2, \ldots, n$

$$y_i = x_i^T \beta + \epsilon_i$$

with x_i^T denoting a row of X. The ϵ_i are independent and identically $N(0, \sigma^2)$ distributed, or the y_i independent $N(x_i^T \beta, \sigma^2)$. We write the density of any ϵ_i as

$$p_{\epsilon_i}(v) = (2\pi\sigma^2)^{-1/2} \exp(-\tfrac{1}{2}\,(v/\sigma)^2)$$

with v a scalar argument. As the ϵ_i are independent, the density of the vector ϵ is obtained by raising this expression to the nth power, or

$$p_{\epsilon}(v) = (2\pi\sigma^2)^{-n/2} \exp(-\tfrac{1}{2}\,(v^T v/\sigma^2))$$

with v now representing a vector of n elements.

As we shall see in Section 7.1, application of Maximum Likelihood theory to this model yields the standard OLS estimator of β,

$$b = (X^T X)^{-1} X^T y$$

with (asymptotic) covariance matrix

$$Vb = \sigma^2 \,(X^T X)^{-1}$$

The derivation is much simplified if we concentrate on the estimation of β, and treat σ^2 as a known constant or as a parameter of no consequence, which happens to come to the same thing. If we do estimate σ^2 along with β, however, we find

$$\hat{\sigma}^2 = \frac{1}{n}\,(y - Xb)^T(y - Xb)$$

This differs from the usual estimate s^2 in that no correction has been made for the number of fitted parameters. But this does not matter for the large samples for which Maximum Likelihood theory holds.

2.2 Generalities

We have a set of observations $\{x, y\}$ and a given *specification* of an econometric model, which identifies y with the realization of a random y with density function

$$p_y(w, \theta, x), \qquad \theta \in \Theta \tag{1}$$

The form of this density function effectively summarizes the specification of the econometric model; it *is* this specification. In its construction lies the true model builder's art. The finished form usually represents a compromise between various considerations: arguments from economic theory, common sense requirements such as invariance to changes in the units of measurement, and the strong attraction of convenient statistical properties. At this stage there is no need to specify the form of (1).

In (1), the symbol w denotes the density's argument, which is of course commensurate with y and $\mathbf{y}$, and x indicates *exogenous* regressor variables. Their values are known since they have been observed or assigned, as in the case of the intercept dummy "1" or of a trend variable. Statistical inference is traditionally concerned with controlled experiments, and if y were the outcome of such an experiment the x would represent the control variables that have been set at will by the experimenter, and that can be reset at the same values if the experiment is repeated. In that context it is natural to treat the x as nonrandom constants or as known parameters of the density (1). For the time being we adopt the same view here, although it quite clearly does not directly apply to the usual data sets of econometric analyses. We return to this issue in Sections 4.4 and 4.5.

The reader may have noticed that we have not indicated the size or format of y and x. Since statistical inference rarely bears on a single pair of scalars they are presumably arrays, but their dimensions need not yet be defined. We postpone this until Section 2.7.

By θ° we denote a vector of l unknown parameters located somewhere in the given parameter space Θ. We assume that any $(l \times 1)$ vector θ can range freely over this space, and that the functions of θ we consider are several times over differentiable in respect of all its elements, at least in the neighborhood of θ°; θ° must be an inner point of Θ. This parameter space is usually the l-dimensional Euclidean real number space, or part of it; we cannot define it at will, for it must satisfy the requirement that (1) is a proper density function for all $\theta \in \Theta$. Further limitations of the admissible parameter values may of course arise from economic theory, but these are immaterial for the statistical argument.

Although θ° is unknown, and although we may conceive of its location anywhere in Θ, it is nevertheless a set of fixed constants, not a (vector) variable. For θ° represents the "true" parameter values, that is, the values that have governed the generation of the observed data and that will also govern any addition to this sample.[3]

The specification (1) defines a *likelihood function*

$$L = L(\theta, y, x) = p_y(y, \theta, x) \tag{2}$$

This is obtained from the density (1) by substituting the observed y for w, and an $(l \times 1)$ vector θ for θ°. The y, being realizations, are known nonrandom constants, and θ is the argument of L; in comparison with (1) the roles have been reversed, and so has the order in which the symbols occur. We recall that θ can vary freely over Θ, and that (2) is differentiable, at least in the neighborhood of θ°.

As a matter of fact we shall be dealing more often with $\log L$ than with L itself. Since (1) is a density, it is positive for all $\theta \in \Theta$, and hence so is (2): Its logarithm always exists. If $\mathbf{y}$ is a discrete random variable, (1) is moreover a probability that cannot exceed unity, (2) follows suit, and $\log L$ is never positive. With continuous $\mathbf{y}$, however, the density function (1) represents a probability only if we integrate it over a (multidimensional) interval dw, which should presumably be geared to the limited precision of the observed y. Since this is never done in practice, with continuous y $\log L$ can take any value. In applications it is, moreover, standard usage to omit all constants that are irrelevant to the problem under review, such as the term π in Normal densities. In general, therefore, the numerical value of $\log L$ does not by itself permit of a direct interpretation.

Although the likelihood function has θ as its argument, it also depends on y, so that for any given θ – say θ^* – it is a sample statistic. Upon restoring the stochastic character of $\mathbf{y}$ this is of course a random variable, too, or

$$\mathbf{L}^* = L(\theta^*, \mathbf{y}, x)$$

with expected value

$$E\mathbf{L}^* = \int_w L(\theta^*, w, x)\, p_y(w, \theta^\circ, x)\, dw$$

The single integral in this expression is symbolic, for in fact w is of course an array like $\mathbf{y}$, and dw is multidimensional. If $\mathbf{y}$ is discrete we

[3] The distinction between the true parameter vector θ° and a variable vector θ of assigned values is essential to the present argument, but it loses much of its importance once the principles of Maximum Likelihood estimation and testing are understood. From Chapter 6 onward it is quietly dropped.

should use summation. But the point to note is that the expectation is taken over the density (1) at the true parameter vector $\theta°$, whatever θ^* may be. While $\theta°$ is given and constant (although unknown), θ^* may vary and EL^* is a function of θ^*.

2.3 Regularity

We recall that $p(w, \theta, x)$ is a density function for any $\theta \in \Theta$ (though not *the* density function of y unless $\theta = \theta°$), so that

$$\int_w p(w, \theta, x)\, dw = 1 \tag{3}$$

This density is *regular of the first and second order* if for all first and second derivatives differentiation in respect of (elements of) θ and integration over w can be carried out in either order with the same outcome: The integral of the derivative is identically equal to the derivative of the integral. This is a property of the specific form of the density function, and if (1) is regular it follows at once from (3) that

$$\int_w p'(w, \theta, x)\, dw = 0 \tag{4}$$

and

$$\int_w p''(w, \theta, x)\, dw = 0 \tag{5}$$

For an analysis of the conditions for regularity see Wilks (1962: 345 f.). In the general analysis that follows, we always take it for granted that we are dealing with regular densities. Since regularity is a mathematical property of the density function, it cannot be assumed, but it can be verified: In any particular application we should check that the basic density (1) is indeed regular, for if it is not, the standard likelihood theory set out below does not apply.

The above results of course also hold for $\theta = \theta°$, and if it is recalled that expectations are always taken over the density with parameters $\theta°$ it is seen that by (4) and (5)

$$E\left(\frac{p'(y, \theta, x)}{p(y, \theta, x)}\right)_{\theta=\theta°} = 0 \tag{6}$$

$$E\left(\frac{p''(y, \theta, x)}{p(y, \theta, x)}\right)_{\theta=\theta°} = 0 \tag{7}$$

2.4 Score vector and information matrix

The *score vector* q is the $(l \times 1)$ vector of first derivatives of log L in respect of (the elements of) θ. We treat log L as a single symbol, and recall that differentiation yields a row vector; moreover, we denote vectors and matrices by a typical element. We find

$$q(\theta) = (\log L')^T = \left[\frac{p'_j(y, \theta, x)}{p(y, \theta, x)}\right] \tag{8}$$

The index j in the last term indicates that the jth typical element of the vector consists of the partial derivative in respect of the jth element of the parameter vector.

While q is a function of θ, it also depends on x and on $\mathbf{y}$, and in view of the random character of the latter we may take its expectation. By (6) we then find

$$E\mathbf{q}(\theta^\circ) = 0 \tag{9}$$

We also consider Q, the $(l \times l)$ Hessian matrix of log L,

$$Q(\theta) = \log L'' = \left[\frac{p''_{jh}(y, \theta, x)}{p(y, \theta, x)} - \frac{p'_j(y, \theta, x)\, p'_h(y, \theta, x)}{p^2(y, \theta, x)}\right] \tag{10}$$

and treat it in the same way in order to define the (Fisher) *information matrix* H,

$$H = -E\mathbf{Q}(\theta^\circ) \tag{11}$$

Applying (7) to (10) and making use of (9) we find

$$H = E\mathbf{q}(\theta^\circ)\mathbf{q}(\theta^\circ)^T = V\mathbf{q}(\theta^\circ) \tag{12}$$

where V denotes a covariance matrix. We take it that both Q and H are nonsingular so that, by (12),

$$H \text{ is positive definite} \tag{13}$$

as befits the covariance matrix of $\mathbf{q}(\theta^\circ)$.

That these matrices are nonsingular is a matter both of the model and of the observed sample. In the model specification we must avoid side relations among the elements of θ, since this may lead to (linear) dependence among the scores, and hence render Q as well as H singular. If such side relations occur, the variation of θ and θ° is restricted to a subspace of H of less than l dimensions, and at least some of the l parameters are unidentified; but this case is easily dealt with by eliminating the redundant parameters. In the second place, $\mathbf{Q}(\theta^\circ)$ depends on the sample observations $\{x, \mathbf{y}\}$ just like log $\mathbf{L}$ and $\mathbf{q}$, and its expected value

H, taken over y alone, is still a function of the sample x. Both $\boldsymbol{Q}$ and its expectation (with reverse sign) H may therefore happen to be singular on account of the particular sample values that have been observed, although this is presumably less likely the larger the sample size. Still, to exclude singularities on this count is a substantive assumption about the observed sample, just like the assumption that there is no perfect multicollinearity (i.e., that the matrix X has full column rank) in the linear regression model.

We now consider the function

$$\psi(\theta) = E \log \boldsymbol{L}(\theta) \tag{14}$$

and its behavior as θ ranges over Θ. Note that ψ still depends on x, though not on y. Because of regularity we have

$$\psi'(\theta)^T = E\boldsymbol{q}(\theta), \qquad \psi''(\theta) = E\boldsymbol{Q}(\theta)$$

By (9), (11), and (13), then,

$$\psi'(\theta^\circ)^T = 0 \tag{15}$$

$$\psi''(\theta^\circ) = -H, \; -H \text{ negative definite} \tag{16}$$

It is easy to see that (15) and (16) are necessary concomitants of $\psi(\theta^\circ)$ being a local maximum of $\psi(\theta)$, but they are also sufficient conditions and thus identify θ° as a (local) maximand of $\psi(\theta)$. To show this we paraphrase Fletcher (1980: I, 11). Consider a Taylor series expansion of $\psi(\theta^\circ + d)$, with d some vector of small deviations. As the first derivative vanishes, by (15), we find

$$\psi(\theta^\circ + d) = \psi(\theta^\circ) + \tfrac{1}{2} d^T \psi''(\theta^\circ) d + o(d^T d) \tag{17}$$

where $o(d^T d)$ denotes a term that is negligibly small relative to its argument $d^T d$. The matrix $-\psi''(\theta^\circ)$ is symmetric and, by (16), positive definite; it can be decomposed as

$$-\psi''(\theta^\circ) = P^T \Lambda P$$

where P is a matrix of orthonormal eigenvectors, with $P^T P = I$, and Λ is a diagonal matrix containing the eigenvalues which are all positive. It follows that

$$-d^T \psi''(\theta^\circ) d \geqq \lambda \, d^T d, \qquad \lambda > 0 \tag{18}$$

where λ is the smallest eigenvalue of $-\psi''(\theta^\circ)$. As a result we may rewrite (17) as

$$\psi(\theta^\circ + d) \leqq \psi(\theta^\circ) - (\tfrac{1}{2}\lambda - o(1)) d^T d \tag{19}$$

The elements of d can be made as small as we please without affecting λ, and we can thus ensure that the term $o(1)$, regardless of its sign, is negligible in comparison to $\frac{1}{2}\lambda$. Hence for sufficiently small d

$$\psi(\theta^\circ + d) < \psi(\theta^\circ) \tag{20}$$

so that $\psi(\theta^\circ)$ is a local maximum.

At the present level of generality we have no means of verifying whether this local maximum is unique, and corresponds to the global maximum of $\psi(\theta)$ over the entire parameter space Θ. For the time being we shall assume that this is indeed the case. Once we are dealing with a particular model specification the issue may be decided by inspection of the behavior of ψ and of related functions, like H, over the parameter space.

Questions and exercises

2.1 Consider the linear regression model of Section 2.1. What is the parameter space? Write down the loglikelihood function, derive q, and verify (9).

2.2 We consider the linear regression model of Section 2.1 and add the simplifying assumption that σ is a known constant, not an unknown parameter that must be estimated. In this case $\theta = \beta$, and up to an additive constant

$$\log L(\beta) = \frac{1}{\sigma^2} \sum_i (y_i - x_i^T \beta)^2$$

Derive q, Q, and H.

2.3 (Continuation.) If the regression equation is specified as

$$y_i = \alpha + (\beta + \gamma)x_i + \epsilon_i$$

β and γ are unidentified; if we have

$$y_i = \alpha + \beta x_i + \gamma z_i + \epsilon_i,$$
$$x_i = \lambda z_i \text{ for all } i$$

the sample data suffer from perfect multicollinearity. Show that in both cases Q, as derived in Exercise 2.2, is singular. Will it remain singular as the number of observations increases indefinitely?

2.4 (Continuation.) Show that in the model of Exercise 2.2 the local maximum defined by (15) will automatically satisfy (16) and will moreover correspond to a unique global maximum.

2.5 The inequality of Cramér–Rao

With no other assumption than regularity we can already obtain a quite powerful and general result by means of the apparatus thus far constructed. This is the Cramér–Rao lower bound for the variance of an estimator. We take the standard case of an unbiased estimator but admit from the outset that it is a vector.

Some definitions are in order. Any set of sample statistics, or any (vector) function of the observed sample $\{x, y\}$ can be taken as an *estimate* of $\theta°$, provided it does not depend on $\theta°$ and can be calculated while $\theta°$ is unknown. An *estimator* is the corresponding function of $\{\boldsymbol{x}, \boldsymbol{y}\}$, and hence a random variable. We assume that the vector function $t\{\boldsymbol{x}, \boldsymbol{y}\}$, or $\boldsymbol{t}$ for short, is an unbiased estimator of $\theta°$, that is

$$E\boldsymbol{t} = \theta° \qquad \text{for all} \quad \theta° \in \Theta \tag{21}$$

Repeating this with the expectation operator written in full gives

$$E\boldsymbol{t} = \left[\int_w t_j(w, x)\, p(w, \theta°, x) dw \right] = \theta°$$

where the vector is once more represented by its typical jth element. Differentiating the last two terms with respect to $\theta°$, making use of the assumed regularity, and equating the results we obtain

$$\left[\int_w t_j(w, x) p'(w, \theta°, x) dw \right] = \left[\int_w t_j(w, x) \frac{p'(w, \theta°, x)}{p(w, \theta°, x)} p(w, \theta°, x) dw \right]$$
$$= E\, \boldsymbol{t}\, \boldsymbol{q}(\theta°)^T = I \tag{22}$$

Now consider the vector

$$\boldsymbol{z} = \boldsymbol{t} - \theta° - H^{-1} \boldsymbol{q}(\theta°) \tag{23}$$

By (21) and (9) we find

$$E\boldsymbol{z} = 0 \tag{24}$$

and, making use of (22), (9), and (12),

$$V\boldsymbol{z} = E\boldsymbol{z}\boldsymbol{z}^T = E((\boldsymbol{t} - \theta°)(\boldsymbol{t} - \theta°)^T) - H^{-1}$$

or again

$$V\boldsymbol{t} = H^{-1} + V\boldsymbol{z} \tag{25}$$

This is the Cramér–Rao inequality for vector estimators. It shows that the covariance matrix of any unbiased estimator $\boldsymbol{t}$ exceeds H^{-1} by $V\boldsymbol{z}$, which is a positive semidefinite matrix since it is itself a covariance matrix, though possibly degenerate.

Speaking loosely, (25) sets a lower bound for Vt at H^{-1}: An unbiased estimator that attains this covariance matrix is *efficient* within its class. The same formulation occurs in the Gauss–Markov theorem of linear regression theory, where the covariance matrix of the *Best* Linear Unbiased Estimator (or BLUE) differs from the covariance matrix of any other linear unbiased estimator by a positive semidefinite matrix – see, for example, Theil (1971: 119). But in either case the meaning of this criterion is not immediately apparent, and an explanation is in order.

This explanation is simple if t and θ° are scalars instead of vectors. In this case all three matrices in (25) reduce to nonnegative scalars, too, and the Cramér–Rao inequality states that the variance of an unbiased estimator cannot be less than $1/H$. It is natural to call an unbiased estimator efficient among all unbiased estimators when its variance attains this lower bound.

When we return to unbiased *vector* estimators t of the parameter vector θ° the difficulty is that there is no immediate intuitive measure of dispersion by which they can be ranked. The first need is for a uniform description of the multivariate dispersion of random vectors, irrespective of the precise nature of their distribution. This is supplied by the *ellipsoid of concentration*, introduced by Cramér (1946: 300). For the $(l \times 1)$ random vector t with expectation θ° and covariance matrix Vt this l-dimensional ellipsoid is traced out in l-dimensional space by the vector s that satisfies the equation

$$(s - \theta^\circ)^T \, Vt^{-1} \, (s - \theta^\circ) = l + 2 \tag{26}$$

A random vector with a uniform distribution over the hyperspace enclosed by this ellipsoid has expectation θ°, as is clear from symmetry considerations, and it also has the same covariance matrix Vt as t. As far as the first and second moments are concerned the ellipsoid of concentration thus serves as a fair characterization of the distribution of t.

A similar representation applies if the unbiased estimator t is (approximately) Normally distributed, for the contour lines of an l-dimensional $N(\theta^\circ, Vt)$ distribution are given by

$$(s - \theta^\circ)^T \, Vt^{-1} \, (s - \theta^\circ) = C \tag{27}$$

with C some constant. Again a $(100 - \alpha)\%$ *confidence region* for θ° is defined by a similar ellipsoid, for this region is bounded by the s which satisfy

$$(s - t)^T \, Vt^{-1} \, (s - t) = \chi^2_\alpha(l) \tag{28}$$

In all three cases we have ellipsoids that are centered at θ° and have Vt^{-1} as the quadratic coefficient matrix. In order to examine their size we consider a ray or straight line through θ° with direction vector r. The points on such a line can be represented as

$$\theta^\circ + dr$$

with d a nonnegative scalar distance parameter. Such a ray cuts the ellipsoids at the point

$$s = \theta^\circ + dr \qquad (29)$$

When we apply this to (26), the distance from θ° to the ellipsoid shell along r is found by solving d from

$$dr^T\, Vt^{-1}\, r\, d = l + 2$$

or

$$d^2 = (l+2)/(r^T\, Vt^{-1}\, r) \qquad (30)$$

Inspection shows that the distance would diminish if Vt^{-1} were augmented by a positive definite matrix, and this for all directions r. If there is an upper bound for Vt^{-1}, exceeding all other coefficient matrices by a positive semidefinite matrix, the corresponding ellipsoid will be completely contained within all other ellipsoids, at worst touching them or coinciding with them. Such an upper bound for Vt^{-1} with a minimal ellipsoid is given by H. This follows from (25), for if A and B are positive definite matrices and $(A - B)$ is positive semidefinite then so is $(B^{-1} - A^{-1})$.[4]

The above argument applies, of course, equally well to (27) and (28). In each case unbiased estimators that are efficient in the Cramér–Rao sense have minimal ellipsoids as just explained. If no efficient unbiased estimator exists, the minimal ellipsoid is still there as a lower bound for all the inefficient estimators.

This general result also sets bounds for certain scalar measures of the performance of (unbiased) estimator vectors. These bounds may also be derived directly from (25).

First consider the l-dimensional *volume* of the ellipsoids under review. Other things being equal, the ellipsoid with coefficient matrix H is contained within an ellipsoid with matrix Vt^{-1}, therefore it cannot have a greater volume. This means

$$c\sqrt{|H|^{-1}} \leqq c\sqrt{Vt} \qquad (31)$$

where we have made use of the formula for the volume enclosed by an

[4] For a proof with $(A - B)$ positive definite, also valid in the semidefinite case, see Madansky (1976: 43).

l-dimensional ellipsoid (Cramér 1946: 118–20). The constant of proportionality c depends on l, the number of dimensions, and on the right-hand side of the quadratic equation concerned; this is different for (26), (27), and (28). It follows from (31) that

$$|H^{-1}| \leqq |V\boldsymbol{t}| \tag{32}$$

This sets a lower limit to the determinant of $V\boldsymbol{t}$, always positive, which is also known as thc *generalized variance* of the vector $\boldsymbol{t}$ and used as a scalar measure of its dispersion. We now know why.

Secondly, any linear combination of the elements of θ° with known coefficients, say $a^T\theta^\circ$, is estimated without bias by $a^T\boldsymbol{t}$. This scalar estimator has a scalar variance

$$V(a^T\boldsymbol{t}) = a^T(V\boldsymbol{t})a$$

It follows at once from (25) that this has a lower bound since

$$a^T H^{-1} a \leqq a^T(V\boldsymbol{t})a \tag{33}$$

When we construct a as a vector of zeroes with a single unit element we obtain the special case of a single element of $\boldsymbol{t}$, or the scalar estimator of a single parameter, say θ_j°. By (33), the scalar variance of this estimator satisfies the inequality

$$H^{jj} \leqq V\boldsymbol{t}_j \tag{34}$$

where H^{jj} stands for the jth diagonal element of H^{-1}.

Efficient or Minimum Variance Unbiased Estimators (MVUE) are of course desirable, but they do not always exist. While we may reduce $V\boldsymbol{z}$ in (25) to the null matrix by equating $\boldsymbol{z}$ in (23) to zero, the result

$$\boldsymbol{t} = \theta^\circ + H^{-1}\,\boldsymbol{q}(\theta^\circ) \tag{35}$$

is a proper estimator of θ° only if θ° happens to vanish from the right-hand side.

2.6 Maximum Likelihood estimation

The Maximum Likelihood estimate (MLE) $\hat{\theta}$ of θ° is the solution of

$$\text{maximize } \log L(\theta, y, x) \qquad \text{for } \theta \in \Theta \tag{36}$$

$\hat{\theta}$ of course satisfies the standard conditions

$$\left[\frac{\partial \log L}{\partial \theta_j}\right]_{\hat{\theta}}^T = q(\hat{\theta}) = 0 \tag{37}$$

$$\left[\frac{\partial^2 \log L}{\partial \theta_j \, \partial \theta_h}\right]_{\hat{\theta}} = Q(\hat{\theta}) \text{ is negative definite} \tag{38}$$

provided there is a unique solution at an inner point of Θ. How this solution is actually found is discussed in Chapter 5.

Since $\hat{\theta}$ is a function of y it is the realization of the corresponding ML estimator $\hat{\theta}(\boldsymbol{y})$ or $\hat{\boldsymbol{\theta}}$. The major attractive properties of this estimator are a matter of its asymptotic behavior as the number of observations increases beyond all bounds. So far we have, however, treated the observed $\{x, y\}$ as a single amorphous whole, and apart from one or two asides we have not mentioned sample size at all. For the asymptotic argument we must change our ways.

2.7 Independent observations

We assume that the observed sample $\{x, y\}$ can be partitioned into n elements $\{x_i, y_i\}$, and that the y_i can be treated as realizations of *independent* random variables $\boldsymbol{y}_i$. Moreover, the same model applies to each element, and the general specification (1) is replaced by the specification of the density function of $\boldsymbol{y}_i$,

$$p_{y_i}(w_*, \theta^\circ, x_i) = p_i(w_*, \theta^\circ, x_i) \tag{39}$$

where w_* has the same dimensions as $\boldsymbol{y}_i$. As before $\boldsymbol{y}_i$ may represent a vector or a matrix, and the elements of this array need not be stochastically independent. Again $\boldsymbol{y}_i$, like x_i, may represent transformations of the original economic variables, including transformations, as used in time series analysis, that are meant to ensure independence.

All the quantities that we have so far introduced for the entire sample $\{x, y\}$ can be redefined for a single individual observation $\{x_i, y_i\}$. As in (2), the likelihood function follows from the density as

$$L_i = L_*(\theta^\circ, y_i, x_i) = p_i(y_i, \theta^\circ)$$

and because of the independence of the $\boldsymbol{y}_i$

$$\log L = \sum_i \log L_i \tag{40}$$

It follows at once that, in self-evident notation,

$$q = \sum_i q_i, \qquad Q = \sum_i Q_i \tag{41}$$

and likewise for mathematical expectations, as in (14) and (11),

$$\psi = \sum_i \psi_i, \qquad H = \sum_i H_i \tag{42}$$

We shall also need *mean expected values* such as

$$\overline{\psi} = \frac{1}{n}\psi = \frac{1}{n}\sum_i \psi_i, \qquad \overline{H} = \frac{1}{n}H = \frac{1}{n}\sum_i H_i \tag{43}$$

We note that all the results we have earlier obtained apply equally to each individual observation $\{x_i, y_i\}$ as well as to the entire sample $\{x, y\}$, since there is nothing in their derivation to distinguish between these two. We also note that the y_i are independent but *not* identically distributed random variables since their density (39) has x_i among its parameters, and these x_i generally differ – indeed, they often must be different to permit estimation at all. Hence the q_i and Q_i are not identically distributed either, and the expected values ψ_i and H_i will in general vary with x_i, too.

2.8 Consistency of the MLE

The distinction of n separate observations and the strong substantive assumption that they are stochastically independent prepare the way for two major theorems about the behavior of the MLE $\hat{\theta}_n$ as the sample size n increases beyond all bounds. These theorems have been proved by different routes for various models under ever weaker conditions, but not at the level of generality of the present setting. Such a proof would anyhow be beyond our scope. We can however loosely sketch the type of argument adduced. This involves allusions to several forms of the Law of Large Numbers and to other convergence theorems, never strictly valid without certain further conditions. For these we refer to Gnedenko (1962). We shall also often invoke Slutsky's theorem: If z converges in probability to ζ, then any continuous function $\psi(z)$ converges to $\psi(\zeta)$ (Cramér 1946: 255; Theil 1971: 361).

The first theorem establishes that $\hat{\theta}_n$ is a *consistent* estimator of $\theta°$ since it converges in probability to it. This is denoted as

$$\hat{\theta}_n \xrightarrow{p} \theta° \tag{44}$$

which means

$$\lim_{n\to\infty} P(|\hat{\theta}_n - \theta°| > \epsilon) = 0$$

for any positive ϵ, however small; the inequality refers to each element of the vectors. To see this we consider the mean expected loglikelihood function $\overline{\psi}(\theta) = (1/n)\,\psi(\theta)$ of (43), and recall that for any given n it will have a maximum at $\theta°$ by (15) and (16). By Tchebychev's version of the weak law of large numbers we have, under certain conditions,

$$\frac{1}{n}\log \boldsymbol{L}(\theta) = \frac{1}{n}\sum_i \log \boldsymbol{L}_i \xrightarrow{P} \overline{\psi}(\theta)$$

at any $\theta \in \Theta$. (Gnedenko 1962: 240; Rao 1973: 112). This implies

$$\max_{\theta\in\Theta} \frac{1}{n}\log \boldsymbol{L}(\theta) \xrightarrow{P} \max_{\theta\in\Theta} \overline{\psi}(\theta)$$

Further conditions are however needed to infer from this that the *maximand* $\hat{\boldsymbol{\theta}}_n$ converges to the maximand $\theta°$, as required in (44). One device is to restrict the parameter space Θ to a countable set like $\{\theta_1, \theta_2, \ldots\}$, but this seems hardly in keeping with the way we handle Θ in general. The classical solution is found in the proof of the MLE's consistency by Wald (1949). Like most of the statistical literature, however, it deals with the case of identically distributed (and scalar) random variables.

The consistency of $\hat{\boldsymbol{\theta}}$ is an attractive property of this estimator in its own right, and it also has a useful corollary. By Slutsky's theorem convergence in probability of $\hat{\boldsymbol{\theta}}$ to $\theta°$ implies similar convergence of any continuous function $\phi(\hat{\boldsymbol{\theta}})$ to $\phi(\theta°)$. The difference

$$|\phi(\hat{\boldsymbol{\theta}}_n) - \phi(\theta°)|$$

can therefore be made as small as we like to any degree of probability short of certainty by sufficiently increasing the sample size. We shall repeatedly consider Taylor series expansions and neglect all but one or two terms on the grounds that such differences, including of course $|\hat{\boldsymbol{\theta}}_n - \theta°|$ itself, are small; we now know that this is legitimate, at least in the limit.

2.9 Asymptotic distribution of the MLE

We expand $q(\hat{\boldsymbol{\theta}}_n)$ in a Taylor series around the true parameter vector $\theta°$ as

$$q_n(\hat{\boldsymbol{\theta}}_n) \approx \boldsymbol{q}_n(\theta°) + \boldsymbol{Q}_n(\theta°)(\hat{\boldsymbol{\theta}}_n - \theta°) \tag{45}$$

Since $q_n(\hat{\boldsymbol{\theta}}_n)$ is zero, by (37), we have

$$\hat{\boldsymbol{\theta}}_n - \theta° \approx -\boldsymbol{Q}_n(\theta°)^{-1}\,\boldsymbol{q}_n(\theta°)$$

or again

$$\sqrt{n}(\hat{\boldsymbol{\theta}}_n - \theta°) \approx \left(-\frac{1}{n}\boldsymbol{Q}_n(\theta°)\right)^{-1} \frac{1}{\sqrt{n}}\boldsymbol{q}_n(\theta°) \tag{46}$$

We here append a suffix n to $\boldsymbol{q}$ and to $\boldsymbol{Q}$ to stress the fact that their distributions vary with the sample size. It is hoped that no confusion will arise with the earlier use of $\boldsymbol{q}_i$ and $\boldsymbol{Q}_i$ for the score vector and Hessian matrix pertaining to a single observation (y_i, x_i).

As n increases beyond all limits three things happen. First, the approximation (45) holds the better since $\hat{\theta}_n$ converges to θ°, as we have just seen. Secondly, by the direct application of Tchebychev's version of the weak law of large numbers

$$-\frac{1}{n}\boldsymbol{Q}_n(\theta^\circ) = -\frac{1}{n}\sum_i \boldsymbol{Q}_i(\theta^\circ) \xrightarrow{P} \overline{H} \tag{47}$$

and by Slutsky's theorem

$$\left(-\frac{1}{n}\boldsymbol{Q}_n(\theta^\circ)\right)^{-1} \xrightarrow{P} \overline{H}^{-1} \tag{48}$$

For the last term of (46) we invoke Liapounov's Central Limit Theorem for nonidentically distributed variables to argue that under certain conditions its distribution converges to the Normal (Gnedenko 1962: 306). By (9) its expectation is zero, and by (12) its variance is

$$E\,\frac{1}{\sqrt{n}}\,\boldsymbol{q}_n(\theta^\circ)\boldsymbol{q}_n(\theta^\circ)^T\frac{1}{\sqrt{n}} = \frac{1}{n}\,H = \overline{H}$$

so that

$$\frac{1}{\sqrt{n}}\,\boldsymbol{q}_n(\theta^\circ) \xrightarrow{L} N(0, \overline{H}) \tag{49}$$

Upon combining this with (46) and (47) we obtain

$$\sqrt{n}\,(\hat{\boldsymbol{\theta}}_n - \theta^\circ) \xrightarrow{L} N(0, \overline{H}^{-1}) \tag{50}$$

This is a strong result. It establishes several major properties of the MLE in addition to its consistency. The MLE is asymptotically Normal, which is of great help for the derivation of (asymptotically valid) tests; it is asymptotically unbiased; and it is asymptotically efficient, since the covariance matrix of its limiting distribution is $\overline{H}^{-1}$, and thus equals the Cramér–Rao lower bound of (25). For estimates from a given sample size we must take account of the terms in n, so that their asymptotic covariance matrix is, from (50),

$$V\hat{\boldsymbol{\theta}} = \frac{1}{n}\,\overline{H}^{-1} = (n\overline{H})^{-1} = H^{-1} \tag{51}$$

2.10 Estimation of the covariance matrix

As a rule we wish to supplement the parameter estimates by an estimate of their (asymptotic) covariance matrix, or at least of that part of it that refers to a particular subset of the parameter estimates. This will permit us to assess (asymptotic) *t*-ratios and (asymptotic) confidence regions. The estimated covariance matrix is moreover needed for a number of test statistics, as we shall see in Chapter 3.

Since the parameter vector θ° in the present formulation contains *all* parameters of the probability density of $\boldsymbol{y}$ of (1), it provides a complete characterization of the model and of all the accessory magnitudes that can be derived from it. The estimation of the asymptotic covariance matrix of $\hat{\theta}$, $V\hat{\boldsymbol{\theta}}$ or V for short, therefore does not call for any new, additional estimates. We can just evaluate the appropriate expression at the estimated parameter values $\hat{\theta}$ we already have, taking $V(\hat{\theta})$ for an estimate of $V(\theta^\circ)$.[5] As we shall see in Section 3.1, a function of MLE provides under quite lenient conditions the MLE of the same function of the parameters. $V(\hat{\boldsymbol{\theta}})$ is thus the ML estimator of V, with all attendant properties, provided of course we have taken the correct expression for $V(\theta^\circ)$.

By (51) this ML estimator of V is

$$\hat{V}_1 = H(\hat{\theta})^{-1} \tag{52}$$

The expression of H is obtained from (11) or (12) (which should give identical results) as

$$H(\theta^\circ) = -E\boldsymbol{Q}(\theta^\circ) = E\boldsymbol{q}(\theta^\circ)\,\boldsymbol{q}(\theta^\circ)^T$$

We can also use approximations for H. These do not yield ML estimators, but if the approximations converge to H the result is still consistent. Thus we may desist from taking expectations and use

$$\hat{V}_2 = -Q(\hat{\theta})^{-1} = -\left(\sum_i Q_i(\hat{\theta})\right)^{-1} \tag{53}$$

Again we may look to (12) and define, by analogy,

$$\hat{V}_3 = \left(\sum_i q_i(\hat{\theta})\,q_i(\hat{\theta})^T\right)^{-1} \tag{54}$$

This form has been warmly advocated because of its simplicity by

[5] We recall the subtle difference in notation between the covariance matrix *of* $\hat{\boldsymbol{\theta}}$, denoted as $V\,\boldsymbol{\theta}$, or V for short, and the same matrix *as a function of* θ, denoted as $V(\theta)$. This use of brackets extends to estimators and estimates, so that we may have $V(\boldsymbol{\theta})$ as the estimator of $V(\theta^\circ)$.

Berndt et al. (1974). Both (53) and (54) are consistent estimators, for they contain sums of independent variates which (upon suitable scaling by n) will converge to the mean expected value $\bar{H}$ of (43). Hence $\hat{V}_2$ and $\hat{V}_3$ converge to H^{-1}.

In particular applications it may turn out that two (or possibly even all three) of these estimators coincide. When they differ, the choice that must be made among them is often influenced by considerations of computational convenience.

Questions and exercises

2.5 In the linear regression model of Section 2.1 the covariance matrix of the asymptotic distribution of $\hat{\beta}$ is

$$E\sqrt{n}(\hat{\beta}-\beta)(\hat{\beta}-\beta)^T\sqrt{n} = \sigma^2(X^TX/n)^{-1}$$

and this is asymptotically efficient in the sense that it meets the Cramér–Rao bound. At the same time $\hat{\beta}$ is identical to the OLS estimate $\boldsymbol{b}$ with

$$V\boldsymbol{b} = \sigma^2(X^TX)^{-1}$$

and this is efficient in the sense of the Gauss–Markov theorem for BLUE (Theil 1972: 119). Compare these two statements about the efficiency of $\hat{\boldsymbol{\beta}} = \boldsymbol{b}$ in respect of the assumptions about the regression disturbances and in respect of the qualifying conditions.

2.6 Consider the linear regression model of Section 2.1 in the special case of Exercise 2.2 with σ^2 a known constant and

$$\log L(\beta) = -\frac{1}{2\sigma^2}\sum_i (y_i - x_i^T\beta)^2$$

Establish $V\hat{\boldsymbol{\beta}}$ according to (51), and examine its estimators (52), (53), and (54).

2.7 Consider the simple regression model of Section 2.1 with $\theta^T = \{\beta\,\sigma^2\}$ and establish $V\hat{\boldsymbol{\theta}}$ according to (51).

2.8 We consider an ordered sequence $z_1, z_2, \ldots, z_n$ that has been observed as the realization of a random $(n \times 1)$ vector $\boldsymbol{z}$, which has an n-dimensional Normal distribution, $\boldsymbol{z} \sim N(0, \Omega)$. In the absence of further assumptions, can any parameters be estimated? What is the sample size of these observations?

2.9 (Continuation.) We now impose the assumption that the z_i represent an autoregressive process

$$z_i = \rho z_{i-1} + \epsilon_i$$

with the ϵ_i independent $N(0, \sigma^2)$ variates. Construct a loglikelihood function in terms of independent random variables. What is the sample size? Discuss.

2.10 A household budget survey yields individual household data on food expenditure (c), disposable family income (m), and farming status ($f = 1$ if farm household, $f = 0$ if nonfarm household). Consider three regression models

1. $c = \alpha_1 + \beta_1 m + \epsilon_1$ for farm households,
   $c = \alpha_2 + \beta_2 m + \epsilon_2$ for nonfarm households,
   ϵ_1 independent $N(0, \sigma_1^2)$,
   ϵ_2 independent $N(0, \sigma_2^2)$.
2. $\left.\begin{array}{l} c = \alpha_1 + \beta_1 m + \epsilon_1 \\ c = \alpha_2 + \beta_2 m + \epsilon_2 \end{array}\right\}$ as above
   ϵ_1, ϵ_2 both independent $N(0, \sigma^2)$
3. $c = \alpha + \beta m + \gamma f + \epsilon$
   ϵ independent $N(0, \sigma^2)$.

What model will yield the highest value of $\log L(\hat{\theta})$?

CHAPTER 3

Tests of simplifying assumptions

This chapter is concerned with three different tests of simplifying assumptions that have been developed in the context of likelihood theory. For the general case only asymptotic distributions of the test statistics have been established. As a preliminary we consider parameter transformations and constrained estimation.

3.1 Invariance of MLE and transformation of parameters

We consider a function of the parameter vector θ, say the scalar function $\psi = \psi(\theta)$. Substitution of the true values θ° yields

$$\psi^\circ = \psi(\theta^\circ)$$

and substitution of the ML estimators $\hat{\theta}$

$$\bar{\psi} = \psi(\hat{\theta})$$

It depends on the nature of the function ψ what properties of the MLE $\hat{\theta}$ extend to $\bar{\psi}$ as an estimator of ψ°. If ψ is continuous, the consistency of $\hat{\theta}$ carries over to $\bar{\psi}$, by Slutsky's theorem; if ψ is moreover differentiable, the distribution of $\bar{\psi}_n$ converges to a Normal distribution: In the notation of Section 2.9

$$\sqrt{n}(\bar{\psi} - \psi^\circ) \xrightarrow{L} N(0, \psi' V\hat{\theta}\psi'^T)$$

where ψ' stands for the row vector of derivatives of ψ (Cramér 1946: 353–4, 366–7). The estimator $\bar{\psi}$ is thus asymptotically equivalent to an ML estimator of ψ°, for it has the same asymptotic distribution.

These results suggest that ML estimation is usually *invariant* under parameter transformations, in the sense that $\psi(\hat{\theta})$ is an ML estimator of $\psi(\theta^\circ)$ because $\hat{\theta}$ is an ML estimator of θ°. According to Zehna, $\psi(\hat{\theta})$ may indeed be regarded as an MLE for *any* function ψ on the grounds that the maximization of log $L(\theta)$ over Θ at $\hat{\theta}$ is matched by the maximization of an "induced likelihood function" over the transformed parameter space Θ^* at $\psi(\hat{\theta})$ (Zehna, 1966). In the absence of further conditions it is however not easy to establish that the "induced likelihood" is the same as the likelihood function that follows from the density function with parameter ψ.

The standard usage is to require that there be a one-to-one correspondence between ψ and an element of θ, or between θ and its vector transformation. We shall follow this usage in the demonstration of the invariance property of ML estimation given below. While the condition may possibly be unduly restrictive, it is certainly in order when we consider the parameter transformation involved in the *reparametrization* of a model. What we have in mind then is to change the representation of the model without altering its material content by transforming the parameter vector θ to η. Clearly the two versions of the model can only be fully equivalent if we can retrieve the first from the second as well as we can construct the second from the first. There must therefore be a one-to-one correspondence between the two $(l \times 1)$ parameter vectors θ and η by the vector functions

$$\eta = g(\theta), \qquad \theta = g^{-1}(\eta) \tag{1}$$

After the transformation from θ to η the true parameter vector is of course $\eta^\circ = g(\theta^\circ)$, and the parameter space is transformed from Θ to Θ^*; when we retain the same symbol we use an asterisk to distinguish the transformed model from the original.

We recall from Section 2.1 that a model is fully described by the (conditional) probability distribution of the dependent variable. For the two models under review to be equivalent they must therefore yield the same distribution of y at given x. For the original formulation we have the density (2.1)

$$p_y(w, \theta^\circ, x), \qquad \theta^\circ \in \Theta$$

and for the transformed model

$$p_y^*(w, \eta^\circ, x), \qquad \eta^\circ \in \Theta^*$$

The latter density can be constructed from the first by the substitution

$$p_y^*(w, \eta^\circ, x) = p_y(\mathrm{w}, g^{-1}(\eta^\circ), x) \tag{2}$$

where we make use of the reverse transformation from (1). This ensures that the two densities are identically equal, or, in full,

$$\begin{aligned} p_y^*(w, \eta^\circ, x) &= p_y^*(w, g(\theta^\circ), x) \\ &= p_y(w, g^{-1}(\eta^\circ), x) = p_y(\mathrm{w}, \theta^\circ, x) \end{aligned}$$

When we pass to loglikelihood functions we have

$$\begin{aligned} \log L^*(\eta) &= \log L^*(g(\theta)) \\ &= \log L(g^{-1}(\eta)) = \log L(\theta) \end{aligned}$$

It follows at once that $\log L^*(\eta)$ is maximized by $g(\hat{\theta})$, or

$$\hat{\eta} = g(\hat{\theta}) \tag{3}$$

This establishes the *invariance property* of ML estimation. Note that the two loglikelihood functions attain the *same* maximum value, or

$$\log L^*(\hat{\eta}) = \log L(\hat{\theta}) \tag{4}$$

Clearly all results of Chapter 2 carry over to this translation of the estimation problem with η°, $\hat{\eta}$, and Θ^* taking the place of θ°, $\hat{\theta}$, and Θ. We illustrate this by some expressions for the correspondence between the two models, or rather between the two representations of the same model.

To begin with we arrange the derivatives with respect to θ of the vector function g of (1) into an $(l \times l)$ Jacobian matrix G, defined by

$$G = G(\theta) = \left[\frac{\partial \eta_i}{\partial \theta_j}\right] \tag{5}$$

The reverse transformation, also of (1), has the inverse Jacobian, or

$$G^{-1} = \left[\frac{\partial \theta_i}{\partial \eta_j}\right]$$

With a proper one-to-one correspondence between θ and η both matrices are regular. The elements are in general functions of the parameters θ (or η), but not of $\boldsymbol{y}$ or of any other random variable.

We consider

$$\log L(\theta) = \log L^*(g(\theta))$$

and differentiate both sides in respect of θ. By the chain rule this yields

$$q(\theta) = G^T q^*(g(\theta)) = G^T q^*(\eta)$$

and hence

$$q^*(\eta) = G^{T-1} q(\theta) \tag{6}$$

It follows that $E\boldsymbol{q}(\theta^\circ) = 0$, from (2.9), implies

$$E\boldsymbol{q}^*(\eta^\circ) = 0 \tag{7}$$

In the same way we may differentiate (6) once more to obtain $Q^*(\eta)$; for $-E\boldsymbol{Q}^*(\eta^\circ)$ we then find, making use of (7) and of (2.11),

$$-E\boldsymbol{Q}^*(\eta^\circ) = H^* = G^{T-1} H \, G^{-1}$$

It follows from this that we have, as in (2.51),

$$V\hat{\eta} = H^{*-1} = G\, V\hat{\theta}\, G^T$$

or, more succinctly,

$$V^* = G\, V\, G^T \tag{8}$$

The ML estimator (3) is thus supplemented by

$$\hat{V}^* = \hat{G}\, \hat{V}\, \hat{G}^{\mathrm{T}} \tag{9}$$

as an estimator of its asymptotic covariance matrix, with

$$\hat{G} = G(\hat{\theta})$$

and $\hat{V}$ any of the three estimators of $V\hat{\theta}$ of Section 2.10.

So much for the main formulae of the ML estimation of η°. It is not hard (but superfluous) to derive by similar arguments that the numerical maximum conditions (2.37) and (2.38)

$$q(\hat{\theta}) = 0, \qquad Q(\hat{\theta}) \text{ negative definite}$$

indeed imply

$$q^*(\hat{\eta}) = 0, \qquad Q^*(\hat{\eta}) \text{ negative definite}$$

There is, however, no need to determine $\hat{\eta}$ from these conditions, for (3), (4), and (9) already permit us to calculate the MLE of η°, the attendant value of the loglikelihood, and the covariance matrix of the estimates from the corresponding results of estimating θ°. We can thus easily move from one representation of the model to another. This can be quite practical. We may for instance adopt any (re-) parametrization that is computationally attractive to establish a set of ML estimates, and then transform these back to the parameters originally of interest. Again a single derived parameter can be regarded as part of a larger transformation, and its ML estimate and variance can be readily obtained from the original estimates. Any model has an endless variety of different parametrizations, but we can provide estimates of them all on the basis of a single set of ML estimates; the numerical search involved in estimation (which may be quite arduous) need never be repeated.

We shall use these possibilities time and again in the sequel.

Questions and exercises

3.1 The Engel function which relates household food expenditure c to household income y has been specified as

$$\mathbf{c}_i = \alpha + \beta y_i + \boldsymbol{\epsilon}_i$$

with the ϵ_i independent Normal $(0, \sigma^2)$ variates. We wish to use the food share $w = c/y$ and the income elasticity of food demand $\mu(y)$, both evaluated at the sample mean income $\bar{y}$, to characterize this function instead of α and β. Determine the function g and the matrix G.

3.2 An Engel function of the form

$$c/y = \alpha + \beta \log y$$

has been fitted by OLS to budget survey data on food expenditure c and income y. We wish to examine the income elasticity of food demand $\mu(y)$ at a given income level y^*. Give an estimate of $\mu(y^*)$ and an expression for the variance of this estimate in terms of the familiar OLS estimates a and b and related sample statistics.

3.3 A macroeconomic import demand function $y = x^T\beta$ has been estimated by OLS, with y the (natural) logarithm of the annual import volume. We consider the prediction $y^* = x^{*T}\boldsymbol{b}$ of y at some given x^*, with $\boldsymbol{b}$ the OLS estimator of β. What is its variance? What is the variance of predicted import volume?

3.2 Nested hypotheses

The remainder of this chapter is concerned with statistical tests of $r < l$ independent equality restrictions on the $(l \times 1)$ parameter vector $\theta°$, which we represent by the implicit side relations

$$g_j(\theta) = 0, \qquad j = 1, 2, \ldots, r \tag{10}$$

The vectors that satisfy these equations form an $(l - r)$-dimensional subspace $\Theta°$ of the parameter space Θ, and we shall consider the null hypothesis that $\theta°$ lies in this subspace. The restrictions under review are thus set within the context of a wider parent model, which provides the maintained hypothesis and defines the alternative hypothesis. Written in full the system is

$$\theta° \in \Theta, \quad H_0 : \theta° \in \Theta°, \quad H_1 : \theta° \in \bar{\Theta}.°, \quad \bar{\Theta}° = \Theta - \Theta°$$

In this classical setting the null hypothesis is sometimes called a *nested* hypothesis, with obvious reference to the relative position of $\Theta°$ and Θ. We earlier stipulated, in Section 2.1, that θ can range freely over Θ, so that functions of θ are several times over differentiable in respect of all its elements, at least in the neighborhood of $\theta°$. This property continues to hold under H_0: Since $\Theta°$and $\bar{\Theta}°$ together form the entire well-behaved parameter space Θ, we can differentiate functions of θ at $\theta° \in \Theta°$ in all directions, including those leading to a passage into the alternative parameter space $\bar{\Theta}°$. We shall make use of this facility in deriving the three tests of the present chapter.

When we compare (10) and (1), we see that each restriction is in some (re-) parametrization equivalent to putting one parameter equal to zero, or suppressing it. This usually means a simplification of the model, and in this sense hypotheses of the form (10) express *simplifying* assumptions, as is reflected by the corresponding reduction in the number of dimensions of the parameter space. Starting from a loosely specified very general model with a surfeit of parameters we may arrange successive simplifications in a definite order so as to nest subspaces of ever smaller dimensionality within one another. In obeisance to the *principle of parsimony* we should then move down along this sequence, paring down the number of parameters and thus gradually carving the final sparse specification out of the overblown parent model in which it is concealed, testing all the while to see how far we can go. There is, of course, much more to this methodological prescription, advocated by some as part of a larger research strategy (Mizon and Hendry 1980). But simplifying assumptions or nested hypotheses and the need for relevant statistical tests do, of course, also arise outside this specific context in the natural pursuit of parsimony.

There are other types of hypotheses than (10) and other statistical tests than the three that will be discussed presently. We may, for instance, wish to consider inequality constraints of the parameters and these cannot be handled like the exact restrictions of (10). Again there are specification tests that are based on a model's predictive performance; in the case of failure, there is no definite maintained hypothesis or parent model to fall back on, and for this reason they do not belong to the present class. The third example is non-nested hypotheses, where the hypotheses under consideration do not together constitute a well-behaved maintained hypothesis; if there is just a pair, rejection of the one does not imply acceptance of the other. Any number of non-nested hypotheses may thus be rejected without a positive conclusion (Deaton 1978; Pesaran 1974).

3.3 Constrained estimation

The computational burden of determining ML estimates usually varies in proportion with the number of independent parameters, and in practice the simplest way of estimating θ° subject to (10) is to eliminate r parameters. This is done by adopting a transformation like (1)

$$\eta = g(\theta)$$

while taking care to define the first r elements of the vector function in such a way that they correspond to the restrictions (10), or

$$g_j(\theta) = 0, \qquad j = 1, 2, \ldots, r$$

The remaining functions $g_j(\theta)$ for $j = r + 1, r + 2, \ldots, l$ can be chosen at will, provided the existence of the inverse transformation

$$\theta = g^{-1}(\eta)$$

is assured. Whenever possible the identity is a popular choice. Under H_0 we now have

$$\eta^\circ = \begin{bmatrix} 0 \\ \mathring{\eta}_* \end{bmatrix}$$

and the remaining $l - r$ elements of the subvector η_* can be estimated without constraint. This will yield an estimator $\hat{\eta}_*$ with covariance matrix $V\hat{\eta}_*$. The constrained estimator of the full parameter vector is then

$$\tilde{\eta} = \begin{bmatrix} 0 \\ \hat{\eta}_* \end{bmatrix}, \qquad \tilde{V}^* = V\tilde{\eta} = \begin{bmatrix} 0 & 0 \\ 0 & V\hat{\eta}_* \end{bmatrix}$$

By (2) and (9) we find for the constrained estimator of the original parameter vector θ°

$$\tilde{\theta} = g^{-1}(\tilde{\eta}), \qquad \tilde{V} = V\tilde{\theta} = G^{-1}\tilde{V}^* G^{T^{-1}}$$

It will be clear that r elements of $\tilde{\theta}$ are redundant, and that the rank of $\tilde{V}$ (and of its estimates) is only $l - r$; but apart from this $\tilde{\theta}$ has all the properties of an ML estimator since it is a function of the MLE $\hat{\eta}_*$.

This is a practical method of estimation, but it is not very helpful when we wish to examine the asymptotic distribution of the constrained estimate; for this purpose we turn to constrained maximization of the likelihood function by the Lagrange Multiplier method. To begin with, we rewrite the restrictions (10) as a vector function

$$g_r(\theta) = 0$$

where the suffix now serves to recall that g_r is an $(r \times 1)$ vector. Likewise we write G_r for the $(r \times l)$ matrix which consists of the top r rows of the matrix G of (5). The new maximand is

$$\log L(\theta) - g_r(\theta)^T \mu$$

with μ a vector of r Lagrange multipliers. Differentiation yields $r + l$ first-order conditions that must be satisfied by the constrained estimators $\tilde{\theta}$ and $\tilde{\mu}$, namely,

$$\left.\begin{aligned} q(\tilde{\theta}) - G_r(\tilde{\theta})^T \tilde{\mu} &= 0 \\ g_r(\tilde{\theta}) &= 0 \end{aligned}\right\} \qquad (11)$$

We examine these estimators under H_0, when they are appropriate; as ML estimators they are consistent, and as the sample size increases $\tilde{\boldsymbol{\theta}}$ will converge to $\theta^\circ \in \Theta^\circ$. We suppose indeed that $\tilde{\boldsymbol{\theta}}$ is sufficiently close to θ° to justify several large-sample approximations, as follows:

$$G_r(\tilde{\boldsymbol{\theta}})^T\tilde{\boldsymbol{\mu}} \approx G_r(\theta^\circ)^T\tilde{\boldsymbol{\mu}} \tag{12}$$

$$q(\tilde{\boldsymbol{\theta}}) \approx \boldsymbol{q}(\theta^\circ) + \boldsymbol{Q}(\theta^\circ)\,(\tilde{\boldsymbol{\theta}} - \theta^\circ) \tag{13}$$

$$g_r(\tilde{\boldsymbol{\theta}}) \approx G_r(\theta^\circ)\,(\tilde{\boldsymbol{\theta}} - \theta^\circ) \tag{14}$$

H_0 is used in the last line where we take it that $g_r(\theta^\circ) = 0$.

Upon substitution of these approximations into (11) and some rearrangement of the terms we obtain a system of $r + l$ simultaneous linear equations

$$\begin{bmatrix} -\boldsymbol{Q}(\theta^\circ) & G_r(\theta^\circ)^T \\ G_r(\theta^\circ) & 0 \end{bmatrix}\begin{bmatrix} \tilde{\boldsymbol{\theta}} - \theta^\circ \\ \tilde{\boldsymbol{\mu}} \end{bmatrix} \approx \begin{bmatrix} \boldsymbol{q}(\theta^\circ) \\ 0 \end{bmatrix}$$

or again

$$\begin{bmatrix} \frac{1}{n}\boldsymbol{Q}(\theta^\circ) & G_r(\theta^\circ)^T \\ G_r(\theta^\circ) & 0 \end{bmatrix}\begin{bmatrix} \sqrt{n}(\tilde{\boldsymbol{\theta}} - \theta^\circ) \\ \frac{1}{\sqrt{n}}\tilde{\boldsymbol{\mu}} \end{bmatrix} \approx \begin{bmatrix} \frac{1}{\sqrt{n}}\boldsymbol{q}(\theta^\circ) \\ 0 \end{bmatrix} \tag{15}$$

We now compound these asymptotic approximations with some convergence theorems already used in Chapter 2. The first is (2.47)

$$-\frac{1}{n}\boldsymbol{Q}(\theta^\circ) \xrightarrow{p} \overline{H}$$

Upon substitution in (15) this gives

$$\begin{bmatrix} \sqrt{n}(\tilde{\boldsymbol{\theta}} - \theta^\circ) \\ \frac{1}{\sqrt{n}}\tilde{\boldsymbol{\mu}} \end{bmatrix} \approx \begin{bmatrix} \overline{H} & G_r(\theta^\circ)^T \\ G_r(\theta^\circ) & 0 \end{bmatrix}^{-1}\begin{bmatrix} \frac{1}{\sqrt{n}}\boldsymbol{q}(\theta^\circ) \\ 0 \end{bmatrix} \tag{16}$$

The other limit theorem is (2.49)

$$\frac{1}{\sqrt{n}}\boldsymbol{q}(\theta^\circ) \xrightarrow{L} N(0, \overline{H})$$

It follows that the $r + l$ vector on the left of (16) is also asymptotically

Normal with zero mean and with covariance matrix

$$\begin{bmatrix} \overline{H} & G_r^T \\ G_r & 0 \end{bmatrix}^{-1} \begin{bmatrix} \overline{H} & 0 \\ 0 & 0 \end{bmatrix} \begin{bmatrix} \overline{H} & G_r^T \\ G_r & 0 \end{bmatrix}^{-1}$$

If we write

$$\begin{bmatrix} \overline{H} & G_r^T \\ G_r & 0 \end{bmatrix}^{-1} = \begin{bmatrix} A & B^T \\ B & C \end{bmatrix}. \tag{17}$$

we find for the covariance matrix of the asymptotic distribution

$$V \begin{bmatrix} \sqrt{n}(\tilde{\theta} - \theta^\circ) \\ \frac{1}{\sqrt{n}} \tilde{\mu} \end{bmatrix} = \begin{bmatrix} A\overline{H}A & A\overline{H}B^T \\ B\overline{H}A & B\overline{H}B^T \end{bmatrix}$$

For the asymptotic covariance matrices of the estimates themselves we must take account of the terms in n; we find

$$V\tilde{\theta} = \frac{1}{n} A\overline{H}A,\; A = \overline{H}^{-1} - \overline{H}^{-1}G_r^T(G_r\overline{H}^{-1}G_r^T)^{-1}G_r\overline{H}^{-1} \tag{18}$$

$$V\tilde{\mu} = n\, B\overline{H}B^T,\; B = (G_r\overline{H}^{-1}G_r^T)^{-1}G_r\overline{H}^{-1} \tag{19}$$

where A and B have been obtained by applying the standard formulae for the inverse of a partitioned matrix to (17).[6] After some simplification this yields

$$\begin{aligned} \tilde{V} = V\tilde{\theta} &= \frac{1}{n}\overline{H}^{-1}(I - G_r^T(G_r\overline{H}^{-1}G_r^T)^{-1}G_r\overline{H}^{-1}) \\ &= H^{-1}(I - G_r^T(G_rH^{-1}G_r^T)^{-1}G_rH^{-1}) \end{aligned} \tag{20}$$

since $H = n\overline{H}$ by (2.43). The matrix in parentheses has the same structure, and hence much the same properties, as the "projection matrix" of the linear regression model in its Generalized Least Squares version (Theil 1971: 241). It is idempotent, as is readily verified, and hence its rank equals its trace (Theil 1971: 29). This trace is the difference of the traces of two terms. The first is a unit matrix of order l, with trace l; the second term is itself idempotent and of rank r, since it includes G_r, and hence of trace r. Altogether the rank of (20) is $l - r$, which is as it should be since the l elements of $\tilde{\theta}$ satisfy the r restrictions of (10).

As for $\tilde{\mu}$, we seldom explicitly determine these estimates, and there is little interest in their asymptotic covariance matrix; for the record we

[6] These formulas can for instance be found in the textbooks of Silvey (1970: 177) and Theil (1971: 17).

mention that (19) leads to

$$V\tilde{\mu} = n(G_r\overline{H}^{-1}G_r^{\mathrm{T}})^{-1} = (G_rH^{-1}G_r^{\mathrm{T}})^{-1} \tag{21}$$

Questions and exercises

3.4 Verify that the three models of Exercise 2.10 are nested, and establish the restrictions in the form of (10) for (a) model 2 relative to 1, (b) model 3 relative to 2, (c) and model 3 relative to 1.

3.5 Consider two rival regression models for the same phenomenon

1. $y_i = \alpha + \beta x_i + \gamma z_i + \epsilon_i$, ϵ_i independent $N(0, \sigma^2)$
2. $y_i = \alpha + \beta x_i + v_i$, $v_i = \rho v_{i-1} + \epsilon_i^*$, ϵ_i^* independent $N(0, \sigma_*^2)$

Are these two models nested? Are they each nested within a third model? Is there a fourth model which is nested both within 1 and within 2?

3.6 Consider the linear regression model

$$y_i = \alpha + \beta x_i + \gamma z_i + \epsilon_i$$

Taking for granted that ML and OLS estimation coincide, what regression equations would you use for constrained estimation under the hypotheses

(a) $\gamma = 0$ (b) $\beta = \gamma$ (c) $\gamma = \beta + 3$ (d) $\gamma = 3$?

3.4 Likelihood Ratio test

This test is based on the likelihood function. If H_0 holds, and hence $\theta^\circ \in \Theta^\circ$, the unconstrained maximum $L(\hat{\theta})$ should be close to the constrained maximum $L(\tilde{\theta})$. We therefore consider the *likelihood ratio*

$$\lambda = L(\tilde{\theta}) \,/\, L(\hat{\theta})$$

As all likelihoods are positive, and as the constrained maximum cannot exceed the unconstrained maximum, $0 < \lambda \leqq 1$. The quantity

$$\boldsymbol{LR} = -2 \log \lambda = 2\left(\log L(\hat{\theta}) - \log L(\tilde{\theta})\right) \tag{22}$$

is therefore always nonnegative, and we shall show that under H_0 it is asymptotically distributed as chi-square with r degrees of freedom, or

$$\boldsymbol{LR} \xrightarrow{L} \chi^2(r) \tag{23}$$

$\boldsymbol{LR}$ can thus serve as a test statistic for H_0.

Once more we examine a Taylor series expansion

$$\log L(\tilde{\theta}) - \log L(\hat{\theta}) \approx q\,(\hat{\theta})^T(\tilde{\theta} - \hat{\theta}) + \tfrac{1}{2}(\tilde{\theta} - \hat{\theta})^T Q(\hat{\theta})(\tilde{\theta} - \hat{\theta}) \tag{24}$$

The first term on the right-hand side vanishes since $q(\hat{\theta}) = 0$ by (2.37); by the consistency of $\hat{\theta}$ and (2.47)

$$-\frac{1}{n}\boldsymbol{Q}(\hat{\theta}) \xrightarrow{p} \overline{H}$$

We simplify (24) accordingly, and substitute the result in (22). This gives

$$\boldsymbol{LR} \approx \sqrt{n}(\tilde{\boldsymbol{\theta}} - \hat{\boldsymbol{\theta}})^T\overline{H}(\tilde{\boldsymbol{\theta}} - \hat{\boldsymbol{\theta}})\sqrt{n} \tag{25}$$

We already know from (16) and (17) that under H_0

$$\sqrt{n}(\tilde{\boldsymbol{\theta}} - \theta°) \approx A\frac{1}{\sqrt{n}}\boldsymbol{q}(\theta°)$$

and from (2.46) and (2.47) that

$$\sqrt{n}(\hat{\boldsymbol{\theta}} - \theta°) \approx \overline{H}^{-1}\frac{1}{\sqrt{n}}\boldsymbol{q}(\theta°)$$

so that

$$\sqrt{n}(\tilde{\boldsymbol{\theta}} - \hat{\boldsymbol{\theta}}) \approx (A - \overline{H}^{-1})\frac{1}{\sqrt{n}}\boldsymbol{q}(\theta°) \tag{26}$$

We now recall once more (2.49)

$$\frac{1}{\sqrt{n}}\boldsymbol{q}(\theta°) \xrightarrow{L} N(0, \overline{H})$$

so that

$$\frac{1}{\sqrt{n}}\overline{H}^{-1/2}\boldsymbol{q}(\theta°) \xrightarrow{L} \boldsymbol{\epsilon} \sim N(0, I) \tag{27}$$

Here $\boldsymbol{\epsilon}$ is a vector of l standard Normal variates that are uncorrelated and hence (since they are Normal) independent. By (26) and (27), moreover,

$$\sqrt{n}(\tilde{\boldsymbol{\theta}} - \hat{\boldsymbol{\theta}}) \approx (A - \overline{H}^{-1})\overline{H}^{1/2}\boldsymbol{\epsilon}$$

Upon substituting this into (25) and making use of (18) for A we finally obtain

$$\boldsymbol{LR} \approx \boldsymbol{\epsilon}^T\overline{H}^{-1/2}G_r^T(G_r\overline{H}^{-1}G_r^T)^{-1}G_r\overline{H}^{-1/2}\boldsymbol{\epsilon} \tag{28}$$

This is a quadratic form in independent standard Normal variates, with a nonstochastic idempotent coefficient matrix that is of rank r because of the order of G_r; and it is therefore distributed as chi-square with r

degrees of freedom (Rao 1973: 186). And this is what we set out to prove in (23).

3.5 Wald's test

This test is based on the functions $g_j(\theta)$ of (10). If H_0 holds the $g_j(\theta^\circ)$ are zero, and the $g_j(\hat{\theta})$ should presumably be close to zero. Suppose for a moment that we adopt the transformation (1), and consider η; then, under H_0, the first r elements of η° are zero, and this can be tested by examining the first r elements of the estimator $\hat{\eta}$, say $\hat{\eta}_r$. The covariance matrix of these elements is the leading $(r \times r)$ submatrix of (9)

$$V^* = GVG^T$$

with $V^* = V\hat{\eta}$ and $V = V\hat{\theta}$. The leading submatrix is then

$$V\hat{\eta}_r = G_r V G_r^T$$

where G_r consists of the top r rows of G, as before. Similarly, since by Section 2.9

$$\sqrt{n}(\hat{\theta} - \theta^\circ) \xrightarrow{L} N(0, \bar{H}^{-1})$$

we also have

$$\sqrt{n}(\hat{\eta}_r - \eta_r^\circ) \xrightarrow{L} N(0, G_r \bar{H}^{-1} G_r^T)$$

Under H_0 $\eta_r^\circ = 0$, and we use this in the quadratic form

$$\sqrt{n}\hat{\eta}_r^T (G_r \bar{H}^{-1} G_r^T)^{-1} \hat{\eta}_r \sqrt{n} = \hat{\eta}_r^T (G_r V G_r^T)^{-1} \hat{\eta}_r \xrightarrow{L} \chi^2(r)$$

The Wald test statistic is the sample counterpart

$$\mathbf{W} = \hat{\eta}_r^T (\hat{\mathbf{G}}_r \hat{\mathbf{V}} \hat{\mathbf{G}}_r^T)^{-1} \hat{\eta} \tag{29}$$

with $\hat{\mathbf{V}}$ some estimator of V (that is $V\hat{\theta}$), and $\hat{\mathbf{G}}_r$ equal to $G_r(\hat{\theta})$. By the consistency of $\hat{\theta}$ and Slutsky's theorem these all converge to the true values, and

$$\mathbf{W} \xrightarrow{L} \chi^2(r) \tag{30}$$

This establishes the asymptotic distribution of Wald's test statistic.

In practice we need not actually perform the transformation since we may use (1) and rewrite (29) as

$$\mathbf{W} = g_r^T(\hat{\theta}) (\hat{\mathbf{G}}_r \hat{\mathbf{V}} \hat{\mathbf{G}}_r^T)^{-1} g_r(\hat{\theta}) \tag{31}$$

We can therefore construct the test statistic from the original unconstrained estimate $\hat{\theta}$ and its covariance matrix estimate $\hat{V}$ with the help of the restriction functions g_r of (10) and their first derivatives which form G_r.

3.6 Lagrange multiplier test

This test is also known as the Rao efficient score test or as the chi-square test (Silvey 1970: 118). It is based on the score vector $q(\theta)$ of the original parametrization. When we evaluate this vector at the constrained estimate $\tilde{\theta}$ the result is $q(\tilde{\theta})$, and under H_0 this should be close to the value of the score vector at the unconstrained estimate, which is of course zero.

In order to examine the asymptotic distribution of $q(\tilde{\theta})$ we once more start off from a Taylor series

$$q(\tilde{\theta}) \approx q(\hat{\theta}) + Q(\hat{\theta})(\tilde{\theta} - \hat{\theta}) \tag{32}$$

and use $q(\hat{\theta}) = 0$ and $Q(\hat{\theta}) \approx -H$, as before. This yields

$$q(\tilde{\theta}) \approx H(\hat{\theta} - \tilde{\theta})$$

or

$$\frac{1}{\sqrt{n}} q(\tilde{\theta}) \approx \overline{H} \sqrt{n}(\hat{\theta} - \tilde{\theta})$$

so that

$$\frac{1}{\sqrt{n}} q(\tilde{\theta})^T \overline{H}^{-1} q(\tilde{\theta}) \frac{1}{\sqrt{n}} = q(\tilde{\theta})^T H^{-1} q(\tilde{\theta}) \approx \sqrt{n}(\hat{\theta} - \tilde{\theta})^T \overline{H}(\hat{\theta} - \tilde{\theta})\sqrt{n} \tag{33}$$

and this by (25) is the Likelihood Ratio test statistic, which we know to be asymptotically chi-square (r) distributed. This will also hold if we replace H in (33) by a consistent estimate, as in the test statistic

$$LM = q(\tilde{\theta})^T \hat{V}(\tilde{\theta})\, q(\tilde{\theta}) \tag{34}$$

This is based on the second expression in (33), and we have replaced H^{-1} by some estimator $\hat{V}$ of $V\hat{\theta}$, evaluated at the constrained estimator $\tilde{\theta}$ – just as the score vectors q here take their *form* from the unconstrained estimation problem, but their *values* from the constrained estimator $\tilde{\theta}$. In order to calculate the test statistic $\tilde{\theta}$ is the only estimate we need determine.

By the first line of (11)

$$q(\tilde{\theta}) \approx G_r(\tilde{\theta})^T \tilde{\mu}$$

so that

$$LM \approx \tilde{\mu}^T \tilde{G}_r\, \hat{V}(\tilde{\theta})\, \tilde{G}_r^T \tilde{\mu}$$

with $\tilde{G}_r = G_r(\tilde{\theta})$. Under H_0 $\hat{V}(\tilde{\theta})$ is of course a consistent estimate of $V\hat{\theta}$ or H^{-1}, so that upon comparison with (21) the LM test statistic may be regarded as a standardized quadratic form in the estimated Lagrange Multipliers. This may explain the usual name of the test.

3.7 Discussion

All we have shown is that *under the null hypothesis* the three test statistics have the same asymptotic distribution; in the alternative case they need not at all have the same asymptotic behavior. Again, in a finite sample the three test statistics usually take different values, and at the present level of generality nothing can be said about their exact distribution, under the null hypothesis or otherwise. Without further knowledge of the finite-sample properties of the tests in a particular application they are of little use, since it is hard to tell what significance levels from an asymptotic distribution mean if the evidence comes from a small sample. In certain applications it has, however, proved possible to derive the exact distribution of one or other of the present test statistics or of its transformation. Failing this, the finite-sample performance of the tests may always be established by simulation studies.

In certain cases the asymptotic test statistic is thus taken as the starting point of a further investigation, as a suggestion for an exact approach. This applies in particular to the Likelihood Ratio test; as it is the oldest of the three it has been studied more intensively than the other two. It was introduced by Fisher in the 1920s and adopted in Neyman and Pearson's testing methodology of a decade later. The next test was that of Wald (1943), and the most recent is the Lagrange Multiplier test (Rao 1948; Silvey 1959).

If we do not have the benefit of further analyses, and a large sample that inspires some confidence in the validity of asymptotic results, the choice between the three tests may be affected by expediency. Each requires different computations. For the LR test we must maximize the likelihood function twice, with and without restrictions; for the Wald test we need unconstrained parameter estimates with their covariance matrix; and for Silvey's test, constrained estimates and their covariance matrix. Some ingredients may be easier to obtain than others.

Questions and exercises

3.7 $z_1, z_2, \ldots, z_n$ are realizations of independent $N(\mu, \sigma^2)$ variates. Establish LR test statistics of (a) $\mu = 0$, (b) $\sigma^2 = 1$, (c) $\mu = 0$ *and* $\sigma^2 = 1$.

3.8 Consider the regression equation

$$y_i = \beta_0 + x_i^T\beta + \epsilon_i$$

where β contains no intercept and x_i no constant. We find

$$\log L(\beta_0, \beta) = -\frac{n}{2} \log \sum_i (y_i - \beta_0 - x_i^T\beta)^2$$

What is the test statistic for $\beta = 0$? Show that it is monotonically related to the familiar F statistic.

3.9 Consider the hypothesis that a single regression coefficient is zero and derive the Wald test statistic, making use of the familiar OLS regression formula for $V\beta$. Compare with the standard t-test.

3.10 For the regression equation

$$y_i = \beta_0 + \beta_1 x_i + \beta_2 z_i + \epsilon_i$$

use the familiar OLS formulas for $V\hat{\beta}$ in establishing Wald and LM test statistics for the hypothesis $\beta_1 + \beta_2 = 0$.

CHAPTER 4

The use of likelihood in econometrics

This chapter is concerned with the justification of likelihood methods in the specific context of econometric analyses. This question prompts responses at various levels. In discussing it we cannot entirely avoid philosophical and ideological issues on which readers must form their own opinions. Some views that bear on the interpretation of the asymptotic argument turn out to have practical implications.

The simplest justification of Maximum Likelihood estimation is the immediate intuitive appeal of assigning values to the unknown parameters that maximize the probability of the events that have in fact occurred. Many people find this idea equally satisfying as the *correspondence principle* of equating population parameters to their sample counterparts, as in the *method of moments.* Maximum Likelihood estimation indeed also falls into this category, for the maximum conditions of Section 2.6 that determine the MLE

$$q(\hat{\theta}) = 0, \qquad Q(\hat{\theta}) \text{ negative definite}$$

exactly match the conditions of (2.15, 2.16) for their expected values at $\theta°$, or, by (2.9) and (2.11, 12)

$$\psi'(\theta°) = E\boldsymbol{q}(\theta°) = 0$$

$$\psi''(\theta°) = E\boldsymbol{Q}(\theta°) = -H \text{ negative definite}$$

We have nothing to add to these arguments, which may or may not appeal to the reader. This also holds for the Likelihood Principle, stated as an axiom by Edwards (1972); but this is in another class, since it is developed by the author into a complete theory of inference of his own.

It can also be claimed that ML estimators and the related tests have heuristic value, since in certain cases they turn out to have much stronger properties than follows from the general argument. In the linear regression model, for instance, the MLE of β coincides with the OLS estimator, which is Best Linear Unbiased. Again, the likelihood tests of Chapter 3 may at times lead the way to tests of known small-sample qualities.

4.1 A Bayesian interpretation

In the Bayesian approach to inference we assign to the unknown parameter θ° a proper probability distribution that reflects the knowledge or ignorance of the analyst. Before embarking on the analysis at issue, the analyst holds certain views about the parameters, and these beliefs are described by this *prior* density $p(\theta)$ of $\boldsymbol{\theta}^\circ$. Since $\boldsymbol{\theta}^\circ$ now technically is a random variable, not a constant, the density function (2.1) of the sample y represents a *conditional* density, and we must rewrite it as

$$p_{y|\theta^\circ}(w|\theta^\circ; x) = p_y(w, \theta^\circ, x) \tag{1}$$

But for the change in interpretation indicated by the vertical bar this is of course exactly the same expression as the density (2.1) and the likelihood (2.2). We continue to treat the x as known nonrandom constants or parameters, as we did throughout Chapters 2 and 3.

By the common algebra of conditional, joint, and marginal distributions we can write

$$\begin{aligned} p(y|\theta^\circ; x)p(\theta^\circ) &= p(y, \theta^\circ; x) \\ &= p(\theta^\circ|y; x)p(y; x) \end{aligned} \tag{2}$$

and hence

$$p(\theta^\circ|y; x) = \frac{p(y|\theta^\circ; x)p(\theta^\circ)}{p(y; x)}$$

Since

$$p(y; x) = Ep(y|\boldsymbol{\theta}^\circ; x)$$

where the mathematical expectation is taken over $\boldsymbol{\theta}^\circ$, $p(y; x)$ does not depend on $\boldsymbol{\theta}^\circ$, and we may replace it by a constant. Hence

$$p(\theta^\circ|y; x) = c\, p(y|\theta^\circ; x)p(\theta^\circ) \tag{3}$$

If prior beliefs about $\boldsymbol{\theta}^\circ$ are vague and uninformative, its distribution will be widely spread and almost uniformly flat, its density nearly constant. Skipping the technical translation of these notions we may say that the term $p(\theta^\circ)$ will then be of little importance for (3), and that the conditional density (1) will predominate. Upon rescaling the right-hand side so that it yields a proper density function with unit integral we obtain

$$p(\theta^\circ|y; x) \approx c' p(y|\theta^\circ; x) \tag{4}$$

On the left we now have the *posterior* distribution of $\boldsymbol{\theta}^\circ$ which represents the analyst's beliefs about the unknown parameters after taking into account the evidence of the observed $\{x,y\}$; and on the left we have the conditional density, which is the same function as the likelihood (2.2). Both show the same behavior as θ° varies over Θ.

The Bayesian analyst may of course wish to summarize the acquired knowledge by a few statistics of location and dispersion rather than by the full posterior distribution itself. Insofar as the approximation (4) holds, the ML estimate will correspond to its mode, and if the posterior distribution is unimodal and symmetric it corresponds to the mean and the median as well. For a measure of dispersion we will turn to the covariance matrix of the posterior distribution, and in specific cases this may again lead to the same expressions as we find for the asymptotic covariance matrix of the MLE. The confidence regions based on the MLE then turn into concentration ellipsoids of the posterior distribution.

This brief discussion hardly does justice to the Bayesian argument; there is obviously much more to it, both in the present context and without. We refer the reader to the literature (Box and Tiao 1973; DeGroot 1975; Zellner 1971). But however interesting and illuminating it may be to rediscover certain likelihood statistics in the Bayesian approach, this is a very roundabout way of justifying the orthodox likelihood methodology.

4.2 Asymptotic behavior

We now turn to the asymptotic properties of the ML estimators of Chapter 2 – consistency, asymptotic unbiasedness, Normality, and efficiency – and to the neat asymptotic distributions of the test statistics of Chapter 3. All this holds in the limit only, and it may well be asked in what sense it is relevant to practical applications, which are inevitably restricted to finite samples.

In statistical writings the standard explanation is that asymptotic results are *approximately* valid in large samples, and that we can make the approximation as close as we wish by increasing the sample size. This presupposes that the observations are generated by a well-defined statistical experiment, and that increasing their number is a practical proposition. In many cases the latter condition is not met, if only for reasons of costs or of time. We may then still derive substantial intellectual satisfaction from considering the hypothetical case. The firm knowledge that the sample statistics would increasingly adopt quite attractive properties if the sample were extended does add to their appeal.

Even if the sample cannot in fact be enlarged, however, we must still specify how we envisage this hypothetical process to take place. In statistics this presents no difficulties since, whatever the phenomenon under review, the model always specifies the probability distribution from which successive observations are drawn. In econometrics, however, the observations consist of pairs $\{x_i, y_i\}$, and while the distribution of y_i for given x_i is determined by the model specification (2.1), we must still indicate how new values of x_i are generated as the sample is extended. The reason for this is that the limit theorems that we have used in Sections 2.8 and 2.9 depend on "certain conditions." Thus the consistency of $\hat{\theta}$ turned on the application of Tchebychev's weak law of large numbers to

$$\frac{1}{n}\sum_i \log \boldsymbol{L}_i(\theta)$$

and this depends on the variance of $\log \boldsymbol{L}_i(\theta)$ being uniformly bounded. Again, in deriving the asymptotic normality of $\hat{\theta}$ we made use of Liapounov's Central Limit Theorem for

$$\frac{1}{\sqrt{n}}\boldsymbol{q}_n(\theta^\circ)$$

and this requires a complicated bound for the mean variance of the individual scores. We refer once more for the details to Gnedenko (1962: 240, 360). We can, of course, verify these conditions only if we know the precise model specification, and hence the functional form of the loglikelihood and of the scores. But both expressions will as a rule be functions of the x_i, and in order to examine their behavior for $n \to \infty$ we must specify how the additional x_i are generated.

Since the hypothetical case of extending the sample is an abstraction anyhow (like all considerations of the infinite), it is sometimes argued that we may make light of the problem, as it can always be resolved by putting forward some imaginary scheme. We shall come across one or two examples below. It is, however, questionable whether this is legitimate; perhaps we should insist that the scheme can in principle be implemented. What "in principle" means is open to interpretation and controversy, but there are cases where the distinction is clear. Tossing coins or casting dice are tedious exercises, and as a statistical experiment they will ultimately break down, as the coins and dice are affected by wear and tear. Yet few people would dispute that these experiments can "in principle" continue forever. Again we may almost indefinitely dig or drill holes in the earth to find out whether they will yield gold or oil. Once a number of hoards of Roman coins of varying age have been discovered we may be tempted to treat these as a sample from all treasure ever buried in the soil; but now we must wait for the next find to increase the sample size, and the principle is wearing thin. In the realm of econometrics we may be asked to visualize a re-run of the economic history of the 1930s, starting from the initial conditions of January 1, 1928. It requires a strong mind to accept this as a feasible statistical experiment.

The issue whether the number of observations can be increased at will is not only relevant to the validity of asymptotic arguments, but it may even decide whether mathematical statistics apply at all. Ever since Laplace, its subject matter is variously described as mass phenomena (Kendall and Stuart 1963: I, 1) or as uncertain phenomena that exhibit a predictable regularity in the long run (Mood, Graybill, and Boes 1974: 2). The real question is, in either case, whether the results of statistical reasoning may be applied by analogy to unique events. On this point opinions differ. Gnedenko limits statistics to uncertain phenomena that can in principle be reproduced infinitely often (1962: 26), but others are less strict. Thus Feller asserts that "practical and useful probability models may refer to non-observable worlds" (1957: I, 4), and Cramér refers to the "hypothetical infinite population of all experiments that might have been performed" under given conditions (1946: 144). Cox and Hinkley write that "with 'unique' data, such as economic time series, repetition under identical conditions is entirely hypothetical. Nevertheless the introduction of probability models does seem a fruitful way of trying to separate the meaningful from the accidental features of the data" (1974: 5).

It is clear that time series of economic aggregates do not constitute a mass phenomenon nor the outcome of an experiment that can ever be repeated. On a severe interpretation, mathematical statistics and classical inference (as opposed to Bayesian methods) do not apply to such data. A substantial part of the accumulated results of applied econometrics would therefore have to be discarded altogether. The contrary view cannot be defended on rational grounds. In the last analysis, it is a matter of belief in the power of analogy, for it has no other support.

Readers must make up their own minds on this question. In the sequel we restrict the discussion to the practical problem of what additional assumptions (if any) are needed to permit hypothetical or real increases in the sample size.

4.3 Statistical models

By a statistical model we mean a model without explanatory or exogenous variables x. The original model specification (2.1) reduces to

$$p_y(w, \theta^\circ) \tag{5}$$

and its counterpart (2.39) for independent individual y_i to

$$p(w_*, \theta^\circ) \tag{6}$$

The observed sample has been drawn, as it were, from a single distribution, and the same density function holds for each of the observations we have, as well as for any additional observations. We may thus conceive of an extension of the sample without making further assumptions.

There are two examples of statistical models for economic data. The first is the analysis of size distributions, such as the income distribution. If we assume random sampling, (6) is the population density and y_i an income taken at random.

The second example is a purely autoregressive model of time series, such as

$$y_t = \beta y_{t-1} + \epsilon_t \tag{7}$$

with the ϵ_t independent $N(0, \sigma^2)$ variates. The issue is complicated by the fact that it is not the observed y_t but the underlying ϵ_t which are independent, but it is quite clear from the model formulation itself how we would extend the sample if we could, namely by drawing additional ϵ_t from the inexhaustible supply of independent Normal variates, and generating further y_t. In principle one might also add to the sample at the other end, and extend the period of observation backward, but this raises conceptual and technical problems. As a rule, the probability density of the sample and hence the likelihood function are taken as conditional on the starting value of the process, and y_0 is therefore not a random variable like the others. We must therefore extend the sample at the other end only.

No new problems arise if y_t is a vector or if the number of autoregressive lags is increased. The case is conceptually simple, although it is of course usually quite impracticable; but we have already dealt with that objection above, and it is immaterial to the present discussion.

As we shall see in the next section, the autoregressive statistical model may be naturally extended to include exogenous variables as well.

4.4 Economic aggregates

Econometrics is sometimes identified exclusively with the regression analysis of time series of macroeconomic aggregates. This traditional pursuit in the spirit of Tinbergen (1939) indeed still constitutes the major part of applied work. Outside likelihood methods, considerations of the asymptotic behavior of these variables already arise when we wish to establish the consistency of the OLS estimator. In the standard model

$$y = X\beta + \epsilon$$

this is

$$\boldsymbol{b} = (X^T X)^{-1} X^T y = \beta + (X^T X)^{-1} X^T \epsilon$$

With the classical assumption of independent and identically distributed disturbances with zero mean and constant variance, the behavior of ϵ with increasing n is clear. For the asymptotic behavior of $\boldsymbol{b}$, however, additional assumptions are needed about X. In the present case, consistency of $\boldsymbol{b}$ requires

$$\lim_{n \to \infty} (X^T X)^{-1} = 0 \tag{8}$$

but this is usually replaced by

$$\lim_{n \to \infty} \frac{1}{n} (X^T X) = Q \tag{9}$$

with Q a positive definite matrix (Malinvaud 1964: 184; Theil 1971: 363). This is unduly restrictive, as the example of a trend variable shows, but it is easier to handle and perhaps easier to understand.

Can we think of a way of extending a sample that meets condition (9)? The question first arose in the Cowles Commission's work on the estimation of simultaneous economic models, and it was answered by a suggestion of Hotelling of a few years earlier (Hotelling 1940; Koopmans and Hood 1953: 119; Theil 1971: 365). This is the idea of keeping X "constant in repeated samples." If the observed values of x form an $(n_\circ \times k)$ matrix $X_\circ$, n is increased by multiples of $n_\circ$ and the entire array $X_\circ$ is reproduced over and over again. As a result

$$\lim_{n \to \infty} \frac{1}{n} (X^T X) = \frac{1}{n_\circ} X_\circ^T X_\circ$$

so that we can, throughout, use the sample values without compunction. In this view the x remain nonrandom variables; it has obviously been inspired by the case where X represents the control variables in a series of controlled experiments. But econometrics does not permit such experiments, least of all where macroeconomic aggregates are concerned, and in that context it is a highly artificial and purely hypothetical case.

A different view is that time series data accrue through the actual passage of calendar time. A time trend regressor would thus take the values $1, 2, \ldots, n_\circ, (n_\circ + 1), \ldots$, and increase beyond all bounds; this meets condition (8), and consistency is assured. On the "constant in repeated samples" view the time trend would run over and over again from 1 to n_0, and then (9) would hold too. The view of macroeconomic time series as continuing chronicles is both natural and realistic. But if this view is adopted, (9) implies assumptions about the future course of the real world: The regressor variables must show stationary behavior, and the same economic structure that is reflected by their variances and covariances must persist indefinitely.

An alternative approach is to regard all economic aggregates at time t as the outcome of a single vast generalized autoregressive vector process. As in the case of (7), current values are completely determined by a set of initial conditions and by the subsequent random shocks administered to the system. In this view the dependent variables $\mathbf{y}_t$ and the exogenous variables $\mathbf{x}_t$ both belong to a random vector $\mathbf{z}_t$, which follows a complex dynamic stochastic process involving independent multivariate random shocks with a given distribution. This is once more enough to define the system's course to infinity.

Since $\mathbf{x}_t$ is now just as much (a realization of) a random variable as $\mathbf{y}_t$ we must change the basic probability density of the sample (2.1) and the density of a single observation (2.39). Since we are dealing with an autoregressive process the latter are no longer independent, and the relation between the two densities is not so simple as in Section 2.7. We deal with these matters in Section 9.1; for present purposes it is sufficient to define

$$\mathbf{z}_t = \begin{bmatrix} \mathbf{y}_t \\ \mathbf{x}_t \end{bmatrix}$$

and to state that the model can always be solved to yield a probability density function of $\mathbf{z}_t$,

$$f_{\mathbf{z}_t}(w_t, \theta^\circ, z_\circ)$$

with $z_\circ$ denoting initial conditions. Since $\mathbf{y}_t$ and $\mathbf{x}_t$ are now generated by the same stochastic process, however, an operational distinction between dependent and exogenous variables is in order, and this has been provided by Engle, Hendry, and Richard (1983). The density above is the *joint* density of $\mathbf{y}_t$ and $\mathbf{x}_t$, and this can always be expressed as the product of the conditional density of $\mathbf{y}_t|x_t$ and of the marginal density of $\mathbf{x}_t$. Now consider the special case that this product can be written as

$$f_{\mathbf{z}_t}(w_t, \theta^\circ, z_\circ) = f_{\mathbf{y}_t}(v_t|x_t, \theta_1^\circ, z_\circ) f_{\mathbf{x}_t}(u_t, \theta_2^\circ, z_\circ) \tag{10}$$

for some appropriate parametrization of the model. The salient feature of this decomposition is that the two densities have no parameters in common, and this defines the $\mathbf{x}_t$ as *weakly exogenous*. Note that this is a relative property: The x_t are exogenous in respect of a particular set y_t. As a result of (10), the likelihood can be similarly partitioned, and the loglikelihood is the sum of two terms in θ_1 and in θ_2, respectively. Maximization of the conditional loglikelihood with the x_t treated as constants therefore yields the same MLE of θ_1° as maximization of the joint loglikelihood. While this requires a little further development for the present autoregressive model, it is immediately obvious in the case of independent observations, as will be demonstrated in the next section.

So much for the perpetual generation of macroeconomic time series. I know of no similar specific models for cross section aggregate data, as in the analysis of a number of countries, states, or regions, or of industries. The "constant in repeated samples" model will hold equally well (or equally badly) as for time series, but there is no hope that the number of observations will grow spontaneously. One would like to think of a sampling framework, but the observed sample usually covers the entire population, and some imaginary superpopulation must be invented to support the notion.

4.5 Genuine samples

In the case of surveys of individuals, households, firms, or the like, the data are a genuine sample from a real population and increasing the sample size presents neither conceptual nor practical problems. Provided sampling takes place "with replacement," an infinite sample can be drawn even from a finite population, and in this process the sample statistics will converge in probability to their population counterpart, as will the sample relationships. Malinvaud has argued with some force that we should acknowledge the essential stochastic character of causal economic relations even in the population (1964: 70). For the purpose of statistical inference, however, it would appear that we can best treat the population with all its characteristic properties as a nonrandom phenomenon, leaving the wider issue of generalizations from a population open. Hence the population is determinate, and the stochastic character of the observations is entirely due to their generation by a randomized sampling scheme. It is the *i*th observation itself that is drawn at random, and consequently the x_i are just as much (realizations of) random variables as the y_i. This calls again for a change in the basic density (2.1) for the sample and in (2.39) for a single independent observation. The model specification, which summarizes the object of the analysis, remains unchanged, but the same function now represents a *conditional* density,

$$p(w_*, x_i, \theta^\circ) = p(w_* | x_i; \theta^\circ) \tag{11}$$

If we wish to consider the probability density of the observation in full we must of course take the *joint* density of $\boldsymbol{x}_i$ and $\boldsymbol{y}_i$,

$$g(w_*, v_*, \theta^\circ, \eta^\circ) = p(w_* | x_i; \theta^\circ) h(v_*; \eta^\circ) \tag{12}$$

Here v_* is the argument of the distribution of $\boldsymbol{x}_i$, and η° is some unknown parameter vector governing its marginal density

$$h(v_*; \eta^\circ) \tag{13}$$

In the case of random sampling the joint and marginal densities correspond of course to the joint and marginal frequency functions of the population.

The conditional and marginal densities of the decomposition (12) once again have no parameters in common. In the sampling context under review this is not a very special and rare conditon; in many cases it is a natural assumption, and in practice, the joint density is frequently constructed in this way. There are examples of this where (11) is an Engel function and (13) an income distribution, and where (11) is a model of individual transport choice and (13) the distribution of the relevant determinants in the population (Aitchison and Brown 1957: 122 ff.; Westin 1974). Both cases are concerned with aggregation, and with population frequency distributions rather than with sample densities as a basis for inference, but the problem is the same.

A moment's reflection will show that separability may not only be assumed in the case of random sampling from the population but also with more complex sampling schemes. The selection procedure may even be related to the values taken by the $\boldsymbol{x}_i$, when we have additional "selection" parameters ζ° and

$$g(w_*, v_*, \theta^\circ, \eta^\circ, \zeta^\circ) = p(w_* | x_i; \theta^\circ) h(v_*; \eta^\circ, \zeta^\circ)$$

But for the substitution of $(\eta^\circ, \zeta^\circ)$ for η° this function does not differ from (12), and both lead to much the same expression if we pass from densities to likelihood functions, take logarithms, and sum over all observations, as in

$$\log L_j(y, x, \theta, \eta, \zeta) = \log L_a(y, x, \theta) + \log L_m(x, \eta, \zeta) \tag{14}$$

As long as we are interested in θ° only it makes no difference whether we estimate these parameters by maximizing L_j or L_a; for the proper interpretation of asymptotic theory we should consider the joint density and the joint likelihood L_j, but the common practice of using the conditional function L_a yields the same results.

This argument does not materially change if the selection rule and its parameters ζ would enter into the conditional density (11), but it no longer holds if the sample selection depends on the endogenous variables y_i and hence on the parameter values θ°. There are some examples of this where y is labor market behavior and the sample is drawn from a special category that reflects a particular behavioral choice, as when the sample is restricted to married women who have in fact joined the labor market, or when the sample is drawn from the unemployment register (Heckman 1974; Ridder 1984). In either case a further analysis brings to light that the parameters θ enter into the marginal density (13), and hence in L_m. As a result, the use of the conditional likelihood for the estimation of θ° is no longer justified by the argument given above, and we must seriously consider the possibility of maximizing the joint likelihood instead. Thus we would be maximizing

$$\log L_j(y, x, \theta, \eta, \zeta) = \log L_a(y, x, \theta) + \log L_m(x, \theta, \eta, \zeta)$$

in respect of θ instead of just the first right-hand term alone. It will be clear that the gain of taking into account the information on θ contained in the observed x by adding $\log L_m$ must be balanced against the need to specify this marginal density and to allow for the additional parameter vectors η and ζ; each further elaboration of the model adds to the danger of misspecification. In Section 12.4 we give an illustration of the case of sampling from the unemployment register for the duration of spells of unemployment, which is taken from Ridder (1984).

CHAPTER 5

Techniques of maximization

We find the MLE $\hat{\theta}$ by maximizing log $L(\theta, y, x)$. This is often done by solving the first-order conditions

$$q(\hat{\theta}, y, x) = 0 \tag{1a}$$

and verifying that

$$Q(\hat{\theta}, y, x) \text{ negative definite} \tag{1b}$$

since this is sufficient for a local maximum, as we have seen in Section 2.4. When we have thus obtained parameter estimates we establish their asymptotic covariance matrix by inserting their values into one or other of the estimating formulas of Section 2.10

$$V_1 = H^{-1} \tag{2}$$

$$V_2 = -Q^{-1} \tag{3}$$

$$V_3 = \left(\sum_i q_i q_i^T\right)^{-1} \tag{4}$$

Some parameters may be more important than others, and the process can sometimes be simplified by concentrating our efforts accordingly.

Traditional models usually yield the MLE as an explicit analytical function of $\{x, y\}$, as in the linear regression model with

$$b = (X^T X)^{-1} X^T y$$

$$s^2 = \frac{1}{n} y^T (I - X(X^T X)^{-1} X^T) y$$

Such formulas provide straightforward instructions for calculating the estimates, although some operations, like the inversion of large matrices, may call for quite advanced algorithms. The distinguishing feature of many newer models is not that estimation requires extensive computation, but that the maximum problem has no explicit analytical solution.

This chapter is concerned with such cases. We concentrate on broad strategy and ignore the tactics of numerical calculation. The maximization of a given function is a problem of applied mathematics, not of statistics, and we may forget that the sample observations $\{x, y\}$ are realizations of random variables.[7] For a fuller treatment we refer to Bard (1974) and to textbooks of optimization (Aoki 1971; Fletcher 1980; Walsh 1975); this mathematical literature, like many standard computer programs, is usually concerned with minimization rather than maximization.

5.1 Stepwise maximization

A common strategy is to partition θ as

$$\theta = \begin{bmatrix} \beta \\ \gamma \end{bmatrix} \tag{5}$$

and to deal with each subvector in turn; we first determine the conditional maximum of $\log L$ over γ for various given β, say

$$\max \log L(\beta) = \max_{\gamma} \log L(\beta, \gamma) \tag{6}$$

and next establish the *maximum maximorum* by optimizing (6) over β. This is illustrated in Figure 1 for scalar β and γ. The first figure traces the contour lines of $\log L$ and the determination of the conditional maxima, and the second figure shows these maxima as a function of β. The maximum of the latter function determines $\hat{\beta}$, and we find $\hat{\gamma}$ as the corresponding conditional maximand of the first stage. The final result is of course the same as that of simultaneous maximization in respect of both arguments (Koopmans and Hood 1953: 156).

At each step we are dealing with a subspace of lower dimensionality than the original parameter space, and this is of some help; but the major gain is that each partial optimization problem can be solved by the techniques that suits it best. Many nonlinear models can thus be treated in part by OLS regression; the money demand function of Section 1.3 is a case in point. This is

$$M = \gamma Y + \frac{\beta}{R - \alpha}$$

and it must be fitted to the money stock M, national income Y, and interest rate R by minimizing the Residual Sum of Squares, or RSS (Konstas and Khouja 1969). For a *given* α this is done by regressing M on

[7] The reader should of course keep this fact constantly in mind. We might recall it from time to time by repeating parts of the argument with the use of boldface type, but it would be very tedious to do so.

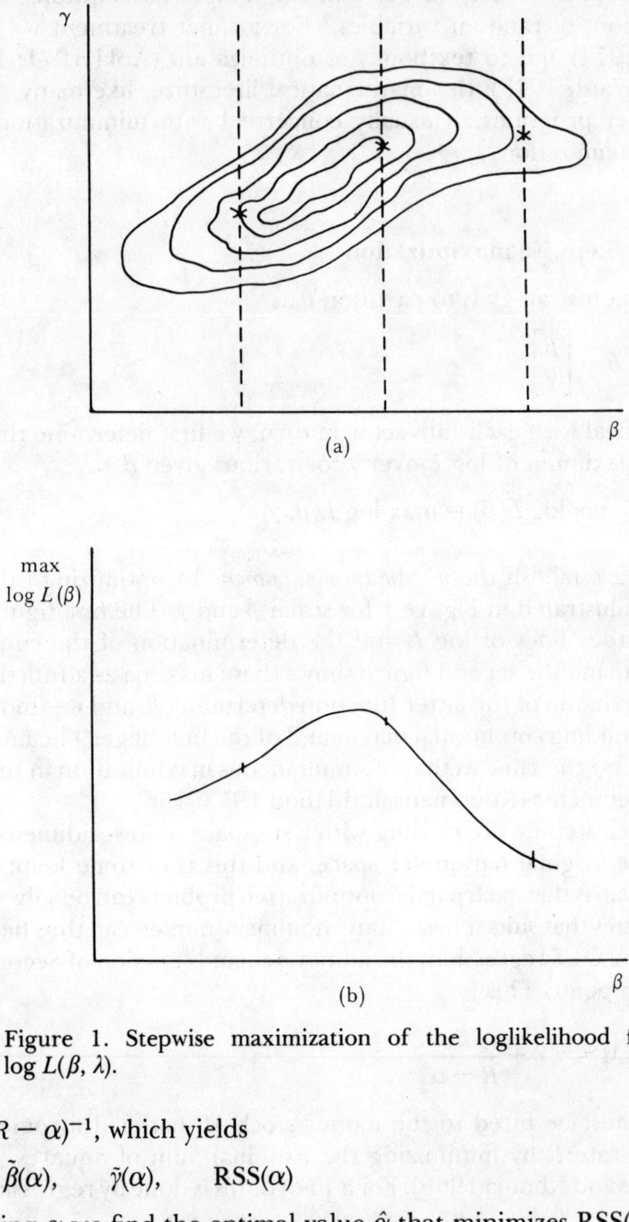

Figure 1. Stepwise maximization of the loglikelihood function $\log L(\beta, \lambda)$.

Y and $(R - \alpha)^{-1}$, which yields

$$\tilde{\beta}(\alpha), \qquad \tilde{\gamma}(\alpha), \qquad \mathrm{RSS}(\alpha)$$

By varying α we find the optimal value $\hat{\alpha}$ that minimizes $\mathrm{RSS}(\alpha)$, and hence

$$\hat{\beta} = \tilde{\beta}(\hat{\alpha}), \qquad \hat{\gamma} = \tilde{\gamma}(\hat{\alpha})$$

The values $\hat{\alpha}$, $\hat{\beta}$, $\hat{\gamma}$ are genuine nonlinear Least Squares estimates, and with a suitable statistical specification they are MLE, too.

This use of OLS regression embedded within the estimation of a nonlinear equation is a valid computational device for finding the parameter estimates. Note, however, that the OLS standard errors do not apply, since they fail to take into account that $\hat{\alpha}$ is just as much (the realization of) a random variable as $\hat{\beta}$ and $\hat{\gamma}$; the joint covariance matrix of all three estimates must still be separately established. This is sometimes overlooked when standard regression programs are being used.

5.2 Concentrating the likelihood function

We again partition θ into β and γ of k and m elements respectively, but now β is of intrinsic interest and γ is not; the latter represents *nuisance parameters* that are necessary for a proper statistical model but of no interest in themselves. In macroeconomic regressions, for instance, the slope coefficients usually have a definite interpretation, but the intercept and the disturbance variance have not. We may still have to estimate γ since we need the result to evaluate the covariance matrix of $\hat{\beta}$, but we do not need the covariance matrix of $\hat{\gamma}$. In these conditions we naturally wish to eliminate γ as far as possible since this reduces the dimensionality of the parameter space and hence simplifies the optimization problem. This is accomplished by the technique of *concentrating* the loglikelihood function, originally due to Koopmans and Hood (1953: 161).

To begin with, we partition the score vector and the Hessian of the original full-scale estimation problem just as we have partitioned θ,

$$q = \begin{bmatrix} q_\beta \\ q_\gamma \end{bmatrix}, \qquad Q = \begin{bmatrix} Q_{\beta\beta} & Q_{\beta\gamma} \\ Q_{\beta\gamma}^T & Q_{\gamma\gamma} \end{bmatrix} \tag{7), (8}$$

We suppose that $\hat{\theta}$ is determined by solving the first-order conditions (1a), and we rewrite these as

$$q_\beta(\theta) = q_\beta(\beta, \gamma) = 0 \tag{9a}$$

$$q_\gamma(\theta) = q_\gamma(\beta, \gamma) = 0 \tag{9b}$$

The m equations of (9b) also reflect the first-order conditions for a *conditional* maximum of $\log L$ in respect of γ for given β, and we assume that they can be solved to give an explicit expression for this optimal $\tilde{\gamma}$ as a function of β, say $h(\beta)$. The existence of this analytical solution is a prerequisite for the concentration technique.

If $h(\beta)$ exists, we have, by its definition,

$$q_\gamma(\beta, h(\beta)) = 0 \qquad \text{for all } \beta \tag{10}$$

Moreover, since $\tilde{\gamma} = h(\beta)$ maximizes $\log L$ for any given β, the MLE must satisfy

$$\hat{\gamma} = h(\hat{\beta}) \tag{11}$$

Differentiating both sides of (10) once more with respect to β we obtain, by the chain rule

$$Q_{\beta\gamma}(\beta, h(\beta))^T + Q_{\gamma\gamma}(\beta, h(\beta))A(\beta) = 0 \tag{12}$$

with A the matrix of first derivatives of the vector function $h(\beta)$ with respect to β,

$$A = \left[\frac{\partial \tilde{\gamma}_i}{\partial \beta_j}\right]$$

In (12) $Q_{\beta\gamma}^T$, A, and the null matrix on the right are all of order $(m \times k)$, and

$$A(\beta) = -Q_{\gamma\gamma}(\beta, h(\beta))^{-1}Q_{\beta\gamma}(\beta, h(\beta))^T$$

or, having regard to (11)

$$A(\hat{\beta}) = -Q_{\gamma\gamma}(\hat{\theta})^{-1}Q_{\beta\gamma}(\hat{\theta})^T \tag{13}$$

After these extensive preliminaries we substitute $\gamma = h(\beta)$ in $\log L(\theta) = \log L(\beta, \gamma)$ and obtain the *concentrated (log) likelihood function*

$$\log L_c(\beta) = \log L(\beta, h(\beta)) \tag{14}$$

Clearly

$$\max_\beta \log L_c(\beta) \leqq \max_\theta \log L(\theta)$$

while by (11) and (14)

$$\log L_c(\hat{\beta}) = \log L(\hat{\beta}, \hat{\gamma}) = \log L(\hat{\theta}) \tag{15}$$

Hence the MLE $\hat{\beta}$ maximizes $\log L_c$, and $\log L_c(\hat{\beta})$ attains the same maximum as $\log L(\hat{\theta})$.[8] It follows that the score vector of the concentrated loglikelihood function satisfies

$$q_c(\hat{\beta}) = 0$$

[8] In practice we must of course allow for differences in the constants that are habitually omitted both from the original and from the concentrated loglikelihood function.

This can be verified by differentiating (14) by the chain rule as

$$q_c(\beta) = q_\beta(\theta) + A^T(\beta)q_\gamma(\theta) \tag{16}$$

or, making use of (11),

$$q_c(\hat{\beta}) = q_\beta(\hat{\theta}) + A^T(\hat{\beta})q_\gamma(\hat{\theta})$$

By (9) the last term vanishes.

We may thus determine $\hat{\beta}$ by maximizing $\log L_c$, and obtain $\hat{\gamma}$ (if it is needed) subsequently from (11). Can we also use the Hessian of $\log L_c$ to estimate the covariance matrix of $\hat{\beta}$, by analogy to (3)? Indeed we can, as Barnett (1976: 357) has shown. Differentiating (16) once more we find the Hessian as

$$Q_c(\beta) = Q_{\beta\beta}(\theta) + Q_{\beta\gamma}(\theta)A(\beta) + \left\{\frac{\partial A(\beta)}{\partial \beta}\right\} q_\gamma(\theta) \tag{17}$$

The term

$$\left\{\frac{\partial A(\beta)}{\partial \beta}\right\}$$

symbolically denotes the derivatives of (the elements of) A in respect of (the elements of) β, and by strict standards we should indicate how these are arranged; but in the present case there is no need to do so. For if $Q_c(\beta)$ is used as an estimate of the covariance matrix, as in (3), it is evaluated at the MLE's $\hat{\beta}$, $\hat{\theta}$, and the last term of (17) then vanishes anyhow since $q_\gamma(\hat{\theta}) = 0$. We may therefore write

$$Q_c(\hat{\beta}) = Q_{\beta\beta}(\hat{\theta}) + Q_{\beta\gamma}(\hat{\theta})A(\hat{\beta})$$

and upon substitution of (13) and some rearrangement this yields

$$-Q_c(\hat{\beta})^{-1} = (-Q_{\beta\beta}(\hat{\theta}) + Q_{\beta\gamma}(\hat{\theta})Q_{\gamma\gamma}^{-1}(\hat{\theta})Q_{\beta\gamma}^T(\hat{\theta}))^{-1} \tag{18}$$

This is precisely the leading $(k \times k)$ submatrix of the inverse of $-Q$ as partitioned in (8), according to the standard formulas for the inverse of a partitioned matrix.[9] Hence $-Q_c(\hat{\beta})^{-1}$ is identical to the estimated covariance matrix of $\hat{\beta}$ that would follow from the use of (3) for the original full parameter vector $\hat{\theta}$.

To sum up, we may use the concentrated likelihood function exactly like the original article for finding $\hat{\beta}$ and for obtaining its estimated covariance matrix by means of the Hessian as in (3). If $\hat{\gamma}$ is required for the latter's evaluation, it is readily obtained from (11).

[9] See footnote 6, page 38, for references.

The derivation of this useful result hinges on the simplification of (17) upon its evaluation at the MLE $\hat{\theta}$, or $(\hat{\beta}, \hat{\gamma})$; it therefore applies to the *estimated* covariance matrix only, and it is, moreover, restricted to the estimate by the estimator (3). If we try to derive a similar result for the estimator (2), which uses the information matrix in lieu of the Hessian, we must take the expectation of (17), and this may present considerable difficulties. In general, estimation of $V\hat{\boldsymbol{\beta}}$ by the quasi information matrix $-E\boldsymbol{Q}_c$ can therefore only be justified by the argument that taking the expectation leads to simpler expressions, which usually yield a fair approximation. But the use of $-E\boldsymbol{Q}_c$ or H_c is of course fully vindicated if the complete information matrix H happens to be block diagonal, that is if $E\boldsymbol{Q}_{\beta\gamma} = 0$. We shall see in Section 6.2 that this is the case for the large class of generalized regression models when we make the natural distinction between parameters of the systematic part and parameters of the random disturbances. This is the usual form of concentration.

By equation (2.40), the original loglikelihood for the entire sample is the sum of n individual loglikelihoods, one for each of the stochastically independent observations. The concentrated loglikelihood cannot be decomposed in the same way, and it is even doubtful whether the concentrated loglikelihood for a single observation is a meaningful concept. In certain cases we may determine a conditional estimate $\tilde{\gamma} = h(\beta)$ for a single observation i, and think of substituting this into $\log L_i$ to establish $\log L_{ci}$. In doing so we would, however, admit n different estimates $\tilde{\gamma}_i$ of γ, and moreover the individual $\log L_{ci}$ will not sum to $\log L_c$. Concentration at the level of individual observations thus does not help to simplify the problem of maximizing $\log L$ in respect of β and γ for the whole sample, as we set out to do.

It follows from the above discussion that there is no point in constructing an analogue to the third estimator of the covariance matrix (4) from the concentrated function; if there are no individual loglikelihoods $\log L_{ci}$, there are no individual scores q_{ci} either. It also follows that, just like (2.40), neither (2.41) nor (2.42) have a counterpart for the concentrated function. Indeed Q_c and H_c cannot in general be expressed as a sum of independent terms in any way whatsoever. As a result, the usual convergence theorems cannot be directly invoked, and the use of Q_c and H_c must be justified by relating them to Q and H.

Questions and exercises

5.1 Consider the linear regression model of Section 2.1 and eliminate σ^2 from the loglikelihood. Verify that

$$\log L_c(\beta) = -\frac{n}{2} \log \sum_i (y_i - x_i^T\beta)^2$$

5.2 (Continuation.) Rewrite the regression equation as

$$y_i = \beta_0 + x_i^T\beta + \epsilon_i$$

where β contains no intercept and x_i no constant. Now concentrate $\log L_c$ of exercise 5.1 further by eliminating β_0.

5.3 For the money demand equation of Section 1.3 we find

$$\log L_c(\alpha, \beta, \gamma) = -\frac{n}{2} \log \text{RSS}$$

with RSS the Residual Sum of Squares. Derive $V\hat{\theta}$ for the three parameters named, and compare with the covariance matrix of $(\hat{\beta}\,\hat{\gamma})$ given by the conditional regression.

5.4 (Continuation.) We estimate the money demand function by the conditional regression method explained previously and find the following results:

α	RSS
−0.05	23.14
0	21.07
0.05	20.03
0.10	21.05

Clearly $\hat{\alpha} = 0.05$. Can you test whether α° is significantly different from zero?

5.3 Grid search: optimization in one dimension

The loglikelihood function can always be maximized by trial and error. We may evaluate it at grid points that cover Θ or a likely area of it, inspect the result, and repeat the process over a selected zone with a finer grid. This can work quite well with one or two parameters, when we can trace the behavior of $\log L$ or sketch its contour lines. All we need is a procedure to compute $\log L(\theta)$ at each θ.

In the case of a single parameter it is easy to see how we can improve on this process. We first consider points on either side of a starting value to find out in what direction $\log L$ increases, and then move that way with ever greater steps as long as $\log L$ keeps rising. As soon as we register a decline the direction is reversed and the step length is reduced. This process is illustrated in Figure 2.

In a slightly more sophisticated approach, we determine the derivative of $\log L$ or the score q in each successive point, and adjust the step

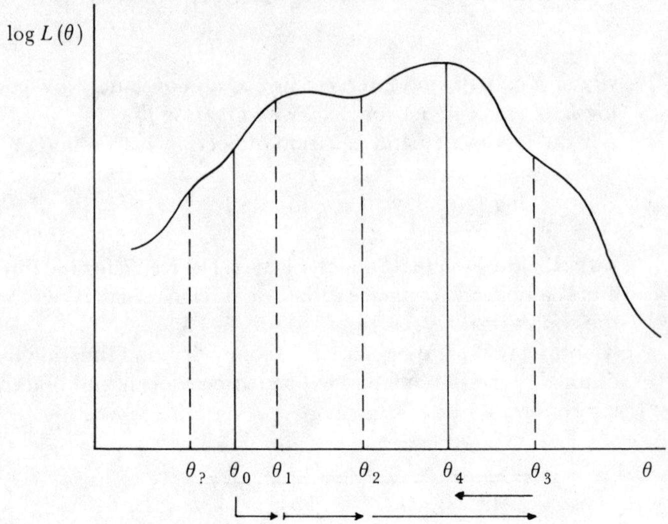

Figure 2. Maximizing log L by systematic trials.

length accordingly. We may even use the second derivative to establish the optimal step from a given point. If α is the scalar argument of log L, $\hat{\alpha}$ is its (unknown) optimal value, α_0 the present value, and

$$\Delta\alpha = \hat{\alpha} - \alpha_0$$

By a Taylor expansion we have

$$q(\hat{\alpha}) \approx q(\alpha_0) + Q(\alpha_0)\,\Delta\alpha$$

where $Q(\alpha_0)$ is the scalar second derivative. Since $q(\hat{\alpha})$ is zero this yields

$$\Delta\alpha \approx -q(\alpha_0)/Q(\alpha_0) \tag{19}$$

We have used a quadratic approximation for log $L(\alpha)$, and unless this happens to hold exactly the process must be repeated.

Obviously there is a variety of iterative methods for finding the maximand, and they all consist of three elements:

a starting value;
a prescription for generating successive values;
a convergence criterion that tells us when to stop.

So far we have considered the second stage only, and then solely for the case of a single parameter. The argument α may, however, also stand for a linear combination of the l elements of a parameter vector θ, and in that case we have been maximizing log L along a straight line in the parameter space Θ. As we have seen, the determination of the optimal movement along such a line presents no great conceptual problems. The choice of the direction of a line through a given point does, however, call for further discussion.

5.4 Directions in Θ

We consider a point θ_j in the l-dimensional parameter space Θ. This point belongs to the iterative sequence $\theta_0, \theta_1, \ldots$. If we vary θ from θ_j over a distance μ in the direction r we obtain

$$\theta_j + \mu r$$

The $(l \times 1)$ *direction vector* r can be normalized without loss of generality, and we set its length at 1, or

$$r^T r = 1 \tag{20}$$

The effect of a small displacement along r on log L is given by the Taylor expansion

$$\log L(\theta_j + \mu r) \approx \log L(\theta_j) + \mu q(\theta_j)^T r$$

so that

$$\frac{\Delta \log L}{\mu} = \frac{\log L(\theta_j + \mu r) - \log L(\theta_j)}{\mu} \approx q^T r \tag{21}$$

is the derivative of log L at θ_j in respect of slight displacements in the direction r. The score vector is always taken in θ_j, and we can omit this argument.

In a direction r_1 that satisfies

$$q^T r_1 = 0 \tag{22}$$

log L does not vary at all. In the case of two dimensions, r_1 is the direction of a tangent to the contour lines of log L in θ_j, and with more dimensions all r_1 lie in the tangent hyperplane.

All other directions $r \neq r_1$ can be written as

$$r = Rq \tag{23}$$

with

$$R = I - qq^T/q^T q + rr^T/r^T q \tag{24}$$

as substitution shows. We call r_2 a *feasible* direction if log L increases along it, that is, if

$$q^T r_2 > 0 \tag{25}$$

This is equivalent to

$$r_2 = Rq, \qquad R \text{ positive definite} \tag{26}$$

It is immediately clear from substitution that (26) implies (25). To show that the reverse holds, too, we consider a quadratic $u^T R u$ with arbitrary u. By (24) this is

$$u^T R u = u^T u \left(1 - \frac{(u^T q)^2}{u^T u \; q^T q}\right) + \frac{(u^T r_2)^2}{r_2^T q}$$

The first term is positive because of the Cauchy–Schwarz inequality, and the second is positive because of (25).[10] $u^T R u$ is positive for all u, and this proves (26).

The *optimal* direction maximizes (21) under the side condition (20); we write the Lagrangean

$$q^T r - \kappa (r^T r - 1)$$

and find the maximand r_3 by differentiation as

$$q - 2\kappa r_3 = 0, \qquad r_3 = \frac{1}{2\kappa} q$$

or, on account of (20),

$$r_3 = (q^T q)^{-1/2} q \tag{27}$$

By (25) we must of course take the positive root. This direction, given by the score vector, is the *gradient* or *direction of steepest ascent.* By (22) it is orthogonal to a tangent hyperplane containing all r_1.

5.5 Choice of a direction

In *direct search* techniques we only make use of the value of log L in various points of the parameter space. In the *relaxation method*, for instance, we select a direction parallel to one of the axes by varying each element of θ_j in turn, and comparing the outcome. It stands to reason that the step length in the favored direction is also determined with regard to log L, as in the iterative search of Section 5.3. Since we only

[10] The Cauchy–Schwarz inequality is $(u^T v)^2 \leq u^T u \cdot v^T v$ for any two commensurate vectors u and v.

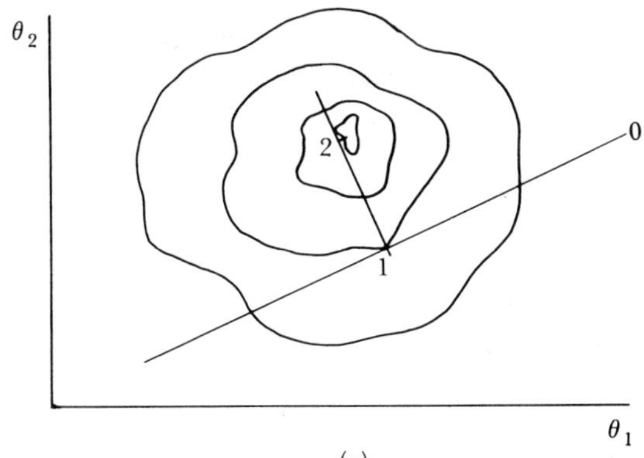

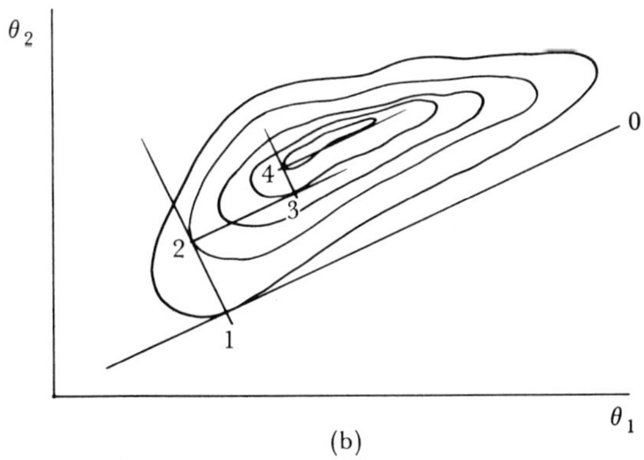

Figure 3. Two examples of orthogonal directions: (a) almost circular contour lines; (b) thin ellipse contour lines.

use directions parallel to the axes, any two consecutive directions are orthogonal.

We may also use the first derivative q to determine the optimal direction, as in the *method of steepest ascent* where the direction taken at θ_j is the gradient at that point. We continue along this line until $\log L$ is at a maximum, and it is then tangent to loglikelihood surface at θ_{j+1}. As we again take the gradient as the next direction, successive directions are once more orthogonal.

Orthogonal consecutive directions work well in some cases, but not in others, as is illustrated in Figure 3. They work well if the likelihood contours are nearly circular, and badly if they are thin ellipses. With more than two dimensions we inspect $-Q(\theta_j)$. If this resembles the unit matrix (apart from a scalar scale factor) the contour surfaces are nearly spherical and the standard methods work well. Their performance can thus at times be improved by simply rescaling the variables so that the implied transformation of the parameters brings about this result. As a rule of thumb it is advisable to have all parameters of roughly the same order of magnitude.

If $-Q(\theta_j)$ is not diagonal, but ill conditioned and verging on the singular, the remedy is not so simple. The thing to do is first to transform the parameter space so as to render the contours of $\log L$ locally near-spherical, then apply orthogonal directions, and finally return by reverse transformation to the original space. We take it that θ_j is sufficiently close to $\hat{\theta}$ for $-Q(\theta_j)$ to be positive definite; it is symmetric as a matter of course. Hence we can always find matrices P and Λ such that

$$PQP^T = -\Lambda, \quad P^TP = I, \quad P^T\Lambda P = -Q$$

with nonsingular P and diagonal Λ. We use these matrices to transform the parameter vector from θ to η by the linear transformation

$$\eta = \Lambda^{1/2}P\theta, \qquad \theta = P^T\Lambda^{-1/2}\eta$$

Hence, in the notation of Section 3.1,

$$G = \Lambda^{1/2}P$$

and

$$-Q^* = -G^{T-1}QG^{-1} = -\Lambda^{-1/2}PQP^T\Lambda^{-1/2} = I$$

as was intended. Consecutive directions d_j, d_{j+1} in the original parameter space are now selected so as to be orthogonal in the transformed space; that is,

$$(\Lambda^{1/2}Pd_j)^T(\Lambda^{1/2}Pd_{j+1}) = 0$$

which implies

$$d_j^TP^T\Lambda Pd_{j+1} = -d_j^TQd_{j+1} = 0 \tag{28}$$

Such direction vectors denote *conjugate directions*.

This can be taken a little further. We always have

$$\theta_{j+1} = \theta_j + \mu d_j$$

with μ the optimal step length, and we also always have approximately

$$q(\theta_{j+1}) \approx q(\theta_j) + Q(\theta_j)\,(\mu d_j)$$

so that

$$\Delta q_j = q(\theta_{j+1}) - q(\theta_j) \approx \mu Q(\theta_j) d_j$$

The condition (28) for optimal consecutive directions can thus also be written as

$$\Delta q_j^T d_{j+1} = 0 \tag{29}$$

This in turn suggests that we construct d_{j+1} as

$$d_{j+1} = q(\theta_{j+1}) + \alpha d_j$$

where α is determined so as to satisfy (29), that is,

$$\alpha = -\frac{\Delta q_j^T q(\theta_{j+1})}{\Delta q_j^T d_j} \tag{30}$$

In summary, we modify the method of steepest ascent by taking into account the previous direction, and we need only know the scores at two consecutive points to construct the next direction from the last. All we need is a first direction in the starting value θ_0 for which we take the gradient. The method is due to Powell (1964).

5.6 Quadratic approximation

We may of course extend the quadratic approximation of (19) to the full case of l dimensions. For θ_j close enough to $\hat{\theta}$ we have the Taylor series expansion

$$q(\hat{\theta}) \approx q(\theta_j) + Q(\theta_j)(\hat{\theta} - \theta_j)$$

or, since $q(\hat{\theta}) = 0$,

$$\Delta\theta_j = (\hat{\theta} - \theta_j) \approx -Q(\theta_j)^{-1} q(\theta_j)$$

Again the process must be repeated unless $\log L$ happens to be exactly quadratic, and we generate successive points by

$$\theta_{j+1} = \theta_j - Q(\theta_j)^{-1} q(\theta_j) \tag{31}$$

Direction and step length are simultaneously determined. This is the method of *Newton* or of *Newton–Raphson,* also known as *quadratic hill climbing.*

There exist several variations on this theme. When we calculate the inverse of the Hessian $-Q^{-1}$ at each step, we automatically have an estimate of $V\hat{\boldsymbol{\theta}}$ upon convergence – see equation (2.53). This suggests that we approximate $-Q$ by its expected value, and use

$$\theta_{j+1} = \theta_j + H(\theta_j)^{-1} q(\theta_j) \tag{32}$$

Instead of $H(\theta)$ we may of course also use the third estimator of $V\hat{\theta}$ from Section 2.10, that is

$$\theta_{j+1} = \theta_j + \left(\sum_i q_i(\theta_j) q_i(\theta_j)^T \right)^{-1} q(\theta_j) \tag{33}$$

This is the method of *scoring*, attributed to Fisher and to Gauss, who employed a similar reasoning in deriving the OLS estimator. Its gain lies in the possibility that the elements of the information matrix are simpler expressions, easier to establish, than those of the Hessian. When the computations are very onerous, the same matrix may be used for several successive quadratic adjustments instead of freshly calculated matrices at each parameter vector. The score vector is of course continually revised.

So far we have assumed that θ_j is sufficiently close to $\hat{\theta}$ for $-Q(\theta_j)$ to be positive definite, so that (31) satisfies the condition (26) for a feasible direction. If this is not so, (31) will lead away from the maximum and not toward it. Some procedures construct $-Q$ or its proxy as AA^T, for some A, thus ensuring feasibility. In other cases we may employ a device that is due to Marquardt (1963). This is to use

$$\theta_{j+1} = \theta_j + (-Q(\theta_j) + \gamma_j B_j^2)^{-1} q(\theta_j) \tag{34}$$

Here B_j^2 is a positive definite matrix, and γ_j is a positive scalar, which is in principle adjusted so as to render the entire expression within brackets positive definite; we set γ_j zero if $-Q$ is already positive definite itself.[11] Just as in the analogous case of *ridge regression* we may use $B^2 = I$.[12] Marquardt himself does, however, recommend the use of a diagonal matrix, composed of the diagonal elements of $Q(\theta_j)$ in absolute value. This will account for the relative variability of the elements of θ, and it also ensures that the method is invariant under simple scale transformations of the parameters, as induced, for example, by rescaling the variables.

Questions and exercises

5.5 A misguided scholar undertakes the estimation of the two parameters β and σ^2 of the simple regression model of Section 2.1 by combining

[11] If the order of Q is small we may use inspection, but with larger orders it is not immediately obvious how we should proceed to establish whether $-Q$ is positive definite or not. On this point see below, Section 5.10.

[12] For ridge regression, see Judge et al. (1980: 417).

stepwise maximization and grid search. The value of the full loglikelihood function is therefore calculated at various β at each of several different σ^2. Sketch the graph of log L as a function of β for two different values of σ^2, and draw some contour lines of log L over the (β, σ^2) plane.

5.6 Establish $q(\beta)$, $Q(\beta)$, and $H(\beta)$ of the linear regression model from the concentrated loglikelihood function of Exercise 5.1. Verify that the iterative schemes of (31) and (32) lead in one step to the OLS estimates, regardless of the starting values β_j.

5.7 (Continuation.) What is the gradient $q(0)$ in this model?

5.8 Is there ever any need for Marquardt's correction (34) in the estimation of β in regression models?

5.7 Two-stage estimation procedures

The search and adjustment procedures so far discussed belong firmly to iterative processes, which reach the MLE $\hat{\theta}$ from arbitrary initial values θ_0 in an unspecified number of steps. The quadratic adjustment of the preceding section does, however, also play an important part in *two-stage estimation* procedures, which merit a brief digression.

The first stage of such a procedure is to obtain a consistent estimate θ_1, usually by a simple method like OLS regression. Clearly this θ_1 must not be confused with the initial value θ_0 of a full iterative process, which may be quite arbitrarily determined by informal methods. The first-stage estimate θ_1 is then adjusted by a quadratic formula like (31), or

$$\theta_2 = \theta_1 + \hat{H}(\theta_1)^{-1} q(\theta_1) \tag{35}$$

where $\hat{H}$ is any consistent estimator of the information matrix H; three examples occur in (31), (32), and (33). This single round of adjustment completes the estimation, for the second-stage estimate θ_2 is the final result, and no further improvements are considered.

This estimator is asymptotically equivalent to the ML estimator, as can easily be shown by following the argument of Harvey (1981: 140). We draw freely on Section 2.9. To begin with, (35) is rewritten as

$$\sqrt{n}(\boldsymbol{\theta}_2 - \theta^\circ) = \sqrt{n}(\boldsymbol{\theta}_1 - \theta^\circ) + nH(\boldsymbol{\theta}_1)^{-1} \frac{1}{\sqrt{n}} q(\boldsymbol{\theta}_1)$$

Upon going rather brutally to the limit, while employing the consistency of $\boldsymbol{\theta}_1$ and of $\hat{H}(\boldsymbol{\theta}_1)$, we obtain

$$\sqrt{n}(\boldsymbol{\theta}_2 - \theta^\circ) \xrightarrow{L} nH^{-1} \frac{1}{\sqrt{n}} \boldsymbol{q}(\theta^\circ) = \bar{H}^{-1} \frac{1}{\sqrt{n}} \boldsymbol{q}(\theta^\circ) \tag{36}$$

with $\overline{H} = n^{-1}H$, as before – see (2.43). We now make use of the $N(0, \overline{H})$ distribution of the last term, from (2.49), and then find

$$\sqrt{n}(\theta_2 - \theta^\circ) \xrightarrow{L} N(0, \overline{H}^{-1}) \tag{37}$$

This is exactly the same asymptotic distribution as that of the MLE $\hat{\theta}$, as given by (2.50). The two estimators have the same asymptotic distribution, and they are therefore asymptotically equivalent.

This surprising property of the two-stage estimator depends on the consistency of the first-stage estimator, and the use of two-stage methods is virtually restricted to regression models where OLS yields consistent but not efficient estimates that can be used for this part.

5.8 Starting values and convergence criteria

We return to fully fledged algorithms for the determination of the MLE. So far we have discussed schemes for local search and adjustment, which must still be supplemented by a starting value θ_0 and by a convergence criterion that brings the process to a stop. We have little to offer on these points beyond some commonsense trivialities.

Most iterative schemes rely on approximations that are only valid in the neighborhood of $\hat{\theta}$, and one must try to respect this condition in setting the starting values. Silly starting values can add considerably to the number of iterations, and hence to costs; they may also make the parameter vector go off in the wrong direction. As we have seen in connection with Marquardt's correction, there may be parameter values at which $-Q$ or H are negative definite, and this may result in movements away from the maximand. For some models, a given set of observations, and a particular procedure, we may trace the *convergence region* of the parameter space Θ. The parameter vector converges to $\hat{\theta}$ from anywhere in this region, and it diverges or converges to a minimand (if $\log L$ has a minimum) from all other points (for an example, see Aitchison and Brown 1957: 77). Even without such protracted retrospective analyses, however, much of the waste and frustration of ill-chosen starting values can be avoided by a little thought. Setting all parameters equal to zero is usually *not* a good idea. A better approximation is easily obtained by reflecting on the various implications of several parameter values, and selecting what seems plausible. This reflection is at all times an excellent exercise, much recommended to model builders. Starting values can also be obtained from related results reported by others, or from coarse exploratory analyses of the data in hand, such as graphical inspection, one or two stages of a grid search, or an application of Least Squares even when it is highly inappropriate. The time and effort devoted to these preliminaries is well spent, not only because they lead to better starting values and quicker results, but also because they provide an exercise in the evaluation and interpretation that must be made of the final estimates.

The *convergence criterion* is applied at each step in the iterative process, which is terminated when its standards are met. This gauge may bear on the increase of $\log L$, a scalar, on the change in the parameter vector, or on the remaining distance between $q(\theta)$ and its optimum value, which is a vector of zeroes. The need to define such a tolerance level numerically brings home the limited precision of the final estimate; it always remains a numerical approximation to the true $\hat{\theta}$, and we should perhaps denote it as $\hat{\hat{\theta}}$. But this lack of exact precision applies of course to *all* calculated values, however simple their calculation, and it has nothing to do with the iterative nature of the algorithms of ML estimation.

Yet the convergence criterion should, in principle, be established with a view toward the desired precision of the final estimates. This precision need not exceed the limits set by the precision of the data, which is usually restricted. The likely standard errors of the estimates provide another yardstick for their precision. But it requires a considerable numerical analysis to translate the required precision of the final result into a convergence criterion, even though the two are obviously related. The common usage is therefore to set convergence criteria at very strict levels, so as to be on the safe side. This is a relatively innocuous habit, as overly narrow convergence criteria are, as a rule, not very costly in terms of the number of iterations.

5.9 Choice of a method

The range of iterative schemes that is available usually offers a payoff between the programming and computing time devoted to a single iteration on the one hand, and the number of iterations on the other. The choice depends on the relative costs of programming and of computing, and on the nature of the analysis. If a particular model is estimated only once there is no point in spending much time and effort on an efficient estimation program, and if iterations require little computing time we need not be concerned over their number. But if we have a large data set that must be processed anew at each iteration, it pays to design an efficient algorithm that needs only a few steps to convergence.

The same commonplace considerations of convenience, time, and cost govern the choice between a specially designed computer program and an existing general purpose ML estimation package. We repeat our recommendation of Section 1.3 to check any new program by running at least one genuine data set on a standard program of proven quality to see whether this gives the same results.

We illustrate the working of a general purpose ML estimation program by a brief sketch of Hall's MAXLIK and of Ridder's GRMAX (Hall, 1981; Ridder 1982).[13] These two programs have been developed independently, and they are built from different strands: GRMAX incorporates several subroutines from the British NAG program library, and MAXLIK largely follows the precepts of Berndt et al. (1974). Yet from the point of view of the lay user both programs offer much the same facilities: The user provides a set of data and a loglikelihood function with a list of parameters, and the program returns ML estimates of the parameters, together with their covariance matrix. Initial values are entered by the user or, in MAXLIK, obtained from the data by a simpler estimation method in a separate procedure. The loglikelihood function is given by the user in the form of a subroutine program; MAXLIK offers some set routines for particular models. MAXLIK assumes independent observations, so that a subroutine that specifies log L_i for a single observation is sufficient to establish the sample loglikelihood; GRMAX can handle any loglikelihood function, including concentrated loglikelihoods that cannot be obtained by summation over the observations. At the end of the process GRMAX offers sundry statistics that can be used for further diagnoses by way of options.

Both programs allow the user a measure of control over the iterative estimation process. The user has a limited choice of maximization methods, sets a limit to the maximum number of iterations, and selects the value of the convergence criterion. All maximization methods make some use of derivatives of the loglikelihood function, and both MAXLIK and GRMAX invite the user to write subroutines for the score vector and for the Hessian matrix or for an approximation to it, like the information matrix. But this is not mandatory: In the absence of subroutines, GRMAX will establish both scores and Hessian by numerical differentiation, and MAXLIK replaces the missing Hessian as a matter of course by its approximation based on the outer product of the individual score vectors, as shown in (2.54). In any case, both GRMAX and MAXLIK will check some or all the subroutines for derivatives by comparing their outcome with its counterpart among the numerically determined derivatives.

[13] We provide token references for this and for other computer programs but these are admittedly of little use. Good programs are never finished, and the constant process of revision and improvement leaves their designers little time for rewriting the manuals.

The facility of numerical evaluation of the derivatives of the loglikelihood function is not just a matter of saving the lazy user the trouble of differentiation at the cost of lengthy computations, but it offers the great advantage that the program will also work if the loglikelihood function or its derivatives do not admit of an analytical representation and involve terms that must be determined, for example, by numerical integration. With an almost universal program that includes such options, access to high-speed computing facilities, and a computing budget to match, virtually any model can be estimated by Maximum Likelihood.

We shall briefly describe some slightly less general ML estimation programs in Section 6.4.

5.10 Local and global maxima

When θ converges smartly to some $\hat{\hat{\theta}}$ we shall usually assume that this is a fair approximation to $\hat{\theta}$, the true maximand of $\log L$. One may well ask, however, how we can make sure (a) that $\log L(\hat{\hat{\theta}})$ is reasonably close to a genuine local maximum, and (b) that this represents a global maximum for the entire parameter space Θ.

The natural way to deal with the first issue is to verify that $\hat{\hat{\theta}}$ meets the conditions for a local maximum

$$q(\hat{\hat{\theta}}) = 0, \qquad -Q(\hat{\hat{\theta}}) \text{ positive definite} \tag{38a,b}$$

These conditions are, however, not quite straightforward. For (38a) the difficulty is that the elements of $q(\hat{\hat{\theta}})$ will never be *exactly* equal to zero; at best they are very small in absolute value. But since we can rescale these derivatives of $\log L$ at will by rescaling the variables, and hence the parameters, we can often make them as small (or as large) as we please without affecting the substance of the estimation result. There is no firm basis by which to judge whether these derivatives are sufficiently "small." One improvement is to replace the derivatives by *likelihood elasticities*

$$s(\hat{\hat{\theta}}) = \left[\frac{\partial \log L}{\partial \log \theta_j}\right]_{\hat{\hat{\theta}}} \tag{39}$$

These are pure numbers, and they at least permit of a sensible comparison and interpretation of the result. The convergence criterion based on q should likewise refer to s or to some other normalization. The question of what constitutes a small value remains unresolved, but it is now at least open to rational discussion. This may bear on s as a whole, that is, on its largest element in absolute value, or on some scalar measure like the vector's length.

The condition (38b) applies to the true Hessian, not to the information matrix or some other approximation. We may employ one or other of several necessary and sufficient conditions to establish whether this given matrix is positive definite or not. Thus we may consider the l eigenvalues or the l principal minors of $-Q$, and check whether they are all positive. Again we may examine the decomposition of $-Q$ into two complementary upper and lower triangular matrices ,which occurs in the course of a Gauss–Doolittle inversion algorithm, and make sure that the diagonal elements of the one are positive when the diagonal elements of the other are 1.[14] With standard computing software the calculation of the principal minors is probably the simplest course as far as programming is concerned.

When we are satisfied that $\hat{\hat{\theta}}$ indicates a local maximum of log L, the question arises whether this is also a global maximum over all of Θ. This is so, and the local maximum is unique, if log L is a *concave function* for all $\theta \in \Theta$. The loglikelihood is concave if

$$\begin{aligned} &\log L(\alpha\theta_1 + (1-\alpha)\theta_2) > \alpha \log L(\theta_1) + (1-\alpha) \log L(\theta_2) \\ &\text{for all } 0 \leq \alpha \leq 1 \text{ and all } \theta_1, \theta_2 \in \Theta \end{aligned} \tag{40}$$

If log L is concave, $-Q(\theta)$ is positive definite over the entire parameter space; the two properties are equivalent. Inspection of log $L(\theta)$ or of $Q(\theta)$ may show whether they hold, as they do for a number of models, such as the linear regression model (see exercises 5.6 and 5.8) and the class of discrete choice models (see Section 10.1). In the absence of such a general proof we can never be sure that log $L(\hat{\hat{\theta}})$ is indeed a global maximum, as no amount of numerical exploration can give us certainty. A grid search over large parts of Θ may suggest that log $L(\theta)$ is well behaved, and reveal no other maxima, yet we can never rule out the existence of a sharp isolated peak of the likelihood surface that is only discovered by chance.

5.11 Some common failures

All empirical studies are subject to reporting and recording errors, faulty transcription, programming mistakes, and computer breakdowns. Iterative methods of ML estimation suffer in addition from specific types of failure. These may be due to technical defects, or to

[14] Fletcher lists these and other conditions (1980: I, 13); see also Gantmacher (1959: I, 304–9, in conjunction with 14–18 and 33–41) or Hadley (1961: 254–63).

deeper problems, and it is important to distinguish between these two causes.

To begin with, the iterative process may fail to converge within a reasonable number of steps. There are a number of unpleasant possibilities. The parameter vector may veer off at ever-increasing speed toward absurd values, while still increasing $\log L$ at each step; it may drift toward a minimum of $\log L$; again it may diverge wildly at alternate trial values. We should monitor the process, or limit the number of iterations at each run, in order to recognize and check these undesirable developments. If they occur right at the start it is probably worthwhile to take another look at the starting values, and if this does not help, at the program and at any matrices that must be inverted. These should be well conditioned. We have already quoted the method of conjugate gradients to deal with moderate near-singularity of the Hessian, and Marquardt's correction as a cure for negative definiteness; there remains the requirement that the diagonal elements should be roughly of the same order of magnitude. We may change the scale or unit of measurement of certain variables or parameters to satisfy this condition. It can make a large difference to the efficiency of the iterative process.

Failure to converge may also occur at the other end of the process. After a promising start the procedure gets bogged down and continues to effect very small improvements in $\log L$ by equally minute changes in the parameters. This will ultimately lead to convergence, if after several hundred iterations; but such cases should surely be classified as failures, and a thorough revision of the algorithm or of the convergence criterion is in order.

The iterative process may also enter a loop or cycle, and keep repeating the same movements of θ over and over; again, substantial changes in the parameter vector may occur in conjunction with an almost constant value of $\log L$. This may be due to technical deficiencies in the algorithm, which lead to ill-conditioned matrices, and it can then be remedied by the various means we have reviewed above. This behavior of the iterative process may, however, also indicate that the loglikelihood surface itself is ill conditioned, and exhibits ridges or plateaus. This corresponds to a singular or near-singular information matrix, and we linked this in Section 2.4 with collinearity of the data or with underidentification of the model. For the analysis in hand it does not matter whether we blame the data for their deficiency, or the model for its pretense: The fact of the matter is that the former are uninformative about the latter. In a longer perspective, however, the distinction between collinearity and lack of identification dictates the analysts' reaction: If there is collinearity, new data that are free from this defect can be collected, but if there is lack of identification, additional extraneous information (or strong a priori assumptions) is needed to resolve the problem.

When the estimates do converge rapidly and we find a local or even a global maximum of $\log L$, the resulting estimates may still be unsatisfactory. Certain coefficients can have the wrong sign or be otherwise unacceptable to economic theory; again the estimates may lie outside Θ and take such values that (2.1) does not represent a probability density. The stock example is that in some models (though not in the regression model) we may end up with a negative estimate of a variance. This is a sign that we should not have relied on unconstrained optimization in the hope that it would come out all right, and that we should instead have imposed the condition $\theta \in \Theta$ from the beginning. In the example given, this is easily done by considering σ instead of σ^2 as the parameter, and disregarding the mirror optimum solution that will occur at $-\hat{\sigma}$. In general, however, we shall have to turn to the theory of optimization subject to inequality constraints. But these techniques (and the statistical properties of their outcome) are beyond our brief.

CHAPTER 6

Generalized classical regression

In the deliberately vague notation of Section 2.2 many econometric models take the form

$$\psi(y, \gamma^\circ) = \phi(x, \beta^\circ) + v \tag{1}$$

where v denotes *disturbances* with a Normal distribution of zero mean. This is an *Additive Normal Disturbance* or AND model. We can define a number of subclasses according to the structure of the three elements of (1); the main classification is by the stochastic specification that determines the course of inference.

A major dichotomy is between models with and without lags. The former take the general form

$$A_L(y_t, \gamma^\circ) = B_L(x_t, \beta^\circ) + v_t$$

We use t instead of i as the index of the observations to indicate that these refer to consecutive periods or moments in time, and thus form an ordered sequence. Both y_t and x_t can be vectors, A_L and B_L are (generalized) lag polynomials, and the v_t are Normal, but not necessarily independent. There is thus room for all sorts of dynamic relations from one period to another, which are characteristic of such models. As time series models they have their origin in statistics, not in economics or econometrics, although they have lately been applied widely to macroeconomic aggregates. Unfortunately, the likelihood theory of Chapter 2 is ill suited to their analysis, and from our point of view they constitute a class apart. There exists a substantial specialist literature in this field, and we shall only briefly touch upon it in Chapter 9.

All other AND models can be written as

$$\psi(y_i, \gamma^\circ) = \phi(x_i, \beta^\circ) + v_i \tag{2}$$

where the ordering of the observations is immaterial; this implies that there are no side relations among the y_i and x_i from one observation to another, and that the v_i are independent. This model can again be simplified in a number of ways, all the way down to the standard OLS regression model. A distinctive feature of these nondynamic AND models is the contrasting treatment of the systematic relationship between the x_i and the y_i on the one hand, and of the random disturbance on the other. Much ingenuity is spent on the specification of the functions ψ and ϕ, which embody all that economic theory has to offer about the phenomena under review. The stochastic component is, however, added on at a later stage, more or less as an afterthought, mainly because it is needed for inference. The disturbance is not an integral part of the model, but it is there to account for its imperfections. Although it primarily represents the effect of neglected variables, it must also take care of approximations in the form of ψ and ϕ, of errors of observation, and of the essential random element that some authors believe to be present in all social and economic phenomena (Malinvaud 1964: 70). As a result the disturbance has no clear and unambiguous interpretation, its additive character is a matter of convenience, and so is its Normal distribution. Apart from some fleeting references to the Central Limit Theorem in the older literature, no constructive arguments in support of this assumption are to be found. It is easy to handle but essentially arbitrary: Small wonder that strong efforts are being made to design robust methods of estimation and testing that can do without such distributional assumptions.

While OLS estimation of the standard linear regression model is robust in this sense, many related models are as yet best dealt with by ML estimation in the AND format. The present chapter deals with Generalized Classical Regression or GCR models, which are a special case of (2) with ψ the identity and the v_i identically distributed. In Section 6.5 we consider the even more restrictive case of scalar y_i and nonlinear ϕ. In Chapter 7 we continue with GCR models, with y_i a vector and ϕ a system of equations that are linear in x_i. Chapter 8 deals with a nontrivial transformation ψ of scalar y_i. Chapter 9 concludes with a brief discussion of models with dynamic elements.

As AND models cover the majority of all econometric models invented over the years, we shall meet a number of familiar regression models in an ML setting.[15]

6.1 Generalized classical regression

Generalized Classical Regression models are of the form

$$y_i = \phi(x_i, \beta^\circ) + \epsilon_i \tag{3}$$

$$\epsilon_i \text{ independent} \sim N(0, \Omega^\circ) \tag{4}$$

[15] As close reading may have revealed we shall not be dealing with the case of heteroskedasticity, when the disturbances, while Normal with zero mean, are independent but not identically distributed.

This differs from (2) on two points. The first is that ψ is the identity. The y_i (like the x_i) may still represent various transformations of economic magnitudes, such as logarithms, index numbers, or first differences, but these should not involve unknown parameters: There is no parameter vector γ. The second point is that the disturbances are independent and identically distributed (IID) as (multivariate) Normal variates with zero mean. This specification is so prevalent that we use the symbol $\boldsymbol{\epsilon}_i$ exclusively for vector or scalar disturbances of this type, as defined in (4). Together these two properties of the GCR model simplify the expression of the sample density, and hence the loglikelihood function, and lead to a particularly simple estimation criterion.

So much for the *classical* regression traits of the model. It is *generalized*, since the dependent or endogenous variables $\mathbf{y}_i$ can be $(g \times 1)$ vectors, and also since the (vector) function ϕ may be nonlinear in the x_i as well as in the parameters. With $(k \times 1)$ vectors of independent or exogenous variables x_i there may be *any* number p of parameters in β°. Since the covariance matrix Ω° is $(g \times g)$ and symmetric, the total number of unknown parameters that make up θ° is $p + \frac{1}{2}g(g+1)$.

While in principle ϕ may be any vector function differentiable in β, the choice is, in practice, restricted by a predilection for simple forms and by commonsense requirements. The model should, for instance, be invariant under changes in the units of measurement of economic magnitudes like quantities, prices, or incomes. We return to this point in Section 6.5.

We shall treat the exogenous x_i as nonrandom variables. Like the stochastic independence of $\boldsymbol{\epsilon}_i$, and hence of the $\mathbf{y}_i$, this is another classical trait of the model, which follows the lines of Chapter 2. By the argument of Section 4.5 exogenous variables may equally well be regarded as (realizations of) random variables, provided it may reasonably be assumed that any $\mathbf{x}_i$ is stochastically independent of any $\boldsymbol{\epsilon}_j$, whether i and j differ or not.

The probability density of a single $\boldsymbol{\epsilon}_i$ is given by the g-dimensional Normal density function

$$p(\epsilon_i) = (2\pi)^{-g/2}\,|\Omega^\circ|^{-1/2}\exp(-\tfrac{1}{2}\epsilon_i^T\Omega^{\circ -1}\epsilon_i) \tag{5}$$

The density of $\mathbf{y}_i$ then follows from (3) by the transformation theorem (Mood et al. 1974: 200). In the present case the multiplicative Jacobian element vanishes, since we have

$$J_i = \left[\frac{\delta\epsilon_{ij}}{\delta y_{ih}}\right] = I, \qquad \mathrm{abs}|J_i| = 1$$

The density of y_i is therefore

$$p_i = p(y_i, \theta^\circ, x_i) = (2\pi)^{-g/2}|\Omega^\circ|^{-1/2} \exp(-\tfrac{1}{2}\epsilon_i^T \Omega^{\circ -1} \epsilon_i) \tag{6a}$$

with

$$\epsilon_i(\beta^\circ) = y_i - \phi(x_i, \beta^\circ) \tag{6b}$$

Because of the stochastic independence of the y_i we have

$$\log L(\theta) = \sum_i \log p_i(\theta) \tag{7}$$

and thus

$$\log L = C - \frac{n}{2} \log |\Omega| - \frac{1}{2} \sum_i e_i(\beta)^T \Omega^{-1} e_i(\beta) \tag{8a}$$

with

$$e_i(\beta) = y_i - \phi(x_i, \beta) \tag{8b}$$

and

$$C = -\frac{ng}{2} \log 2\pi \tag{8c}$$

Note the difference between the *disturbances* $\epsilon_i(\beta^\circ)$ and the *residuals* $e_i(\beta)$, with β° the true parameter vector and β some assigned value. Note also the distinction between the *optimal* or *ML residuals* $\hat{e}_i = e_i(\hat{\beta})$, with $\hat{\beta}$ the ML estimate of β°, and all other nonoptimal *trial residuals* $e_i(\beta)$.[16]

At times we find it convenient to reparametrize the model by substituting

$$\Gamma = \Omega^{-1} \tag{9}$$

as we are free to do by the argument of Section 3.1. The density function (6a) must then be rewritten as

$$p_i = p(y_i, \eta^\circ, x_i) = (2\pi)^{-g/2}|\Gamma^\circ|^{1/2} \exp(-\tfrac{1}{2}\epsilon_i^T \Gamma^\circ \epsilon_i) \tag{10a}$$

and, as before,

$$\epsilon_i(\beta^\circ) = y_i - \phi(x_i, \beta^\circ) \tag{10b}$$

As a rule, we shall of course partition the parameter vectors in either

[16] As we shall increasingly consider particular models as vehicles of estimation, the need to distinguish between the true parameters θ° and the working values θ will gradually disappear, and so will its typographical expression.

case as

$$\theta = \begin{bmatrix} \beta \\ \omega \end{bmatrix}, \qquad \eta = \begin{bmatrix} \beta \\ \gamma \end{bmatrix} \tag{11}$$

where ω and γ stand for some vector arrangement of the $\frac{1}{2}g(g+1)$ unknown elements of Ω and Γ respectively. For present purposes there is no need to specify the precise nature of this rearrangement.

The density of the Generalized Classical Regression model is regular in the sense of Section 2.3, and we shall verify its regularity of the first order by examining the derivatives of (10), taking the subvectors β and γ in turn.

If we arrange the derivatives of the scalar p_i in respect of (the elements of) β in a column vector, we obtain

$$\left[\frac{\partial p_i}{\partial \beta_j}\right]^T = -p_i \phi'(x_i, \beta)^T \Gamma\, \epsilon_i \tag{12}$$

where

$$\phi'(x_i, \beta) = \left[\frac{\partial \phi_j(x_i, \beta)}{\partial \beta_k}\right]$$

denotes the $(g \times p)$ matrix of first derivatives of the $(g \times 1)$ vector function ϕ in respect of the p elements of β. As in equation (2.4) we must now take the integral over the domain of y_i of (elements of) (12), and this gives

$$-\int_{y_i} p_i \phi'(x_i, \beta^\circ)^T\, \Gamma \epsilon_i\, dy_i = -E\phi'(x_i, \beta^\circ)^T\, \Gamma \boldsymbol{\epsilon}_i$$

This is zero since $E\boldsymbol{\epsilon}_i = 0$.

For the derivatives in respect of γ we take the liberty of returning to Γ itself and of arranging the derivatives of (10) in respect of the elements of Γ in a corresponding matrix defined as

$$D_i = \left[\frac{\partial p_i}{\partial \gamma_{jk}}\right]$$

We make use of

$$\frac{d|\Gamma|}{d\Gamma} = |\Gamma|\Gamma^{-1} = |\Gamma|\Omega \tag{13}$$

in the differentiation of (10),[17] and then find

$$D_i = p_i(\Omega^\circ - \epsilon_i \epsilon_i^T) \tag{14}$$

The integral of each element of D_i over the domain of y_i is, in rather cavalier notation,

$$\int_{y_i} p_i(\Omega^\circ - \epsilon_i \epsilon_i^T) dy_i = E(\Omega^\circ - \epsilon_i \epsilon_i^T) = \Omega^\circ - E\epsilon_i \epsilon_i^T$$

and this is zero by the definition of Ω°.

We have thus established regularity of the first order. The present model's density is also regular of the second order for most ϕ, but we shall not pursue the matter further.

6.2 Score vector and information matrix

We partition the score vectors like the parameter vectors in (11) as

$$q = \begin{bmatrix} q_\beta \\ q_\omega \end{bmatrix}, \qquad q^* = \begin{bmatrix} q_\beta^* \\ q_\gamma^* \end{bmatrix}$$

The information matrix is partitioned in the same way. Since regularity obtains we may use (2.12); for the original model in terms of Ω, not Γ, we then find

$$H = -E\boldsymbol{Q}(\theta^\circ) = E\boldsymbol{q}\boldsymbol{q}^T = \begin{bmatrix} E\boldsymbol{q}_\beta \boldsymbol{q}_\beta^T & E\boldsymbol{q}_\beta \boldsymbol{q}_\omega^T \\ E\boldsymbol{q}_\omega \boldsymbol{q}_\beta^T & E\boldsymbol{q}_\omega \boldsymbol{q}_\omega^T \end{bmatrix} \tag{15}$$

For the sequel we need only certain parts of q and certain properties of H. First consider q_β. We may differentiate (8) or use (7), (12), and (9) to obtain

$$q_\beta = -\sum_i \phi'(x_i, \beta)^T \Omega^{-1} e_i \tag{16}$$

For q_ω we examine (8) and find that a typical element of the score vector takes the form

$$\frac{\partial \log L}{\partial \omega_{hk}} = -\frac{n}{2} b - \frac{1}{2} \sum_i e_i^T B\, e_i \tag{17}$$

[17] This follows at once from the definition of the inverse in terms of cofactors and of the determinant. Note that we do not explicitly recognize that Γ, like Ω, is symmetric; the result is the same, whether we do or not. For a treatment of the same problem that does respect symmetry see Magnus and Neudecker (1980: 432).

with

$$b = \frac{\partial \log |\Omega|}{\partial \omega_{hk}}, \quad \text{a scalar}$$

and

$$B = \frac{\partial \Omega^{-1}}{\partial \omega_{hk}}, \quad \text{a } (g \times g) \text{ matrix}$$

It is not necessary to go into further detail for we shall use (17) only to show that the partitioned information matrix (15) is block diagonal.

To do this we consider a typical element of the off-diagonal block $E\boldsymbol{q}_\beta \boldsymbol{q}_\omega^T$, both scores being of course evaluated at the true parameter vector, so that we must substitute $\boldsymbol{\epsilon}_i$ for e_i before taking the expectation. By (16) and (17) we find

$$\begin{aligned} H_{jhk} &= E\boldsymbol{q}_{\beta(j)}\boldsymbol{q}_{\omega(hk)} \\ &= E\left(\sum_i \phi_j'(x_i, \beta^\circ)^T \Omega^{\circ -1} \boldsymbol{\epsilon}_i \left(\frac{n}{2} b + \frac{1}{2} \sum_i \boldsymbol{\epsilon}_i^T B \boldsymbol{\epsilon}_i\right)\right) \end{aligned} \tag{18}$$

If we carry out the multiplication this is the sum of two terms. Upon some slight rerrangement the first is

$$\frac{n}{2} b \sum_i E\phi_j'(x_i, \beta^\circ)^T \Omega^{\circ -1} \boldsymbol{\epsilon}_i$$

and this is zero since $E\boldsymbol{\epsilon}_i = 0$. The second term can also be rearranged; it is the product of two sums in $\boldsymbol{\epsilon}_i$, but since the $\boldsymbol{\epsilon}_i$ are stochastically independent and have expectation zero the expected value of all cross-products is zero. Upon omitting these terms there remains

$$\frac{1}{2} \sum_i E\phi_j'(x_i, \beta^\circ)^T \Omega^{\circ -1} \boldsymbol{\epsilon}_i \boldsymbol{\epsilon}_i^T B \boldsymbol{\epsilon}_i$$

This is the expected value of a linear expression in third powers of elements of $\boldsymbol{\epsilon}_i$, or a linear expression in the third moments of $\boldsymbol{\epsilon}_i$, and since the $\boldsymbol{\epsilon}_i$ are multivariate Normal with zero mean these are zero.

Thus both terms are zero, (18) vanishes, and (15) is block diagonal, or

$$H = \begin{bmatrix} E\boldsymbol{q}_\beta \boldsymbol{q}_\beta^T & 0 \\ 0 & E\boldsymbol{q}_\omega \boldsymbol{q}_\omega^T \end{bmatrix} = \begin{bmatrix} H(\beta) & 0 \\ 0 & H(\omega) \end{bmatrix} \tag{19}$$

Note that we have used properties of expected values in deriving this result, and that we have *not* shown the Hessian Q to be block-diagonal.

A major implication of this result is that the asymptotic covariance matrix of the MLE $\hat{\theta}$ is block-diagonal, too, for by (2.51) it is given by H^{-1}. Hence

$$V\hat{\theta} = \begin{bmatrix} V\hat{\beta} & 0 \\ 0 & V\hat{\omega} \end{bmatrix}$$

or

$$V\hat{\beta} = H(\beta)^{-1}, \qquad V\hat{\omega} = H(\omega)^{-1}$$

The estimators $\hat{\beta}$ and $\hat{\omega}$ are asymptotically uncorrelated, or, as they are asymptotically Normal, they are *asymptotically independent*, element by element.[18]

6.3 Concentrating the likelihood function

We assume that the ML estimates can be obtained by solving the first-order conditions

$$q(\hat{\theta}) = 0, \qquad \text{or} \quad q^*(\hat{\eta}) = 0$$

As we have argued in Section 5.9, this is sufficient for a global maximum, provided the Hessian Q is negative definite (and $-Q$ positive definite) for all $\theta \in \Theta$. Whether this is in fact the case depends on the form of the vector function ϕ, and by strict standards this should be verified by inspection; in practice it is however often taken for granted.

From the two equivalent conditions

$$q(\hat{\theta}) = 0, \qquad q^*(\hat{\eta}) = 0$$

we have

$$q_\beta(\hat{\theta}) = q^*_\beta(\hat{\eta}) = 0, \quad q_\omega(\hat{\theta}) = 0, \quad q^*_\gamma(\hat{\eta}) = 0$$

To see the implications of the last equality we once more arrange the derivatives of log L in respect of (the elements of) Γ in a $(g \times g)$ matrix, and upon equating this element by element to zero we find from (7) and (14)

$$\sum_i (\hat{\Omega} - \hat{e}_i \hat{e}_i^T) = 0 \tag{20}$$

18 This is of course a generalization of the classical result that the mean and variance of a sample from a Normal distribution are stochastically independent.

so that

$$\hat{\Omega} = \frac{1}{n} \sum_i \hat{e}_i \hat{e}_i^T \tag{21}$$

If we determine the *conditional* maximum of log L in respect of Ω at given β we likewise find

$$\hat{\Omega}(\beta) = \frac{1}{n} \sum_i e_i(\beta)\, e_i(\beta)^T \tag{22}$$

with

$$e_i(\beta) = y_i - \phi(x_i, \beta)$$

trial residuals for an assigned value β.[19]

We thus have an analytical expression (22) for the conditional ML estimate of $\Omega°$ at some given β. Moreover Ω perfectly fits the description of a set of auxiliary parameters of secondary importance. The stage is thus set for *concentration* of the likelihood function as explained in Section 5.2.

When we rewrite (8a) as

$$\log L_c(\beta) = C - \frac{n}{2} \log |\hat{\Omega}(\beta)| - \frac{1}{2} \sum_i e_i(\beta)^T \hat{\Omega}(\beta)^{-1} e_i(\beta) \tag{23}$$

with

$$e_i(\beta) = y_i - \phi(x_i, \beta)$$

and

$$C = -\frac{ng}{2} \log 2\pi$$

we already have a concentrated loglikelihood as a function of β alone. But the real gain of concentration lies in the further simplification of the last term on the right-hand side, say

$$W = \sum_i e_i(\beta)^T \hat{\Omega}(\beta)^{-1} e_i(\beta)$$

which is the sum of n scalars. A scalar is equal to its trace, and the trace of

[19] We must exclude the possibility that there is a β for which one or more of the functions $\phi_j(x_i, \beta)$ give a perfect fit to the y_{ji} concerned, for in that case at least one element of $e_i(\beta)$ would be zero for all i, and $\hat{\Omega}(\beta)$ would be singular. This will not do since we shall need its inverse. The case is however unlikely to arise in practice unless the number of observations is very small.

a product is invariant to certain orderly permutations of the order of multiplication, so that

$$W = \sum_i \operatorname{tr}\left(e_i(\beta)^T \hat{\Omega}(\beta)^{-1} e_i(\beta)\right) = \sum_i \operatorname{tr}\left(\hat{\Omega}(\beta)^{-1} e_i(\beta) e_i(\beta)^T\right)$$

$$= \operatorname{tr} \hat{\Omega}(\beta)^{-1} \sum_i e_i(\beta) e_i(\beta)^T$$

We now make use of (22) and obtain

$$W = \operatorname{tr} \hat{\Omega}(\beta)^{-1} n \, \hat{\Omega}(\beta) = n \operatorname{tr} I = ng \tag{24}$$

As a result we may rewrite the concentrated loglikelihood function (23) as

$$\log L_c(\beta) = C_c - \frac{n}{2} \log \left| \sum_i e_i(\beta) \, e_i(\beta)^T \right| \tag{25a}$$

with

$$e_i(\beta) = y_i - \phi(x_i, \beta) \tag{25b}$$

and

$$C_c = -\frac{ng}{2} (\log 2\pi + 1) + \frac{n}{2} \log n \tag{25c}$$

The additive constant can of course be disregarded in maximizing $\log L_c$, but note that it differs from C of (8a). This must be borne in mind when comparing loglikelihoods from different sources.

It follows from (25a) that in the quite wide class of generalized classical regression models ML estimation of β is equivalent to minimizing the residual determinant, that is, the generalized variance of the residual vector.[20] This is a natural extension of the Least Squares principle from scalar to vector residuals.

In the sequel we restrict the discussion as a matter of course to the estimation of β from the concentrated likelihood function; after the event we can always obtain $\hat{\Omega}$ from (21), thus completing the estimation of the full parameter vector θ of the model. It follows that we can readily

[20] While we have excluded exact singularity of $\Omega(\beta)$ for any β in footnote 19, there remains the danger that Ω is *near-singular*. If the number of observations is small relative to the number of parameters in β, there is a definite risk that the estimates minimize $|\Omega|$ by conspiring to render the residuals of a single equation (almost) zero, without any regard to the fit of the others. This will reduce $\hat{\Omega}$ to near-singularity and bring $|\hat{\Omega}|$ close to zero. There is nothing in the ML estimation procedure to prevent all efforts thus being concentrated, as it were, on fitting a single equation out of a set. The possibility was first noticed by Kloek, as Deaton and Muellbauer report (1980b: 318).

evaluate any desired sample statistic, and in particular an estimator of the limited covariance matrix $V\hat{\beta}$.

Two out of the three covariance estimators of Section 2.10 can be adapted to this end by simply treating the concentrated likelihood like a full likelihood. The first estimator is thus the analogue of (2.52)

$$V_1\hat{\beta} = H_c^{-1} \tag{26}$$

This has been justified in Section 6.2 by the demonstration that in the present GCR model H is block-diagonal. The second estimator is the analogue of (2.53)

$$V_2\hat{\beta} = -Q_c^{-1} \tag{27}$$

This formula was shown, in Section 5.2, to be generally valid for the concentrated likelihood of any model. In practice, the information matrix provides the simpler estimator, and we shall give an expression for (26) below, in (32).

As for the third estimator (2.54)

$$V_3\hat{\theta} = \left(\sum_i q_i q_i^T\right)^{-1}$$

we have already argued in Section 5.2 that it has no sensible counterpart for the concentrated loglikelihood.

So much for $V\hat{\beta}$. As a rule we take no interest in the asymptotic covariance matrix of $\hat{\omega}$, the elements of $\hat{\Omega}$. This is determined by the properties of the multivariate Normal distribution, but it may of course be obtained by the standard method of working out the relevant elements of the full information matrix H. If this is done it turns out that the submatrix $V\hat{\omega}$ depends only on ω itself, not on β. This stands to reason since the estimates of the two sets of parameters are stochastically independent.

Questions and exercises

6.1 Consider the GCR model (3), (4) for the special case that (i) y_i and x_i are scalars and (ii) $\phi(x_i, \beta) = \beta x_i$. This is the simplest version of the standard linear regression model. Show directly from $EQ_{\beta\omega}$ that H is diagonal.

6.2 In the standard linear regression model for scalar y_i $\Omega = \omega$, a scalar (also known as σ^2), and $\hat{\omega} = (1/n)S$, with S the residual sum of squares. Derive $V\hat{\omega}$ and consider the asymptotic t-ratio of $\hat{\omega}$.

6.3 (Continuation.) In the standard linear regression model we know the small-sample result that S/ω° is $\chi^2(n-p)$ distributed, with p the number of regression coefficients. What is the variance of the OLS estimator $\hat{\omega}^* = S/(n-p)$? What is its asymptotic t-ratio?

6.4 Verify (20) directly from (8) for the case of scalar y_i.

6.4 Estimation

The change from $\log L(\theta)$ to $\log L_c(\beta)$ is an aid to understanding certain properties of the MLE $\hat{\beta}$; it certainly simplifies matters when $\hat{\beta}$ is obtained by purely numerical methods; but it does not make all that much difference in the algebra of determining $\hat{\beta}$ from the first-order maximum conditions. By (22) and the equivalent of (13) we find from (25a)

$$q_c(\beta) = \sum_i \phi'(x_i, \beta)^T \Omega(\beta)^{-1} e_i(\beta) \tag{28}$$

If we equate this to zero, the MLE $\hat{\beta}$ must satisfy

$$\sum_i \phi'(x_i, \hat{\beta})^T \hat{\Omega}^{-1} y_i = \sum_i \phi'(x_i, \hat{\beta})^T \hat{\Omega}^{-1} \phi(x_i, \hat{\beta}) \tag{29a}$$

with

$$\hat{\Omega} = \frac{1}{n} \sum_i \hat{e}_i \hat{e}_i^T \tag{29b}$$

and

$$\hat{e}_i = y_i - \phi(x_i, \hat{\beta}) \tag{29c}$$

The same system will be obtained if we start off from the original likelihood function (8) and equate all $p + \frac{1}{2}g(g+1)$ elements of $q(\hat{\theta})$ to zero. If (29a) can be easily solved for $\hat{\beta}$ at a given $\hat{\Omega}$ – as in the case of linear ϕ – these equations at once suggest a simple iterative scheme: From a given starting value β_0 we calculate (29c), hence (29b), and then β_1 from (29a). But in the absence of further particulars of ϕ we cannot give general instructions on how to solve (29).

Having obtained $\hat{\beta}$ – and also $\hat{\Omega}$ – we shall wish to assess its covariance matrix. Of the two estimators (26) and (27), the first is by far preferable, if only because of its relatively simple form. We first derive

$$H_c = E\boldsymbol{q}_c(\beta^\circ)\boldsymbol{q}_c(\beta^\circ)^T$$

as in (2.12). Adapting (28) by the substitution of the true parameters and the true disturbances we obtain

$$H_c = E\left\{\left(\sum_i \phi'(x_i, \beta^\circ)^T \Omega^{\circ -1} \boldsymbol{\epsilon}_i\right)\left(\sum_i \boldsymbol{\epsilon}_i^T \Omega^{\circ -1} \phi'(x_i, \beta^\circ)\right)\right\}$$

Because of the stochastic independence of the ϵ_i all cross-products vanish, and we retain

$$H_c = E\left(\sum_i \phi'(x_i, \beta^\circ)^T \, \Omega^{\circ -1} \epsilon_i \epsilon_i^T \Omega^{\circ -1} \, \phi'(x_i, \beta^\circ)\right) \tag{30}$$

or, since $E\epsilon_i\epsilon_i^T = \Omega^\circ$,

$$H_c = \sum_i \phi'(x_i, \beta^\circ)^T \Omega^{\circ -1} \phi'(x_i, \beta^\circ) \tag{31}$$

It follows that

$$\hat{V}\hat{\beta} = \left(\sum_i \phi'(x_i, \hat{\beta})^T \hat{\Omega}^{-1} \phi'(x_i, \hat{\beta})\right)^{-1} \tag{32}$$

Again this expression permits of no further simplification or interpretation as long as ϕ has not been specified. But since we now have established general expressions for H_c as well as for q_c we may use these in another iterative scheme for the determination of $\hat{\beta}$, namely the scoring method of Section 5.6.

Both the iterative schemes we have outlined require the calculation for all i of the vector function $\phi(x_i, \beta)$ and of the matrix of its first derivatives $\phi'(x_i, \beta)$ at each consecutive trial vector β. With the exception of a few primitive search procedures this will hold for most iterative methods of determining $\hat{\beta}$, and it certainly applies to the standard general purpose computer programs that have been designed to deal with Generalized Classical Regression models, if under a different name. The user of the Time Series Processor, or TSP, program package must write a subroutine for $\phi(x_i, \beta)$ only; the program takes care of the derivatives of this function that enter into the scores vector and the information matrix (University of Western Ontario 1978).[21] Deaton's Non-Linear Full Information Maximum Likelihood program (NLFIML) requires subroutine inserts for both $\phi(x_i, \beta)$ and $\phi'(x_i, \beta)$, and so does Wymer's RESIMUL (Deaton 1976; Wymer 1978). No doubt there exist other programs operating on the same principles. Once they have been set up they are fed a data set, initial values β_0, and an indication of the required precision of the convergence criterion. The program returns ML estimates $\hat{\beta}$ together with their covariance matrix, the value of the loglikelihood, and a multitude of optional other statistics, all evaluated at $\hat{\beta}$. The stochastic independence and identical Normal distribution of the additive disturbances is throughout taken for granted. We shall see that these programs can also be used for

[21] See footnote 13 on page 74.

some AND models outside the GCR class, which may be estimated by the same algorithm in spite of conceptual differences.

6.5 Scalar nonlinear regression: choice of a function

A simple special case of the GCR model (3), (4) is that y_i is a scalar while ϕ is nonlinear in x_i and in β, as in the money demand function of Sections 1.3 and 5.1

$$\phi(x_i, \beta) = \beta_1 x_{1i} + \frac{\beta_2}{x_{2i} - \beta_3}$$

The general formulation of such a model is

$$y_i = \phi(x_i, \beta) + \epsilon_i \tag{33a}$$

Since the y_i and ϵ_i are scalar, Ω reduces to a scalar ω which is usually denoted as σ^2, so that

$$\epsilon_i \text{ independent} \sim N(0, \sigma^2) \tag{33b}$$

Even with the reduction to scalar y_i we do not often come across such nonlinear functions; on the whole, the form of $\phi(x_i, \beta)$ and its behavior over the domain of x_i is not a major issue. As far as the *empirical fit* of the model to the observed scatter (y_i, x_i) is concerned, a linear approximation usually does as well as any other function of x_i with the same number of parameters. In many economic data sets the range of variation of both x and y is limited, and when it is not, as with family budgets and other survey data, the fit is usually uniformly bad. We may moreover introduce various types of curvature by the prior transformation of x and y into logarithms, ratios, or shares, writing the regression equation linear in these transforms. The main advantage of these conversions is that they do not increase the number of parameters, unlike the traditional extension of the linear approximation into a polynomial as in

$$\phi(x_i, \beta) = \beta_0 + \beta_1 x_i + \beta_2 x_i^2 + \cdots$$

where x_i is scalar, too. For the purpose of estimation this is linear in the x and in β, as the powers of x_i can be treated just like any other exogenous variable. But this straightforward method of dealing with nonlinearities at the expense of additional parameters has gone out of fashion.

Apart from the matter of fit, there may be theoretical considerations that exclude linear specification of the relation between x and y, in particular in money demand and in production functions. These considerations may also lead to a parametric transformation of the y_i, as in the model discussed in Chapter 8. But there are also considerations that limit the choice of a nonlinear function. If the y_i and x_i represent economic magnitudes like stocks or flows of money or goods, or their ratios (like prices and index numbers), inference should be invariant under changes in the arbitrary units of measurement of these variables. This does not mean that upon rescaling the observations the parameters or their estimates should remain the same, but that they should change in the appropriate manner. Significance statements and other substantive statements should not be affected.

The essential condition for this is that upon scale changes in the variables, ϕ will determine the same density function of $\mathbf{y}$ as before, though possibly with a changed parameter vector θ^* instead of θ. As we argued in Section 2.1 the density of $\mathbf{y}$ *is* the model: It summarizes all we can say about $\mathbf{y}$, and it determines the likelihood function and hence the course of the statistical analysis. In the present case, $\mathbf{y}$ consists of independent y_i, and we therefore need only consider a single element, as in

$$y_i \sim N(\phi(x_i, \beta), \sigma^2) \tag{34}$$

Let y_i and x_i be rescaled as wy_i and $\bar{w}x_i$, with w a scalar and $\bar{w}$ a diagonal matrix of known constants, and apply (33) again.[22] This gives

$$y_i \sim N(w^{-1}\phi(\bar{w}x_i, \beta^*), w^{-2}\sigma^{*2}) \tag{35}$$

Invariance requires that y_i has the same density, or the same distribution, in either representation, in other words that (34) and (35) are identical for all i, that is for all observed x_i or indeed for *any* regressor vector x. The question is thus whether ϕ admits of a unique parameter vector $\theta^* = \{\sigma^* \quad \beta^*\}$ corresponding to $\theta = \{\sigma \quad \beta\}$ such that

$$w^{-1}\phi(\bar{w}x, \beta^*) \equiv \phi(x, \beta) \tag{36}$$

and

$$w^{-2}\sigma^{*2} \equiv \sigma^2$$

The last condition is trivial; the first hinges on the form of ϕ, as was to be expected. Clearly a converse scale operation must also be permitted, or

$$\phi(x, \beta^*) \equiv w\,\phi(\bar{w}^{-1}x, \beta) \tag{37}$$

Changes of scale should thus be absorbed in the parameter vector. Since both (36) and (37) must hold for all x and all β, it is necessary and sufficient that ϕ can be rewritten as in

$$\phi(x, \beta) = \beta_0\phi(\bar{\beta}_1 x, \beta_2) \tag{38}$$

[22] While y_i is scalar x_i may be a vector. A bar over a vector symbol indicates the distribution of its elements over a diagonal matrix, designated by others by the "hat" notation.

where β_0 is a scalar, $\bar{\beta}_1$ a diagonal matrix of coefficients of the elements of x, and β_2 stands for any other parameters, which may or may not depend on β_0 and β_1. Power sums and products like

$$\phi(x, \beta) = \beta_0 + \beta_1 x_1^\gamma + \beta_2 x_2^\delta + \cdots$$

or

$$\phi(x, \beta) = \beta_0 x_1^\gamma x_2^\delta \tag{39}$$

satisfy this requirement, and this may in part account for their popularity.

Even with a Cobb–Douglas function like (39), however, we need not have a nonlinear estimation problem, since we can take logarithms of all variables before introducing the additive Normal disturbance. The issue is then whether there are other grounds than computational convenience for the choice between two specifications that differ only in the stochastic part; the traditional form has a multiplicative disturbance, as in

$$y_i = \beta_0 x_{1i}^\gamma x_{2i}^\delta \exp(\epsilon_i)$$

while the alternative has an additive disturbance for the same y_i,

$$y_i = \beta_0 x_{1i}^\gamma x_{2i}^\delta + \epsilon_i$$

These two statistical specifications of the same function have been shown to give estimators of the elasticities and predictions of y with different properties, and they also give different estimates in applications to the production function (Bodkin and Klein 1967; Goldberger 1968). Yet other problems in the formulation and estimation of production function are more pressing than the precise location of the disturbance in this simple Cobb–Douglas approach.

6.6 Scalar nonlinear regression: estimation

We illustrate the operation of the formulas of Section 6.3 for the simple case of the scalar nonlinear regression model (33). The concentrated loglikelihood function (25a) now reads

$$\log L_c(\beta) = C_c - \frac{n}{2} \log \sum_i e_i(\beta)^2 \tag{40}$$

where C_c is the constant (25c) with $g = 1$. Maximizing the concentrated loglikelihood is thus equivalent with the familiar precept of minimizing the residual sum of squares with respect to β, as is maximizing the original likelihood.

The ML estimator thus coincides with an estimator based on the *Least Squares principle.* The properties of such an estimator have been studied for the model

$$y_i = \phi(x_i, \beta) + v_i \tag{41a}$$

$$v_i \text{ IID with } Ev_i = 0,\ Ev_i^2 = \sigma^2 \tag{41b}$$

This is less restrictive than (33) since the disturbances need not be Normal. Jennrich and Malinvaud show that under fairly weak conditions the LSE of (41) is consistent and asymptotically Normal with the same covariance matrix as the MLE of (33) (Jennrich 1969; Malinvaud 1970). The asymptotic efficiency of this estimator cannot be assessed, since there is no such thing as an information matrix for the model (41). Consistency and asymptotic Normality are thus also established for the MLE of (33), since they are a special case of the LSE of (41); with the results of Jennrich and Malinvaud there is no need to go through the type of proof we have adumbrated in Chapter 2 to derive these properties for the ML estimators of (41), as we should otherwise be compelled to do. And for *this* model we do have the information matrix, which confirms the asymptotic efficiency of the MLE of the GCR model.[23] The Least Squares estimation of (41) is an example of *Quasi Maximum Likelihood* estimation, insofar as it was suggested by the ML treatment of (33): Maximum Likelihood is used as a heuristic device as it gives an estimator for a particular case that may turn out to be more widely applicable.

The reduction of y_i to a scalar leads to some minor changes in the earlier formulas for the numerical determination of $\hat{\beta}$, as the scalar σ^2 may cancel out where the matrix Ω does not. Instead of (29a) we now find a simpler set of p equations that determines $\hat{\beta}$, namely

$$\sum_i \phi'(x_i, \hat{\beta})^T y_i = \sum_i \phi'(x_i, \hat{\beta})^T \phi(x_i, \hat{\beta}) \tag{42}$$

This can be solved by the iterative scoring process without the need to evaluate $\sigma^2(\beta)$ at each step. It is only after convergence that we require

$$\hat{\sigma}^2 = \frac{1}{n} \sum_i \hat{e}_i^2$$

in order to evaluate the covariance matrix (32); that is

$$\hat{V}\hat{\beta} = \hat{\sigma}^2 \left(\sum_i \phi'(x_i, \hat{\beta})^T \phi'(x_i, \hat{\beta}) \right)^{-1} \tag{43}$$

[23] Jennrich indicates a proof of the asymptotic efficiency (1969: 640). While the discussion here as well as in most of the literature refers to scalar y_i and a single equation, we take it that the generalization to the multivariate GCR model presents no difficulties.

Questions and exercises

6.5 Section 6.6 contains the first precise instructions for estimation other than by OLS. As an exercise we propose the estimation of the nonlinear money demand function

$$M/Y = \beta_0 + \frac{\beta_1}{R - \beta_2}$$

with M the money stock, Y (national) income, and R the rate of interest. Specify the system (42), examine the scoring scheme for the solution of these three equations, write a computer program, and estimate the parameters and their variances from the data sets given below.

We propose this demand function, and not Konstas and Khouja's of Sections 1.2 and 5.1, because the latter presents considerable numerical difficulties. This one is more tractable; even so, we suggest that initial parameter values are obtained by a careful regression scan of the equation for different values of β_2. Since this is a minimum rate of interest, it is not hard to think of a reasonable range; a margin on either side should also be explored.

The MLE of β_2 is negative for both data sets, so that there is no liquidity trap in the sense intended by economic theory. While a negative β_2 is an acceptable empirical result – it does not make the equation nonsense – the reader may wish to test $H_0: \beta_2 = 0$ by one (or more) of the tests of Chapter 3.

We give two sets of data on the variables

M money supply,
Y gross national product,
R short-term rate of interest,

all represented by annual aggregate or mean values for the United States. The first set is the original data sample used by Konstas and Khouja (Table 1), as well by Kliman and Oksanen and by Spitzer, as explained in Section 1.3; the data have been published by Konstas and Khouja (1969: 777), who say they took them from *Long-Term Economic Growth 1860–1965* (U.S. Department of Commerce 1966). The definitions are as follows:

M Currency plus demand deposits, amount outstanding, billions of dollars, 1958 prices.
Y Gross National Product, billions of dollars, 1958 prices.
R U.S. Treasury bill yields, with periods to maturity from three to six months, percentages.

The data error reported by Spitzer (1976) occurred in an alternative interest rate series, not reported here.

Table 1. *Konstas and Khouja's data.*

Year	*M*	*Y*	*R*
1919	40.1	146.4	5.37
1920	38.3	140.0	7.50
1921	40.8	127.8	6.62
1922	43.6	148.0	4.52
1923	44.8	165.9	5.07
1924	46.7	165.5	3.98
1925	49.7	179.4	4.02
1926	50.5	190.0	4.34
1927	51.8	189.8	4.11
1928	52.0	190.9	4.85
1929	52.2	203.6	5.85
1930	51.7	183.5	3.59
1931	53.1	169.3	2.64
1932	51.5	144.2	2.73
1933	49.6	141.5	1.73
1934	50.7	154.3	1.02
1935	59.6	169.5	.76
1936	67.9	193.0	.75
1937	68.3	203.2	.94
1938	68.1	192.9	.81
1939	77.3	209.4	.59
1940	88.2	227.2	.56
1941	96.6	263.7	.54
1942	103.0	297.8	.66
1943	126.1	337.1	.69
1944	145.7	361.3	.73
1945	165.2	355.2	.75
1946	157.9	312.6	.81
1947	149.9	309.9	1.03
1948	141.1	323.7	1.44
1949	140.6	324.1	1.49
1950	142.3	355.3	1.45
1951	139.3	383.4	2.16
1952	143.1	395.1	2.33
1953	145.0	412.8	2.52
1954	145.4	407.0	1.58
1955	147.2	438.0	2.18
1956	144.7	446.1	3.31
1957	140.3	452.5	3.81
1958	138.4	447.3	2.46
1959	140.6	475.9	3.97
1960	136.4	487.7	3.85
1961	136.9	497.2	2.97
1962	138.2	529.8	3.26
1963	140.5	551.0	3.55
1964	143.5	580.0	3.97
1965	144.9	614.4	4.38

Table 2. *More recent data on money demand.*

Year	M	Y	R
1950	213.0	534.8	1.218
1951	208.8	579.4	1.552
1952	216.1	600.8	1.766
1953	217.6	623.6	1.931
1954	218.9	616.1	.953
1955	220.9	657.5	1.753
1956	216.6	671.6	2.658
1957	210.5	683.8	3.267
1958	209.6	680.9	1.839
1959	212.6	721.7	3.405
1960	208.8	737.1	2.928
1961	211.3	756.6	2.378
1962	212.0	800.3	2.778
1963	215.0	832.5	3.157
1964	220.2	876.4	3.549
1965	224.7	929.3	3.964
1966	227.6	984.8	4.881
1967	229.7	1011.4	4.321
1968	235.4	1058.1	5.339
1969	237.9	1087.6	6.677
1970	234.6	1085.6	6.458
1971	238.3	1122.4	4.348
1972	245.0	1185.9	4.071
1973	248.8	1255.0	7.041
1974	241.7	1248.0	7.886
1975	230.6	1233.9	5.838
1976	229.9	1298.2	4.989
1977	232.9	1369.7	5.265
1978	227.5	1438.6	7.221
1979	220.2	1479.4	10.041
1980	210.3	1474.0	11.506
1981	184.2	1502.6	14.077
1982	175.4	1476.9	10.686

We also give a more recent data set (Table 2). The variables are defined as follows:

M Currency plus demand deposits, billions of dollars, 1972 prices. Nominal values from *Business Statistics* (U.S. Department of Commerce 1978), *Survey of Current Business*, various issues; deflation by implicit GNP deflator from

Survey of Current Business (December 1980: 17 and later issues).

Y Gross National Product, billions of dollars, 1972 prices; from *Survey of Current Business* (December 1980: 17 and later issues).

R Yield on U.S. government securities, three-month bills (rate on new issues), percentages; from *Business Statistics* and *Survey of Current Business*, various issues.

The series for M and Y in the two data sets can be linked by the GNP deflator for 1958 of 66.04 (1972 = 100); they still differ because of data revision after 1966. The series for R differ by definition.

CHAPTER 7

Systems of linear regression equations

This chapter is concerned with the simultaneous estimation of several linear regression equations that are related by the correlations of their disturbances, by side relations among their coefficients, or by both. Since we maintain the assumption of IID Normal disturbances, this is a special case of the Generalized Classical Regression model of Section 6.1.

$$y_i = \phi(x_i, \beta) + \epsilon_i$$

$$\epsilon_i \text{ independent} \sim N(0, \Omega)$$

In the present instance the vector function ϕ is linear in x_i, so that for the jth element we have

$$y_{ij} = x_{ij}^T\beta_j + \epsilon_{ij} \tag{1}$$

Here x_{ij} is a vector of regressor variables at the ith observation, and β_j the corresponding coefficient vector. While both refer specifically to the jth equation, the same identical regressor may appear repeatedly in several or in all x_{ij}; the intercept variable, 1, is a case in point. Different β_j may also have elements in common; more generally, there may be interrelations among the coefficients of different equations. In this case the linear coefficients of the g equations are constrained, and they can be expressed in terms of a smaller number of free or independent parameters. To handle this we proceed as in Chapter 3, and first transform the elements of all β_j into an equal number of other parameters, say γ, as in

$$\gamma = g(\beta) \tag{2}$$

where β is a rearrangement of the β_j for $j = 1, 2, \ldots, g$ into a single $(p \times 1)$ vector, and $g(\ )$ is a one-to-one transformation. Restrictions on β can now be expressed, as in (3.10), by

$$g_m(\beta) = 0, \qquad m = 1, 2, \ldots, r \tag{3a}$$

or equivalently, as in Section 3.3, by

$$\gamma = \begin{bmatrix} 0 \\ \gamma_* \end{bmatrix} \tag{3b}$$

The $p - r$ elements of γ_* constitute the independent parameters that ultimately determine the systematic part of y.

With n observations on g linear equations like (1), the model can be represented in matrix notation in several ways.[24] We here adopt the following definitions:

$$X_i = \begin{bmatrix} x_{1i}^T & 0 & \cdots & 0 \\ 0 & x_{2i}^T & \cdots & 0 \\ \cdots & \cdots & \cdots & \cdots \\ 0 & 0 & \cdots & x_{gi}^T \end{bmatrix} \tag{4a}$$

$$\beta = \begin{bmatrix} \beta_1 \\ \cdots \\ \beta_j \\ \cdots \\ \beta_g \end{bmatrix} \tag{4b}$$

If there are k_j regressors in the jth equation, p is the sum of these numbers over j, and X_i is $(g \times p)$ while β is $(p \times 1)$. Note that p will usually exceed k, the overall number of different regressor variables in the model, since some (or all) of these can appear in more than one equation.

The complete model now can be written as

$$y_i = X_i \beta + \epsilon_i \tag{5a}$$

$$\epsilon_i \text{ independent} \sim N(0, \Omega) \tag{5b}$$

with or without restrictions on β. The *classical* trait of this model is that the disturbances are IID Normal. Hence all results from Chapter 6 for the GCR model apply: We may use the score vector and information matrix from Section 6.2, concentrate the likelihood function as in Section 6.3, and use the estimators of Section 6.4.

Among the econometric applications of this statistical model we shall meet several models that originally have been developed as offshoots of the great Linear Model of traditional econometrics. In that tradition, Maximum Likelihood estimation is used only when more robust methods fail, while we here employ it as a matter of course. This unfamiliar approach to familiar results may confuse the reader. We try to clarify matters in Section 7.2.

[24] Phillips and Wickens list three different matrix representations of the same linear model (1981: 116).

7.1 Seemingly unrelated regression equations and the single regression equation

In this section and the next we assume that β of (5) is not subject to any restrictions. In particular there are no parameter restrictions across the g regression equations, which therefore seem to be unrelated. If $g = 1$, we have a single equation only, and the model reads

$$y_i = x_i^T \beta + \epsilon_i \tag{6a}$$

$$\epsilon_i \text{ independent} \sim N(0, \sigma^2) \tag{6b}$$

with y_i, ϵ_i, 0, and σ^2 all scalars. But for the additional assumption that the disturbances are Normal this is the standard OLS regression model, the simplest of them all.

From the viewpoint of economic analysis the usual regression equation with a handful of regression variables is a very incomplete representation of reality, and the effect of many neglected variables must be taken up by the disturbances. If we consider regression equations for g similar economic variables with coincident observations, these are likely to have at least some neglected determinants in common, even though they may have no other links. The disturbances therefore will be correlated across equations. As Zellner first demonstrated, the efficiency of the estimators can be improved by taking this correlation into account (1962). Following his terminology, the model of (5) without restrictions on β is known as a set of *Seemingly Unrelated Regression Equations* or SURE.[25] The standard example is that the investments by General Electric and by Westinghouse for the same years are related to other variables that are specific to either firm; the two equations will then certainly share some neglected macroeconomic factors. Other cases readily come to mind, and it could be argued that *all* economic regression equations with coincident observations may be expected to be disturbance-related. SURE estimation techniques have indeed been very widely adopted.

We must warn, however, that here (and elsewhere) the neglected variables interpretation of the disturbances should not be pressed too hard. Statistical inference after all requires that the effects of the observed regressor variables and of the disturbances can be disentangled. This is achieved by treating the first as nonrandom and the second as a random variable, as we do here, or by imposing stochastic indepen-

[25] Zellner did not assume Normality of the disturbances. In referring to the literature we cannot always keep track of the fine distinction between regression models with and without the assumption of Normally distributed disturbances, which brings them within the domain of ML estimation.

dence if the x_i, too, are regarded as (realizations of) random variables. In (5) all elements of $\boldsymbol{\epsilon}_i$ must therefore be uncorrelated with all elements of X_i, and it is a moot point whether this assumption is realistic when X_i is extended to cover the regressors of several equations. Without this condition, however, the neglect of variables constitutes misspecification, and this can have serious consequences if we assume (as we must) that in the passage to the limit the omitted variables behave just like the observed regressors, and are for instance "constant in repeated samples." This case has been treated by P. Rao (1974).

Maximum Likelihood estimation of β in the SURE model, that is, (5) without restrictions, follows at once from the formulas of Chapter 6, which are considerably simplified by the substitution of

$$\phi'(x_i, \beta) = X_i \tag{7}$$

as follows from (5). By (6.29) the full set of equations that determines $\hat{\beta}$ is

$$\sum_i X_i^T \hat{\Omega}^{-1} y_i = \sum_i X_i^T \hat{\Omega}^{-1} X_i \hat{\beta} \tag{8a}$$

or

$$\hat{\beta} = \left(\sum_i X_i^T \hat{\Omega}^{-1} X_i \right)^{-1} \left(\sum_i X_i^T \hat{\Omega}^{-1} y_i \right) \tag{8b}$$

with

$$\hat{\Omega} = \frac{1}{n} \sum_i \hat{e}_i \hat{e}_i^T \tag{8c}$$

and

$$\hat{e}_i = y_i - X_i \hat{\beta} \tag{8d}$$

As before, we must exclude the possibility of a perfect fit of any one equation, which would render $\hat{\Omega}$ singular.[26] As with so many problems this is largely a matter of sample size. Clearly, we must have a sufficient number of observations relative to the number of regressors so that

$$\sum_i X_i^T \hat{\Omega}^{-1} X_i$$

is nonsingular. But the whole issue of sample size in relation to the number of regressors and of parameters is more complex. We return to it at greater length in Section 7.7.

The nonsingularity condition also applies to the single equation model of (6), where Ω reduces to the scalar σ^2; but its form is modified. As σ^2 cancels out in the single equation analogues of (8a) and (8b), the

[26] See footnote 19, page 87.

estimate of β is determined by a single set of equations, namely

$$\hat{\beta} = \left(\sum_i x_i x_i^T\right)^{-1} \left(\sum_i x_i y_i\right) \tag{9}$$

The y_i are scalars, and (9) is the familiar OLS estimator in an unfamiliar guise. The requirement that the inverse on the right-hand side exists corresponds to the well-known rank condition on X in the standard matrix notation, which we shall recall shortly. Note that there is no need to exclude a perfect fit: Since σ^2 cancels out, $\hat{\sigma}^2$ does not enter into the estimator, and we need not worry about the case $\hat{\sigma}^2 = 0$.

The last simplification also applies to (8a) and (8b) if it is assumed that Ω is diagonal, and $\hat{\Omega}$ is similarly restricted. It is easy to see that the large system of equations (8a) then falls apart into g subsets that yield the OLS estimators of the separate regression equations. This is trivial, for with a diagonal covariance matrix the seemingly unrelated regressions are truly unrelated, and can therefore be estimated one at a time. Another special case, which also causes (8a) to collapse to a set of OLS estimation equations, is that the same regressor variables occur in each regression equation, so that the x_{ji} of (4a) are identical. But this is not so easily derived from first principles, and it is best proved in the matrix notation we encounter below (Theil 1971: 309).

Unless we have one of these special cases, the set of equations (8) must be solved by iteration. An obvious scheme is to iterate between (8c) and (8d), which yield Ω for a given β, and (8b), which gives β for a given Ω. This corresponds to the quadratic approximation methods of Section 5.3, applied to the concentrated loglikelihood function. The process is usually started by taking OLS estimates of the β_j of each separate regression equation for the starting values of β.

After convergence the covariance matrix of $\hat{\boldsymbol{\beta}}$ is found as in (6.32) as

$$\hat{V}\hat{\boldsymbol{\beta}} = \left(\sum_i X_i^T \hat{\Omega}^{-1} X_i\right)^{-1} \tag{10}$$

The reader may verify that in the present model (6.26) and (6.27) yield identical expressions. Because of (7) the Hessian of the full loglikelihood of linear models is block-diagonal, and not just the Information matrix, as in the GCR model of Section 6.2.

7.2 The Generalized Least Squares model

We may extend the matrix notation of (4a) to all n observations by arranging the regressor variable values for each equation in the n rows of a matrix X_j

$$X_j = \begin{bmatrix} x_{1j}^T \\ \cdots \\ x_{ij}^T \\ \cdots \\ x_{nj}^T \end{bmatrix} \tag{11}$$

and these matrices in

$$\overline{X} = \begin{bmatrix} X_1 & 0 & \cdots & 0 \\ 0 & X_2 & \cdots & 0 \\ \cdots & \cdots & \cdots & \cdots \\ 0 & 0 & \cdots & X_g \end{bmatrix} \tag{12}$$

We recall that the x_{ij} consist of k_j elements, and that we have denoted the sum of the k_j over j by p. The matrices X_j are thus $(n \times k_j)$, and $\overline{X}$ is $(ng \times p)$. Again some columns may appear repeatedly in several or all X_j, like the intercept column, 1. We likewise redistribute the n observations of y_i in an $(ng \times 1)$ vector y, defined as

$$y = \begin{bmatrix} y_{11} \\ \cdot \\ \cdot \\ \cdot \\ y_{n1} \\ \cdots \\ y_{1j} \\ \cdot \\ \cdot \\ \cdot \\ y_{nj} \\ \cdots \\ y_{1g} \\ \cdot \\ \cdot \\ \cdot \\ y_{ng} \end{bmatrix} \tag{13}$$

The vector $\boldsymbol{\epsilon}$ is constructed in the same way from the $\boldsymbol{\epsilon}_i$. Finally, we define

$$\overline{\Omega} = \Omega \otimes I_n \tag{14}$$

where we make use of Kronecker matrix multiplication.[27]

[27] For the Kronecker multiplication of matrices and its properties, see for instance Theil (1971: 303–6).

After these preliminaries, the original model (5) can be summarized in the standard form

$$y = \overline{X}\beta + \epsilon \tag{15a}$$

$$\epsilon \sim N(0, \overline{\Omega}) \tag{15b}$$

As exercise 7.3 shows, some of the estimating equations like (8a) and (8b) now also admit of an elegant and simple notation, but others, like (8c), do not. So much for the new notation of the SURE model. In the case of a single equation, as in (6), g equals 1, $\overline{X}$ collapses to X_1, and the Kronecker product (14) is trivial; we may write the model as

$$y = X_1 \beta + \epsilon \tag{16a}$$

$$\epsilon \sim N(0, \sigma^2 I_n) \tag{16b}$$

With or without the Normal distribution of the disturbances this is the standard matrix formulation of the simple regression model. The OLS estimator (9) at last takes the familiar form

$$\hat{\beta} = (X_1^T X_1)^{-1} X_1^T y \tag{17}$$

and (12) reduces to

$$V\hat{\beta} = \sigma^2 (X_1^T X_1)^{-1} \tag{18}$$

We return to more general models. The SURE model (15) is a special case of the *Generalized Least Squares* or GLS model. With Normality added this reads as

$$y = X\beta + \epsilon \tag{19a}$$

$$\epsilon \sim N(0, W) \tag{19b}$$

Here X is *any* matrix of regressor variables, not necessarily of the form of $\overline{X}$ of (12), and W is *any* covariance matrix, not necessarily structured like $\overline{\Omega}$ of (14). But as we shall see the imposition of some structure of one kind or another on W is a prerequisite for estimation.

Like the matrix formulation of the OLS model, the GLS variant is due to Aitken (1935). In the original version it is assumed that W is known, at least up to a multiplicative scalar constant. This constant vanishes from the estimator of β

$$\hat{\beta} = (X^T W^{-1} X)^{-1} (X^T W^{-1} y) \tag{20}$$

if not from its covariance matrix

$$V\hat{\beta} = (X^T W^{-1} X)^{-1} \tag{21}$$

Both expressions follow from Maximum Likelihood theory, but they can also be derived from the small-sample theory underlying OLS estimation, and this is what Aitken did. When the GLS model reached econometrics in the late 1940s, it was soon recognized that in most applications the covariance matrix W is not known and must be estimated along with β. On closer consideration this is, however, a matter of degree. When y is $(ng \times 1)$, with g possibly equal to 1, W is $(ng \times ng)$, and in general this would add another $\frac{1}{2}ng(ng+1)$ unknown parameters to the p elements of β. With n observations on g regressands and on at most p regressors, estimation of such numbers of parameters is plainly impossible. We must therefore impose a simple structure on W, and in turn regard this as known; this will reduce its elements to functions of a much smaller number of parameters, preferably independent of the sample size n so as to avoid technical difficulties in the application of asymptotic theory. In empirical applications W is usually introduced with the express purpose of modeling certain salient properties of the disturbances that cannot be overlooked, and its structure is known from the beginning. Apart from the SURE specification (14), W may reflect various types of heteroskedasticity or of autoregressive patterns of the disturbances of economic time series. But the SURE model and its trivial OLS variant are the only GLS covariance structures that imply IID disturbances, and thus the only cases where the results on ML estimation from Chapter 6 apply as a matter of course. For the GLS model (19) with another simplifying structure of the covariance matrix, the MLE of β and of the underlying parameters of W must be established by another route. This has been done by Oberhofer and Kmenta (1974) and by Magnus (1978), and we refer the reader to their work. Our approach happens to intersect with GLS theory here, and does so again when we discuss autoregressive disturbances in Chapter 9; but these fleeting glimpses will have to do, and we shall not discuss ML estimation of the GLS model as such.

The application of ML methodology to GLS models came fairly late; at first the general prescription was to proceed in two stages, as follows: First estimate β by OLS, establish the parameters of W from the residuals, construct an estimate of W, and insert this into (20) in order to obtain the final estimate of β in the second stage (Cochrane and Orcutt 1949; Zellner 1962). This is the first step of the iterative process as sketched in Section 7.1, but since the first-stage OLS estimator is consistent it is also a two-stage procedure as described in Section 5.7. The resulting estimates are therefore asymptotically equivalent to the MLE that we would obtain after continuing the process until convergence.

Questions and exercises

7.1 Verify that the information matrix of the full loglikelihood function of the SURE model (5) is block-diagonal (see also Section 6.2).

7.2 After concentration the information matrix of the SURE model (5) is always positive definite, regardless of β, so that the first-order conditions for a maximum are sufficient for a global maximum (see Section 5.10). Show that this is so.

7.3 Write (8b) in the matrix notation of (15), and verify that X must have full column rank. What condition must be met by the X_j of (12)?

7.4 If Ω happens to be diagonal, the ML estimate (8b) of β in the SURE model coincides with OLS estimates of the β_j. Are the OLS estimates of the standard errors of the estimated coefficients also equal to the estimates based on (10)?

7.3 Sum-constrained dependent variables

The dependent variables of a set of regression equations are sometimes subject to an equality constraint dictated by economic theory, as in *demand systems,* which describe consumer demand by commodity or the derived input demand of producers. In either case the *sum* of the dependent variables is given. In the theory of consumer behavior, the budget restriction and the assumption of nonsatiation together prescribe that expenditure by commodity must add up to disposable income, which is regarded as a nonrandom exogenous regressor. A similar restriction applies to input costs in respect of total outlay. The observed values of the dependent variables identically satisfy the constraint, and this must also be reflected in the statistical model. This requirement complicates the estimation problem.

We consider a set of $g + 1$ linear regression equations like (1), but with the same set of k regressor variables entering each equation. This is the general form of a demand system. The sum of the dependent variables is given for all i. The precise form of this constraint varies, of course, with the definition of the variables: Expenditures add up to income, budget shares sum to one, first differences or deviations from the mean of budget shares sum to zero. This form is immaterial for the nature of the estimation problem, and for convenience we take the case that the $g + 1$ dependent variables add to zero. They form a vector y_i^*, and by this assumption

$$\iota^T y_i^* = 0 \qquad \text{for all } i \tag{22}$$

with ι a vector of unit elements.

Since the regression equations have a common $(k \times 1)$ regressor vector x_i, (1) is replaced by

$$y_{ij}^* = x_i^T \beta_j + \epsilon_{ij}, \qquad j = 1, 2, \ldots, g+1 \tag{23}$$

Instead of (4a) and (4b) we define a $((g+1) \times k)$ matrix B^*

$$B^* = \begin{bmatrix} \beta_1^T \\ \cdots \\ \beta_j^T \\ \cdots \\ \beta_{g+1}^T \end{bmatrix} \tag{24}$$

The system of regression equations (23) can now be rewritten as

$$y_i^* = B^* x_i + \epsilon_i^* \tag{25a}$$

$$\epsilon_i^* \text{ independent} \sim N(0, \Omega^*) \tag{25b}$$

Logic demands that (22) does not only hold for all the observed y_i^*, but also for any y^* that might conceivably be generated by (25a) for any x and any ϵ^*. This implies

$$\iota^T B^* = 0^T \tag{26}$$

and

$$\iota^T \epsilon^* = 0 \tag{27}$$

Clearly, one element of y_i^* as well as the attendant regression equation is redundant, as our count of their number as $g+1$ already suggests. This can be demonstrated by a return to the first principles of Section 2.2. We partition the last elements of $\mathbf{y}_i^*$ and ϵ_i^* and the last row of B* off, as in

$$y_i^* = \begin{bmatrix} y_i \\ \mathring{y}_i \end{bmatrix}, \quad \epsilon_i^* = \begin{bmatrix} \epsilon_i \\ \mathring{\epsilon}_i \end{bmatrix}, \qquad B^* = \begin{bmatrix} B \\ \mathring{\beta}^T \end{bmatrix} \tag{28}$$

The probability density function of (2.1) can now be written as

$$p(y_i^*, \theta, x_i) = p(\mathring{y}_i | y_i, \theta, x_i) \cdot p(y_i, \theta, x_i) \tag{29}$$

where θ represents the model's parameters: the elements of B^* and of Ω^*. The first term on the right-hand side is the *conditional* density of the last element $\mathring{y}_i$ for given y_i. But by (22) $\mathring{y}_i$ is determinate when y_i is known, and this conditional probability density is degenerate and takes the value 1 for the observed value of $\mathring{y}_i$. As a result

$$p(y_i^*, \theta, x_i) = p(y_i, \theta, x_i) \tag{30}$$

We may thus omit one element from y_i^* without affecting its density function, and this carries over to its likelihood and to the likelihood of the entire sample.

As for the parameters, the last row of B^* is determined by the others because of (26), and Ω^* is singular by (27) since

$$\Omega^* = E\, \epsilon_i^*\, \epsilon_i^{*T}$$

As a matter of fact, (27) implies that the rows and columns of Ω^* all sum to zero. The last row and column can therefore always be determined from the remainder, that is, from

$$\Omega = E\, \epsilon_i\, \epsilon_i^T \tag{31}$$

The singular covariance matrix causes no end of trouble if we attempt ML estimation of the coefficients of the entire system (25a), but the problem can be solved quite simply by dropping the last equation. By (28) and (31) we then have

$$y_i = Bx_i + \epsilon_i \tag{32a}$$

$$\epsilon_i \text{ independent} \sim N(0, \Omega) \tag{32b}$$

As we have seen, the likelihood of this model is the same as that of the entire system, and it is therefore a valid basis for estimation and inference in general. We have already indicated how the full $\hat{B}^*$ can be obtained from $\hat{B}$, and $\hat{\Omega}^*$ from $\hat{\Omega}$, and it is just another exercise in algebra to extend the covariance matrix of the linear coefficients to the last row of $\hat{B}^*$ which has been obtained by reconstruction.

Although it is clear that the argument is valid for the deletion of any of the $g + 1$ equations, the reader may wish to be reassured that the estimates of the complete system are indeed identically the same regardless of the choice of the omitted equation. Barten has shown that the likelihood function based on any g residuals can be rewritten as a single function of the full residual vector e_i^*, so that it is indeed immaterial what equation is deleted (1969: 24–7). Direct application of (6.25a) to the full system (24) would give

$$\log L_c^* = C_c^* - \frac{n}{2} \log \left| \sum_i e_i^*(\beta)\, e_i^*(\beta)^T \right|$$

as the concentrated loglikelihood, but this expression is undefined as the determinant is zero since the residuals sum to zero at each i,

$$\iota^T e_i^*(\beta) = 0$$

By an adaptation of Barten's argument we find for the concentrated loglikelihood function based on g residuals

$$\log L_c = C_c - \frac{n}{2} \log \left| \sum_i e_i(\beta) e_i(\beta)^T \right|$$

$$= C_c + n \log(g+1) - \frac{n}{2} \log \left| \sum_i e_i^*(\beta) e_i^*(\beta)^T + \iota\iota^T \right| \tag{33}$$

The point to note is of course that in the second expression all $g + 1$ residuals appear in a symmetric fashion.[28] Hints on the derivation of this result are given in exercise 7.6.

In the approach of the present section we can make the same point by showing that we may exchange the $(g + 1)$th equation, which has been originally omitted, by (say) the gth equation. This is accomplished by multiplying both sides of (32a) by the matrix A,

$$A = \left[\begin{array}{cccc|c} & I_{(g-1)} & & & 0 \\ & & & & \cdots \\ & & & & 0 \\ \hline -1 & -1 & \cdots & -1 & -1 \end{array}\right]$$

This will transform y_i and ϵ_i as desired, and it will effect the appropriate substitutions among the linear coefficients as AB replaces B. It is not very hard to verify that neither the likelihood nor the concentrated likelihood are affected by the change, so that statistical inference is invariant under the choice of the omitted equation.

The above argument holds regardless of further restrictions on the coefficients in B, and it can even be adapted to nonlinear equations. In the linear case under review, (32) can be rewritten by the substitution of

$$X_i = I_g \otimes x_i^T, \qquad \beta = \text{vec } B^T$$

The vec operator arranges the columns of a matrix into a single vector, and is used here to reverse B's construction of (24). As a result, (32) turns into

$$y_i = X_i\beta + \epsilon_i \tag{34a}$$

$$\epsilon_i \text{ independent} \sim N(0, \Omega) \tag{34b}$$

This is the same model as (5): If there are no restrictions on B (as opposed to B^*!), and hence not on β, it is the SURE model of Section 7.1. Since the same regressors occur in all equations – as we have assumed

[28] This is somewhat similar to the remedy for matrices that are not positive definite of Section 5.6.

from the beginning – ML estimation is identical to OLS estimation of each equation separately.

In this particular case of linear equations, identical regressors, and no restrictions, we therefore need not have bothered about the adding-up constraints at all: OLS can be applied with impunity to all $g + 1$ equations of the original system (23), and the resulting estimates automatically satisfy (26) provided (22) holds for the sample data. The true interest of the present analysis is that its principles remain valid in more complicated cases, which are reviewed in the next section.

7.4 Restrictions on the linear coefficients

The main motive for the analysis of complete demand systems is that one may use or test restrictions on the coefficients that stem from the economic theory of optimizing behavior. For consumer demand, this tradition was started nearly 20 years ago by Barten (1964); for derived input demand, it is of a more recent date since the system approach holds no attraction as long as there are only two inputs, like labor and capital. In both cases economic theory describes the agents' behavior as maximization under certain side conditions, and in both cases this leads to a number of restrictions on the elements of B^* or B of (25a) and (32a) respectively. In the standard case of consumer demand systems, as reviewed in the preceding section, expenditure on $g + 1$ commodities is related to income or total expenditure and to all $g + 1$ prices. Apart from the adding-up constraints economic theory suggests restrictions on the coefficients of each equation separately, like homogeneity, and restrictions on coefficients from different equations, like symmetry of the substitution effects. Similar constraints can be formulated for input demands. Economic theory also specifies inequality constraints, like concavity or negativity conditions for the substitution matrices, but the statistical treatment of such hypotheses is beyond our brief. We do not deal with the substance of these theoretical restrictions, and refer for the theory of consumer demand to the surveys by Barten (1977) and by Deaton and Muellbauer (1980a: 25–55), for the derived input demands to Berndt and Christensen (1973), or more generally to the review by Diewert (1974).

We shall also take it for granted that the economic theory and the concomitant restrictions are indeed relevant to the data in hand. As a matter of fact we do feel some misgivings about the usage of applying microeconomic considerations to macroeconomic variables, since the conditions for the implied aggregation are seldom met. But this is not the place to debate this issue; our primary concern is the technique of constrained estimation of a linear system, with demand systems merely providing a fashionable example.

To begin with, we recall that we have already given an expression for r restrictions on the linear coefficients of a system of g equations in (3a). As in Section 3.3, we denote the constrained ML estimate as $\tilde{\beta}$ and require that it satisfies

$$g_m(\tilde{\beta}) = 0 \qquad \text{for } m = 1, 2, \ldots, r \tag{35}$$

with $r < p$. The form of these restrictions varies with their content and also with the precise specification of the equation system; for consumer demand systems, for example, there exist several rival parametrizations, and the form of the Slutsky symmetry theorem differs accordingly. For present purposes the main technical distinction is between independent linear restrictions and the rest; linear restrictions can be written as

$$R\tilde{\beta} - \bar{r} = 0 \tag{36}$$

with R an $(r \times p)$ matrix of rank r and $\bar{r}$ an $(r \times 1)$ vector, both known.

Two alternative courses for the constrained estimation of β of (5) are open to us. The first is to extend the maximization problem by the addition of a Lagrangean term to the concentrated loglikelihood function. This has the advantage that the linear coefficients of the original system are treated symmetrically, and that the full set is estimated directly. At first sight it does, however, complicate matters by increasing the number of unknowns that must be estimated to $p + r$, by the addition of r Lagrange multipliers. With linear restrictions in the present linear system the technique can nevertheless be handled with elegance, as Deaton's use of it in an analysis of consumer demand shows (1974). The other approach to estimation is to eliminate as many parameters as we have restrictions, and to rewrite the concentrated loglikelihood as a function of only $p - r$ new parameters like γ^* of (3b). This requires that the β can indeed be expressed unequivocally in the γ^*. If the concentrated loglikelihood is analytically intractable in other respects, so that it must be maximized by numerical search, we have the advantage that the parameter space is reduced to $p - r$ dimensions; afterward, there is the chore of reconstituting the corresponding estimates of β from $\hat{\gamma}^*$. The method can, however, also be quite useful if the algebra is straightforward, as is demonstrated in Magnus's application to input demand for capital, labor, and energy (1979).

We shall briefly sketch both techniques. For the *first* approach we consider the linear restrictions of (36) imposed on an otherwise unconstrained linear system like (5).[29] We largely follow the same line as in Section 3.3. The Lagrangean to be maximized is

$$\log L_c(\beta) - (\beta^T R^T - \bar{r}^T)\,\mu \tag{37}$$

with

$$\log L_c(\beta) = C_c - \frac{n}{2}\log\left|\sum_i e_i(\beta)\, e_i(\beta)^T\right|$$

as in (6.25). The first order conditions for a maximum of (37) now yield the same system of $p + r$ equations as (3.11), namely

$$\left.\begin{aligned} q_c(\tilde{\beta}) - R^T\tilde{\mu} &= 0 \\ R\,\tilde{\beta} &= \bar{r} \end{aligned}\right\} \tag{38}$$

When we substitute the score vector of $\log L_c$ that was equated to zero in (8a), we obtain

$$\left.\begin{aligned} \left(\sum_i X_i^T\tilde{\Omega}^{-1}y_i\right) - \left(\sum_i X_i^T\tilde{\Omega}^{-1}X_i\right)\tilde{\beta} - R^T\tilde{\mu} &= 0 \\ R\,\tilde{\beta} &= \bar{r} \end{aligned}\right\} \tag{39a}$$

with

$$\tilde{\Omega} = \frac{1}{n}\sum_i \tilde{e}_i\tilde{e}_i^T \tag{39b}$$

and

$$\tilde{e}_i = y_i - X_i\tilde{\beta} \tag{39c}$$

The disturbance covariance matrix must thus be estimated from the residuals as calculated from the *constrained* ML estimate $\tilde{\beta}$. Upon rearrangement we obtain

$$\begin{bmatrix} \sum_i X_i^T\tilde{\Omega}^{-1}X_i & R^T \\ R & 0 \end{bmatrix}\begin{bmatrix} \tilde{\beta} \\ \tilde{\mu} \end{bmatrix} = \begin{bmatrix} \sum_i X_i^T\,\tilde{\Omega}^{-1}y_i \\ \bar{r} \end{bmatrix} \tag{40}$$

[29] If we wish to treat all the $g + 1$ equations of a demand system symmetrically, we must start off from (33) and add an *additional* Lagrangean term to the maximization of

$$C_c - \frac{n}{2}\log\left|\sum_i e_i^*(\beta)e_i^*(\beta)^T + \iota\iota^T\right|$$

subject to

$$\iota^T e_i^*(\beta) = 0$$

We define

$$Q = \sum_i X_i^T \tilde{\Omega}^{-1} X_i, \qquad S = (R\, Q^{-1}\, R^T)^{-1}$$

$$P = \sum_i X_i^T \tilde{\Omega}^{-1} y_i$$

and once more use the standard formula for the inverse of a partitioned matrix. This yields

$$\tilde{\beta} = (I - Q^{-1}R^T SR)Q^{-1}P + Q^{-1}R^T S\bar{r} \tag{41}$$

The covariance matrix of this estimator follows from (3.20) with G_r now equal to R and H^{-1}, the covariance matrix of the unconstrained estimator, given by (10) as Q^{-1}. This gives

$$V\tilde{\beta} = Q^{-1}(I - R^T SRQ^{-1}) \tag{42}$$

We note that the determination of $\tilde{\beta}$ from (41) again calls for an iterative algorithm since the matrices on the right-hand side depend on $\tilde{\Omega}$, as given in (39). Note that $\tilde{\Omega}$ differs from $\hat{\Omega}$ of (8), so that there is no point in trying to relate $\tilde{\beta}$ directly to $\hat{\beta}$.

A simple case arises when we can treat one equation by itself, either because we only have one equation or because the restrictions bear on a single equation at a time while we are moreover prepared to disregard the interdependence of disturbances across equations. This simplifies the expression for $\tilde{\beta}_j$; we consider (41) for $g = 1$, and find that $\tilde{\Omega}$ is replaced by $\tilde{\sigma}_j^2$. This term cancels out: When we multiply Q, S, and P by $\tilde{\sigma}_j^2$ we obtain

$$Q_* = \sum_i x_i x_i^T, \quad S_{*j} = (R_j Q_*^{-1} R_j^T)^{-1}, \quad P_{*j} = \sum_i x_i y_{ij}$$

Note that by (9) we have for the jth equation

$$\hat{\beta}_j = Q_*^{-1}\, P_{*j}$$

Substitution of all this in (41) and rearrangement gives

$$\tilde{\beta}_j = \hat{\beta}_j - Q_*^{-1} R_j^T S_{*j}(R_j \hat{\beta}_j - \bar{r}_j) \tag{43}$$

This simplification is of course only possible with restrictions "within equations," not "across equations," and even then only if we neglect interdependence among the disturbances.

In the *second* approach to constrained estimation, we eliminate as many parameters as there are restrictions, and thus express all p elements of β as a function of the $p - r$ elements of γ_* of (3b). We consider the case of a general, possibly nonlinear vector function[30]

$$\beta = f(\gamma_*) \tag{44}$$

with a $(p \times (p - r))$ matrix F of first derivatives

$$F(\gamma_*) = \left[\frac{\partial \beta_h}{\partial \gamma_{*j}}\right] \tag{45}$$

Upon substitution of (44) the model (5) now reads

$$y_i = X_i\, f(\gamma_*) + \epsilon_i \tag{46a}$$

$$\epsilon_i \text{ independent} \sim N(0, \Omega) \tag{46b}$$

This is a straightforward nonlinear model with unconstrained parameters γ_*, and the treatment of the GCR model of Chapter 6 applies. By the chain rule we have

$$\phi'(x_i, \gamma_*) = X_i F(\gamma_*) \tag{47}$$

When we substitute this into (6.29) we obtain

$$\sum_i \tilde{F}^T X_i^T \tilde{\Omega}^{-1} y_i = \sum_i \tilde{F}^T X_i^T \tilde{\Omega}^{-1} f(\hat{\gamma}_*) \tag{48a}$$

with

$$\tilde{F} = F(\hat{\gamma}_*) \tag{48b}$$

$$\tilde{\Omega} = \frac{1}{n} \sum_i \tilde{e}_i \tilde{e}_i^T \tag{48c}$$

and

$$\tilde{e}_i = y_i - X_i f(\hat{\gamma}_*) \tag{48d}$$

This set of equations determines the MLE $\hat{\gamma}_*$; its covariance matrix follows from (6.32) as

$$V\hat{\gamma}_* = \left(\sum_i \tilde{F}^T X_i^T \tilde{\Omega}^{-1} X_i \tilde{F}\right)^{-1} \tag{49}$$

We shall not bore the reader by recounting how the constrained estimate $\tilde{\beta}$ and its covariance matrix of rank $p - r$ can be obtained once the system (48) has been solved by some appropriate algorithm. This may consist of numerical search in a $(p - r)$-dimensional parameter space for

[30] According to the usage of Section 3.2 we should be writing $\beta = g^{-1}(\gamma_*)$, but in the present case this notation is rather awkward.

the maximum of the concentrated loglikelihood function

$$\log L_c = C_c - \frac{n}{2} \log \left| \sum_i e_i(\gamma_*) e_i(\gamma_*)^T \right| \tag{50}$$

or of an iterative scheme along the lines of Section 5.6.

The estimating equations are simplified if the restrictions are linear, and especially if they are homogeneous linear as in

$$R\beta = 0 \tag{51a}$$

with R a $(r \times p)$ matrix of known constants. We may now rewrite (2) and (3) as

$$\begin{bmatrix} R_1 & R_2 \\ 0 & A \end{bmatrix} \begin{bmatrix} \beta_1 \\ \beta_2 \end{bmatrix} = \begin{bmatrix} 0 \\ \gamma_* \end{bmatrix} \tag{51b}$$

where R has been partitioned so that R_1 is square and A is some convenient nonsingular square matrix of order $p - r$. We require the r restrictions to be linearly independent so that R has rank r, and select R_1 accordingly. Using partitioned inversion we may then solve (51) for β as a linear function of γ_*, say

$$\beta = F\, \gamma_* \tag{52}$$

with F a $(p \times (p - r))$ matrix determined by R and A. In many cases the choice of F is immediately obvious, without the need to select A and to perform the derivation. Take, for instance, the symmetry of (compensated) cross-price elasticities in the theory of consumer demand. With a suitable parametrization of the demand equations this imposes equality on pairs of elements of β. The easiest course is then to construct F as a unit matrix of order $p - r$ with additional rows, with a 1 in one position and zeros elsewhere.

When we have F, substitution into (48a) yields

$$\hat{\gamma}_* = \left(\sum_i F^T X_i^T \tilde{\Omega}^{-1} X_i F \right)^{-1} \left(\sum_i F^T X_i^T \tilde{\Omega}^{-1} y_i \right)$$

and this is (8b) but for the replacement of X_i by a rearrangement into $p - r$ columns in $X_i F$. We may indeed proceed in this manner from the start, form matrices $Z_i = X_i F$, and by (52) specify the model as

$$y_i = X_i F \gamma_* + \epsilon_i = Z_i\, \gamma_* + \epsilon_i \tag{53}$$

This expression looks very much like the SURE model of (5), and since γ_* is not constrained the estimation formulas (8) and (10) appear in order, with Z_i substituted for X_i. These formulas do indeed apply, but since Z_i does not have the particular "row-diagonal" structure of X_i shown in (4a), it is not a proper case of the SURE model. Inspection will show that the special case of identical regressors no longer permits OLS estimation, as it does in the SURE case.

Questions and exercises

7.5 Why do we insist throughout Section 7.3 that all $g + 1$ equations of (23) must have the same regressor variables?

7.6 (Barten 1969): Consider a square symmetric matrix D of order $g + 1$

$$D = \left[\begin{array}{ccc|c} & & & -1 \\ & I_g & & \cdots \\ & & & -1 \\ \hline -1 & \cdots & -1 & -1 \end{array}\right]$$

Verify that $|D| = -(g + 1)$, and that

$$D \left[\begin{array}{ccc|c} & & & 0 \\ & \Omega & & \cdots \\ & & & 0 \\ \hline 0 & \cdots & 0 & 1 \end{array}\right] D = \Omega^* + \iota\iota^T$$

so that

$$|D||\Omega||D| = |\Omega^* + \iota\iota^T|$$

or

$$|\Omega| = (g + 1)^{-2}|\Omega^* + \iota\iota^T|$$

Verify that this applies to (33).

7.7 c_{ij} is expenditure on commodity $j, j = 1, 2, \ldots, (g + 1)$, and x_i is total expenditure of household i, so that

$$\sum_j c_{ij} = x_i$$

Consider $g + 1$ linear Engel functions

$$c_{ij} = \alpha_j + \beta_j x_i$$

Show that OLS estimates $\hat{\alpha}_j$ and $\hat{\beta}_j$ automatically satisfy

$$\sum_j \hat{\alpha}_j = 0, \qquad \sum_j \hat{\beta}_j = 1$$

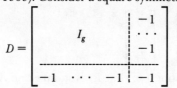

7.8 Consider a demand system that describes the demand for $g + 1$ commodities as a function of a commodity intercept, income (or total expenditure), and $g + 1$ prices. How many parameters are there in B^* and in B? How many *additional* restrictions follow successively from imposing (a) homogeneity of demand and (b) symmetry of compensated price effects?

7.5 Simultaneous linear equations

In the present context, systems of simultaneous linear equations constitute a digression: As far as ML estimation is concerned, they provide just another example of the estimation under constraints of Section 7.4. The single point of specific interest is the identifying role of the parameter restrictions. But it is a historic example, as simultaneous equations gave rise to the first thorough application of likelihood theory to economic models in the work of the Cowles Commission in the early 1950s.[31]

The economic model consists of g simultaneous linear equations that jointly determine g dependent variables. This is a traditional model of long standing in economic theory, where it is applied to the macroeconomic process as well as to the operation of a simple demand and supply schedule. Upon the addition of an independent Normal disturbance vector the structure equations laid down by economic theory form the linear system

$$Ay_i + \Gamma x_i = v_i \tag{54a}$$

$$v_i \text{ independent} \sim N(0, W) \tag{54b}$$

We here use the same matrix arrangement as in (25a). With g equations and g jointly dependent variables in y_i, A is $(g \times g)$, and, with k exogenous variables in x_i, Γ is $(k \times g)$.

These parameter matrices are subject to several restrictions. In the *normalization* of the system, g elements of A are equated to unity – one in each equation, that is, one in each row of A, to be selected at will. Secondly, the specification of the economic structure according to theoretical considerations sprinkles both A and Γ with zeros. Traditionally, no other restrictions are entertained.

The system can be rewritten in its *reduced form* as

$$y_i = Bx_i + \epsilon_i \tag{55a}$$

$$B = -A^{-1}\Gamma \tag{55b}$$

$$\epsilon_i = A^{-1}v_i \tag{55c}$$

[31] See Section 1.4.

$$\boldsymbol{\epsilon}_i \text{ independent} \sim N(0, \Omega) \tag{55d}$$

$$\Omega = A^{-1}WA^{T-1} \tag{55e}$$

The equations (55a) and (55b) correspond exactly to (32), and this was shown in (34) to be equivalent to the SURE model of (5). But while there were no restrictions on B of (32) and on β of (34), we here have restrictions because of (55b) in conjunction with the given pattern of zeros and ones in A and of zeros in Γ.

At first sight we may apply the techniques of Section 7.4, with γ_* representing some vector arangement of the free elements of A and Γ that are neither zero nor one. The structural coefficients are then estimated directly by numerically solving the system (48). In effect we express the entire equation system in terms of the unconstrained structural parameters of A and Γ which form γ_*, and thus obtain a straightforward nonlinear GCR model of Chapter 6. This course reflects that it is the structural model, and not the reduced form that is the prime object of estimation. This approach results in the Full Information Maximum Likelihood or FIML method of estimation of simultaneous equations of Koopmans, Rubin, and Leipnik (1950: 110–237). Goldberger explains the method in a simpler guise (1964: 252–6).[32]

In the present case the transformation of B of (55b) to γ_* depends on the theoretical specification of the economic model. We must therefore pay attention to certain technical conditions that were automatically met in the earlier case of Section 7.4, where the transformation from β to γ_* merely serves as a technical device for eliminating constraints on β. These conditions refer to the identification of the structural coefficients, and they now turn up in the requirement of Section 2.4 that the information matrix must be singular for ML estimation to be feasible. This matrix here is, as in (49),

$$\sum_i F^T X_i^T \Omega^{-1} X_i F = F^T \left(\sum_i X_i^T \Omega X_i \right) F \tag{56}$$

We here make use of the fact that F of (45) carries no observation index i; in this respect it is immaterial whether we consider the true value or some estimate, say

$$F = F(\gamma_*) \quad \text{or} \quad \hat{F} = F(\hat{\gamma}_*)$$

The information matrix (56) is of course of the same order as γ_*, that is,

[32] The term FIML is nowadays employed as a general appellation for ML estimation that respects all the relevant theoretical restrictions, and not just for the estimation of simultaneous equations in this manner.

the number of nontrivial structural coefficients in the model. For (56) to be nonsingular, F must therefore be of full column rank, and by (45) this requires that β has at least as many elements as γ_*. There are $g \times k$ reduced form coefficients in B, and hence in β; when we allow for normalization there are at most $g \times (g-1)$ coefficients in A, and $g \times k$ in Γ, or $g \times (g+k-1)$ structural coefficients in γ_* altogether. Estimation is thus impossible unless the latter number is reduced by $g \times (g-1)$ zeros among the elements of A and Γ. With more than this minimum number of zeros, equation (55b)

$$B = -A^{-1}\Gamma$$

implies constraints on the elements of B. We arrive at the same identification condition when we ask whether the last expression permits a unique solution for the nontrivial elements of A and Γ from a given B.

This requirement that there are at least $g \times (g-1)$ zeros or exclusion restrictions in the structural equations is nothing else than a modelwide count of the *order condition for identification:* It is simply the sum of the numbers of zeros that are necessary for the identification of the coefficients of each separate equation. The *rank* condition for a single structural equation is not so readily extended to the entire system, nor so easily linked to the rank of (56). We do not pursue the matter further, nor do we consider other types of identifying restrictions.[33]

Outside textbooks, FIML estimation of systems of simultaneous equations has for a long time been restricted to a few showpiece examples. At the time of its inception the method was hardly computationally feasible, and soon afterward it was overtaken by the simpler if less efficient method of Two-Stages Least Squares. The arrival of more powerful computers did little to revive the method, for it appears that the standard methods of maximizing the loglikelihood function run into insurmountable numerical difficulties with systems of more than 10 or 12 equations. For macroeconomic models this is of course very little. Recently, however, Parke has designed an algorithm that is much more successful in the FIML estimation of larger systems (Parke, 1982).

7.6 Tests of coefficient restrictions

We now return to the SURE model for a system of free linear regression equations of Section 7.1, and to its constrained counterpart of Section 7.4. The difference lies in the restrictions on the linear regression coefficients, that is, on the systematic part of the model, not on its

[33] For a full survey see Fisher (1966).

stochastic specification. Such restrictions, suggested by the economic theory of such systems as demand systems, do of course call for statistical tests. Inasmuch as they reduce the number of free parameters, they are simplifying assumptions in the sense of Chapter 3, and therefore amenable to the three statistical tests outlined in that chapter. All we have to do is to substitute specific expressions, based on the concentrated log-likelihood functions of the present models, in the general formulas. This leads to expressions that look simple, are easy to calculate, or both. We only contrast the case of r independent constraints of Section 7.4 with the completely free model of Section 7.1. In practice, testing often continues with *additional* constraints, once the first set of restrictions has been accepted. For that case we can however hardly improve on the general formulas of Chapter 3.

Wald's test of Section 3.5 has the test statistic (3.31)

$$W = g_r(\hat{\theta})^T(\hat{G}_r\hat{V}\hat{G}_r^T)^{-1}g_r(\hat{\theta})$$

Apart from the r restrictions

$$g_r(\beta) = 0$$

and the matrix G_r of their first derivatives we need only know the unconstrained estimate $\hat{\beta}$ and its covariance matrix $\hat{V}$. Apart from the substitution of (10) there is little to do; the general form of W is

$$W = \hat{g}_r^T\left\{\hat{G}_r\left(\sum_i X_i^T\hat{\Omega}^{-1}X_i\right)^{-1}\hat{G}_r^T\right\}^{-1}\hat{g}_r \tag{57}$$

and for linear restrictions like (36)

$$W = (R\hat{\beta} - \bar{r})^T\left\{R\left(\sum_i X_i^T\hat{\Omega}^{-1}X_i\right)^{-1}R^T\right\}^{-1}(R\hat{\beta} - \bar{r}) \tag{58}$$

Like the other two test statistics, this is asymptotically chi-square distributed with r degrees of freedom under the null hypothesis that the theoretical constraints do hold for the observations under review.

The second test we reconsider is the Likelihood Ratio test of Section 3.4 with its test statistic (3.22)

$$LR = 2(\log L\,(\hat{\theta}) - \log L\,(\tilde{\theta}))$$

From (6.25) and (50) we at once obtain

$$LR = n\left(\log\left|\sum_i \hat{e}_i\hat{e}_i^T\right| - \log\left|\sum_i \tilde{e}_i\tilde{e}_i^T\right|\right) \tag{59}$$

or, by (6.22) and (48c)

$$LR = n\,(\log|\hat{\Omega}| - \log|\tilde{\Omega}|) \tag{60}$$

The Lagrange Multiplier test of Section 3.6 has the test statistic (3.34)

$$LM = q(\tilde{\theta})^T \hat{V}(\tilde{\theta})\, q(\tilde{\theta})$$

where the score vector and covariance matrix are defined for the unrestricted estimator $\hat{\theta}$ but evaluated at the constrained estimate $\tilde{\theta}$. Employing (6.28) for the scores and (10) for $\hat{V}$ we obtain

$$LM = \left(\sum_i X_i^T \tilde{\Omega}^{-1} \tilde{\epsilon}_i\right)^T \left(\sum_i X_i^T \tilde{\Omega}^{-1} X_i\right)^{-1} \left(\sum_i X_i^T \tilde{\Omega}^{-1} \tilde{\epsilon}_i\right) \qquad (61)$$

While the three tests are asymptotically equivalent, the test statistics may and do differ for finite samples. By examining the original (not the concentrated) likelihood of the Generalized Least Squares model (19), Breusch has established that in any finite sample

$$W \geqq LR \geqq LM \qquad (62)$$

by an elegant proof from first principles (1979). This holds for linear restrictions and also for additional linear restrictions against a maintained hypothesis that already includes such constraints. Since the SURE model can be rewritten in the GLS format, Breusch's ordering applies to all the linear models of this chapter.

Questions and exercises

7.9 Sketch an overall test of the identifying restrictions of an (over-)identified simultaneous equations model. What must be concluded about the structural coefficients if the restrictions are rejected?

7.10 Can you test whether Ω is diagonal or not in the SURE model? Can this test still be performed if all equations contain the same set of regressor variables?

7.11 Consider the regression equation

$$y_i = \beta x_i + \gamma z_i + \epsilon_i$$

and the hypothesis $\beta = \gamma$. Examine the three test statistics and see whether you can verify (62).

7.7 Shortcomings of data sets and of models

We have repeatedly pointed out that singularity or near-singularity of the Hessian Q or of the information matrix H leads to an effective breakdown of Maximum Likelihood estimation. This may be due to properties of the data set or of the model; in practice the cause is not always immediately clear. We shall therefore review the main forms of singularity that may arise with the models of the present chapter. The example we take up is the estimation of the $p - r$ parameter vector γ_* of a constrained linear system from its concentrated loglikelihood, as in Section 7.4; the unconstrained linear system turns up as a special case.

We begin with some numerical considerations. As has been argued in Section 5.10, determination of the ML estimate is impossible if the Hessian of the maximand is singular at values of γ_* close to $\hat{\gamma}_*$. In practice, exact singularity is a rare exception, if only because the determinant is computed as a real-valued variable of such high precision that it almost never equals zero. But this only means that, for practical purposes, near-singularity of Q has equally ill effects on the ML estimates – it is just harder to detect.[34]

In order to simplify the analysis we take yet another step away from the singularity of Q, and replace Q by H. The model under review is (46), its concentrated loglikelihood is (50), and the score vector is obtained by substituting (47) into (6.28); this yields

$$q_c = \sum_i F^T X_i^T \Omega^{-1} e_i \tag{63}$$

Because of the concentration, F, Ω, and e_i are all three functions of γ_*, and if we derive Q_c by further differentiation the general result is an unwieldy expression of three terms, none of which vanishes, not even at $\hat{\gamma}_*$. At first sight this lessens the chance that Q_c is singular, as linear restrictions on its elements are unlikely to occur; in practice, this relief is an artefact. There is no reason why Q_c should not be *numerically* near-singular or ill conditioned, although admittedly it is very hard to establish from its formula when this will be so. It is for this reason that we take the information matrix H_c as its proxy; with change of sign, this provides a reasonable approximation to Q_c.

For the model (46) with concentrated loglikelihood (50) the information matrix is found by substitution of (47) into (6.31) as

$$H_c = \sum_i F^T X_i^T \Omega^{-1} X_i F \tag{64}$$

This matrix H_c, like γ_*, is of order $p - r$; F is the $(p \times (p - r))$ matrix of first derivatives of (45), X_i is the $(g \times p)$ matrix of (4a), with its curious "row-diagonal" design, and Ω is $(g \times g)$. Both F and Ω are functions of

[34] Since the determinant of the information matrix is affected by scale transformations of the parameters (which may be induced by scale transformations of the variables), its value is not a good criterion of near-singularity. The standard method of numerical analysis to establish the extent and nature of near-singularity is Singular Value Decomposition of the matrix; see Belsley, Kuh, and Welsch (1980).

γ_*; for Ω we have

$$\Omega(\gamma_*) = \frac{1}{n} \sum_i e_i(\gamma_*)\, e_i(\gamma_*)^T$$

with

$$e_i(\gamma_*) = y_i - X_i\, f(\gamma_*)$$

F depends on γ_* by its definition in (45). We finally note that (64) can be rewritten, as in (56), as

$$H_c = F^T \left(\sum_i X_i^T \Omega^{-1} X_i \right) F \tag{65}$$

and that we may also employ the notation of (12) and (14) to write

$$H_c = F^T \bar{X}^T \bar{\Omega}^{-1} \bar{X} F \tag{66}$$

where $\bar{X}$ is $(ng \times p)$ and Ω is of order np.

We shall consider the two latter expressions evaluated at $\hat{\gamma}_*$, or at the constrained estimate $\tilde{\beta}$; that is

$$\tilde{H}_c = \tilde{F}^T \left(\sum_i X_i \tilde{\Omega}^{-1} X_i \right) \tilde{F} \tag{67}$$

and

$$\tilde{H}_c = \tilde{F}^T \bar{X}^T \tilde{\bar{\Omega}}^{-1} \bar{X} \tilde{F} \tag{68}$$

Before we actually examine these expressions for singularity we note two special cases. While F is in general a function of γ_*, it is a matrix of known constants in the case of linear restrictions on β. And if we consider a SURE set of linear equations without constraints on the coefficients we may rewrite the above formulas with $r = 0$, $\gamma_* = \beta$, and $F = I_p$.

We begin with two possible defects of the sample x, namely insufficient sample size and multicollinearity. The *sample size n* must again meet two conditions. In the first place, for $\tilde{H}_c$ to have full rank, $\bar{X}$ in (68) must have rank $p - r$, too. Inspection of (12) shows that this requires

$$n \geqq (p - r)/q \tag{69a}$$

and in the absence of restrictions

$$n \geqq p/g \tag{69b}$$

Secondly, $\tilde{H}_c$ may be affected by loss of rank of $\tilde{\Omega}$ brought about by a perfect fit of one of the g equations. In the absence of restrictions this means that for all $j = 1, 2, \ldots, g$ the data set matrices

$$[y_j \; X_j] \tag{70}$$

of (13) and (12) must have full column rank $k_j + 1$, where k_j is the number of regressors in the jth equation. This leads to the condition

$$n \geqq \max_j (k_j + 1) \tag{71}$$

We now recall from Section 7.1 that p is the sum of the k_j over j from 1 to g. As the maximum exceeds the mean, condition (71) is stronger than (69b), and implies it.[35]

In the presence of possibly nonlinear restrictions, which may link coefficients across equations, the analysis is not so straightforward, and almost no general conclusions have been established. An exception is Brown's analysis of FIML estimation of an otherwise identified and estimable simultaneous equations model (1981). Brown finds that the number of observations must at least equal the count of all variables in the entire model, both jointly dependent and predetermined. This follows from the condition that the complete data matrix has full rank. This matrix, as suggested by (54), is

$$[Y^* \; X^*] = \begin{bmatrix} y_1^T & x_1^T \\ \cdot & \cdot \\ \cdot & \cdot \\ \cdot & \cdot \\ y_n^T & x_n^T \end{bmatrix}$$

and it is of order $(n \times (g + k))$. We thus obtain

$$n \geqq g + k$$

This is of course a direct generalization of the condition (71), which followed from a consideration of (70).

A second possible defect of the sample x is multicollinearity: Even with a sufficient number of observations, $\overline{X}$ of (68) may not have rank $p - r$, or p in the unrestricted case, because of linear dependence among the columns of one or more of the $\overline{X}_j$ of (12). The matrix $\tilde{\Omega}$ is not affected. Near-dependence of columns of one or more $\overline{X}_j$ is of course equally damaging, as it induces near-singularity, but it is not so easily detected.

Multicollinearity, like a near-perfect fit of one equation affecting the

[35] Even with a sufficient number of observations the danger of a nearly perfect fit of one of the equations does of course remain. We noted the possibility earlier in footnote 20, page 88.

rank of $\tilde{\Omega}$, may be a transient phenomenon, a fortuitous trait of a particular data set, which may be expected to vanish as the sample size is increased. But multicollinearity of a causal and structural character will persist, and it precludes estimation from any sample.

Lack of identification occurs if different admissible parameter vectors θ° define identically the same probability density (2.1) of the sample observations; it follows that there is no unique maximand of the likelihood function, so that ML estimation is impossible. The description just given implies that identification is a property of the model. Its absence can again be related to the singularity of the information matrix, as has been done by Rothenberg (1971). It is clear that we must now examine the true information matrix, not its sample estimate; but while H_c of (65) and (66) has been obtained by taking the expectation of $-\boldsymbol{Q}_c$ at the true parameter vector over $\boldsymbol{y}$, this expectation is still conditional upon the observed x. As a result the x_i enter as fixed constants in H_c, and if singularity of this information matrix were the issue, undersized samples would rank as a cause of underidentification. But this is confusing, and it is much better to concentrate on the properties of the model, not the sample, by considering an information matrix $\overline{H}_c$ that is obtained by taking the expectation of $-\boldsymbol{Q}_c$ over both $\boldsymbol{y}$ and $\boldsymbol{x}$. This leads to

$$\overline{H}_c = F^T M_x F \tag{72}$$

with M_x defined as

$$M_x = E(\mathbf{X}_\cdot^T \Omega^{-1} \mathbf{X}_\cdot) \tag{73}$$

$\mathbf{X}_\cdot$ is a random variable, the regressor matrix (4a) for a single observation; the X_i are realizations of $\mathbf{X}_\cdot$. The expression is equivalent to

$$M_x = E\left(\frac{1}{n}\sum_i \mathbf{X}_i^T \Omega^{-1} \mathbf{X}_i\right)$$

but it avoids considerations of sample size. In view of the arguments of Sections 2.4, 2.8, and 2.9 we might also have defined a corresponding probability limit M_x^*

$$\frac{1}{n}\sum_i \mathbf{X}_i^T \Omega^{-1} \mathbf{X}_i \xrightarrow{P} M_x^* \tag{74}$$

which would be again equivalent to M_x under suitable assumptions.

In any event, M_x is a $(p \times p)$ matrix, and it must least have rank $p - r$ to ensure that $\overline{H}_c$ is nonsingular. As we have argued at length in Sections 4.4 and 4.5, traditional macroeconomic data permit no definite assertions about the distribution of regressor variables or about their behavior with increasing sample size, whereas genuine samples of survey data offer slightly better prospects. In either case, M_x or M_x^* is usually given full rank p by assumption. Note that the only danger of rank reduction below $p - r$ would lie in severe structural and hence persistent multicollinearity.

With this assumption about the rank of M_x, identification hinges on the rank of F, just as it did in the special case of the identification of the structural coefficients of simultaneous equations of Section 7.5. Here F is $(p \times (p - r))$ and for $\overline{H}_c$ to be nonsingular it must be of rank $p - r$ at the unknown true parameters $\mathring{\gamma}_*$, and hence at any admissible γ_*. Whether this is the case or not is a matter of inspection. With nonlinear restrictions, or nonlinear $f(\gamma_*)$ of (44), F will usually have full column rank. With linear restrictions F is a matrix of constants and its existence, like its rank, requires that the r restrictions are independent – see (51). For a set of unconstrained linear regression coefficients we of course have $F = I_p$. The coefficients of a SURE model without constraints are therefore always identified.

CHAPTER 8

The transformation of Box and Cox

We consider another subclass of the Additive Normal Disturbance models introduced in Chapter 6, namely,

$$\psi(y_i, \gamma) = \phi(x_i, \beta) + \epsilon_i \tag{1a}$$

$$\epsilon_i \text{ independent} \sim N(0, \sigma^2) \tag{1b}$$

This corresponds to the general form (6.1) with the additional assumption of IID disturbances. In accordance with the practice of applied work we consider the simple case of a scalar y_i instead of a dependent vector variable.

This model differs from the scalar nonlinear regression model (6.33) of Section 6.5 only in the parametric transformation of the y_i. When we construct the density of the dependent variable, the Jacobian no longer vanishes, as it did in the transition from (6.5) to (6.6), and we must add it on to the likelihood. The loglikelihood of (1) is therefore

$$\log L = C - \frac{n}{2} \log \sigma^2 - \frac{1}{2} \sum_i e_i(\beta, \gamma)^2/\sigma^2 + \sum_i \log J_i(\gamma) \tag{2a}$$

with

$$e_i(\beta, \gamma) = \psi(y_i, \gamma) - \phi(x_i, \beta) \tag{2b}$$

and

$$J_i(\gamma) = \text{abs}\left(\frac{\partial \epsilon_i}{\partial y_i}\right) \tag{2c}$$

The Jacobian term enters $\log L$ additively and does not contain σ^2; we may therefore concentrate the likelihood in respect of that parameter exactly as before, in Section 6.3, and this yields

$$\log L_c = C_c - \frac{n}{2} \log \sum_i e_i^2(\beta, \gamma) + \sum_i \log J_i(\gamma) \tag{3}$$

ML estimates of β and γ are obtained by maximizing this function, and whether this is much different from the familiar prescription of minimizing the residual sum of squares depends on the form of ψ and on the chances of simplifying the last term of (3). Practical applications of the present model are largely confined to the use of a Box–Cox transformation for ψ, no doubt because under certain conditions this dispenses with the Jacobian altogether. Other parametric transformations of y_i are seldom employed; Ringstad's study of production functions is an exception (1974).

The reason for this neglect is that there is no need to complicate the stochastic specification in order to use a complex functional form for the relation between x and y. Instead of (1) we may write

$$y_i = \psi^{-1}(\phi(x_i, \beta), \gamma) + \epsilon_i \tag{4}$$

and this is a nonlinear regression model of Section 6.5. If we equate ϵ_i to its expected zero value, the systematic relation of y_i to x_i is the same in the models (1) and (4); the only difference lies in the role of the disturbance, and in the distribution of the y_i. But as we have argued at some length at the start of Chapter 6, and again in Section 6.5, the position of the disturbance in econometric models is often determined by convenience. While the Box–Cox transformation of the y_i is convenient enough (as we shall see), there are many examples of production function studies which use (4) instead of (1).

8.1 The transformation of Box and Cox

Univariate statistical analyses often require at least approximate Normality of the variate concerned, and this can be promoted by such standard devices as taking logarithms of positive quantities that have a positively skewed distribution. As a generalization, Box and Cox proposed the parametric transformation

$$z^{(\lambda)} = \frac{z^{\lambda} - 1}{\lambda}, \qquad \lambda \neq 0 \tag{5}$$

for positive z (1964). By l'Hôpital's rule we have

$$\lim_{\lambda \to 0} z^{(\lambda)} = \log z$$

so that the definition

$$z^{(0)} = \log z \tag{6}$$

is the natural complement of (5). For $\lambda = 1$ the transformation induces only a simple shift in z which affects the location but not the shape of its distribution. As λ varies over (0, 1) the transformation thus covers the range from $\log z$ to $z - 1$, or z itself, with something new in between. If λ

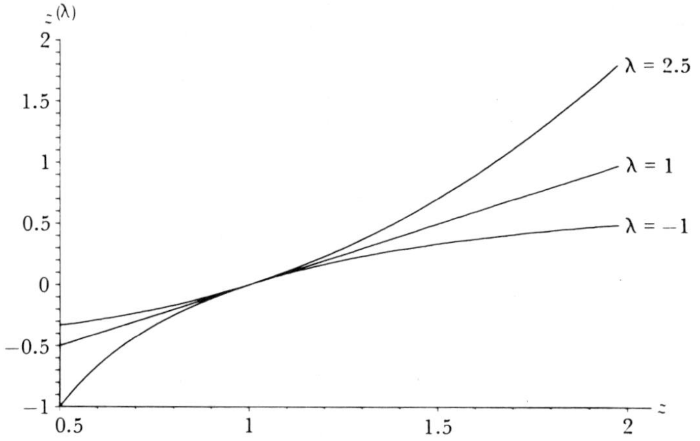

Figure 4. Behavior of the Box–Cox transform for various values of λ.

is not set in advance but determined by estimation we must of course also be prepared for values outside this range. We illustrate the course of (5) for selected values of λ in Figure 4.

In the specification of an econometric relation like

$$y_i^{(\lambda)} = \alpha_0 + \alpha_1 x_i^{(\lambda)} + \alpha_2 z_i^{(\lambda)} + \epsilon_i \tag{7}$$

the Box–Cox transformation offers a generalization of the traditional linear and loglinear regression equations at the cost of only a single additional parameter. For most economic variables – quantities, prices, incomes – the restriction to positive values is no impediment. This flexible functional form was first adopted by Zarembka in an analysis of the demand for money, where functional form matters (1968). The next generalization is of course to have different transformation parameters for the different variables, as in the money demand studies of White (1972) and, later, of Mills (1978) and of Boylan and O'Muircheartaigh (1981).

Several years before the study of Box and Cox, and for entirely different motives, essentially the same generalization had been introduced by economic theorists working in that other field where functional form matters, production function theory.[36] We refer of course to the Constant Elasticity of Substitution or CES production function, introduced because of dissatisfaction with the restrictive character of the loglinear Cobb–Douglas function, which implies an elasticity of

[36] The first to use the CES production function were Arrow, Chenery, Minhas, and Solow (1961).

substitution of 1. In the simple variant with constant returns to scale the CES function is

$$Y_i = A\left(\delta L_i^{\lambda} + (1-\delta)K_i^{\lambda}\right)^{1/\lambda} \tag{8}$$

with Y output, L labor, and K capital. This is a reparametrization of a specification like (7)

$$Y_i^{(\lambda)} = \alpha_0 + \alpha_1 L_i^{(\lambda)} + \alpha_2 K_i^{(\lambda)} \tag{9}$$

provided we impose the restriction

$$\alpha_0 = (\alpha_1 + \alpha_2 - 1)/\lambda \tag{10}$$

so that $Y \to 0$ if $L \to 0$ and $K \to 0$, as logic and homogeneity demand. The parameter α_0 has now disappeared, and we obtain (8) by putting

$$A = (\alpha_1 + \alpha_2)^{1/\lambda},\ \delta = \alpha_1/(\alpha_1 + \alpha_2)$$

The elasticity of substitution of the CES function (8) is

$$1/(1-\lambda)$$

For $\lambda = 0$ we recover the Cobb–Douglas production function as a special case with an elasticity of substitution of 1, and for $\lambda = 1$ we would have a linear production function with an infinite elasticity of substitution. In economic theory this is an absurdity, and even the intermediate cases are seldom discussed; interest centers on elasticities of substitution of less than unity, with negative values of λ.[37]

When we add an IID Normal disturbance to (8) we have a straightforward (if complicated) nonlinear regression equation, as in (4); when we add the same disturbance to (9) we have the mildly novel estimation problem of (7). The denouement is that with the Box–Cox transformation of the y, the Jacobian (2c) can usually be made to vanish altogether, as we shall now show.

8.2 Estimation

We turn briefly to the estimation of a model where the dependent variable is subject to a Box–Cox transformation, or

$$y_i^{(\lambda)} = \phi(x_i, \beta) + \epsilon_i \tag{11}$$

In principle, the specification of ϕ on the right-hand side is immaterial.

[37] Most economists revert the sign, and use $-\rho$ instead of λ in the definition (8) of the CES production function. The elasticity of substitution is then given by

$$\sigma = 1/(1+\rho)$$

and the issue is then whether ρ is significantly greater than zero.

When flexibility of the functional form is the issue, however, it will naturally consist of a regression equation in Box–Cox transforms of the independent variables, as in

$$y_i^{(\lambda)} = \alpha_0 + \alpha_1 X_{1i}^{(\mu)} + \alpha_2 X_{2i}^{(\nu)} + \cdots + \epsilon_i \tag{12}$$

By (11) and (5),

$$J_i(\lambda) = \text{abs}\left(\frac{\partial \epsilon_i}{\partial y_i}\right) = \text{abs}\left(\frac{\partial y_i^{(\lambda)}}{\partial y_i}\right) = y_i^{\lambda - 1} \tag{13}$$

so that the concentrated loglikelihood follows from (3) as

$$\log L_c = C_c - \frac{n}{2} \log \sum_i e_i(\beta, \lambda)^2 + (\lambda - 1) \sum_i \log y_i \tag{14a}$$

with

$$e_i(\beta, \lambda) = y_i^{(\lambda)} - \phi(x_i, \beta) \tag{14b}$$

With normal computational resources it should not be too difficult to obtain the MLE $\hat{\lambda}$, $\hat{\beta}$ by maximizing (14a). Zarembka already noted, however, that the process can be simplified by rescaling the y_i (1968). We should replace y_i by

$$y_i^* = w y_i \tag{15a}$$

so that

$$\sum_i \log y_i^* = 0$$

or

$$w = \exp\left(-\frac{1}{n} \sum_i \log y_i\right) \tag{15b}$$

In other words, we should divide the y_i by their geometric sample mean. The last term of (14a) is now identically zero, and Maximum Likelihood is once again equivalent to minimizing a residual sum of squares. Note that by (14b) this still depends on λ. The advantage is merely that we can now employ standard algorithms that operate on the RSS.

This raises the question whether such a rescaling of the y_i does not affect inference. Multiplication of the y_i by w (or by any other constant) changes the dependent variable of (11) by an affine transformation, for

$$y_i^{*(\lambda)} = w^{\lambda} y_i^{(\lambda)} + w^{(\lambda)} \tag{16a}$$

so that

$$y_i^{(\lambda)} = w^{-\lambda} y_i^{*(\lambda)} - w^{(-\lambda)} \tag{16b}$$

By the argument spelled out in Section 6.5, adapted to the present case, invariance of the statistical analysis requires that the function ϕ can absorb this change in its parameters; the equivalent of (6.36) is that ϕ must permit a reparametrization so that for any x

$$w^{-\lambda}\,\phi(x, \beta^*) - w^{(-\lambda)} = \phi(x, \beta) \tag{17}$$

Clearly linear equations in the elements of x_i or in function of these elements, like (12), meet the case, provided they contain an intercept term.

This line of reasoning confirms the analysis of Schlesselman (1971), who arrives at the same conclusion. If the condition (17) is met, the convenient scaling (15) will not affect the result. As in Section 6.5 this does not mean that the parameters and their estimates are unchanged, but that they vary in accordance with their dimensions; dimensionless parameters like λ are not affected. If parameters and estimates do change, the latter's covariance matrix changes correspondingly, and significance statements are the same.

With or without rescaling of the y_i, the maximization of (14) is a fairly standard problem; an account of various approaches to its solution has been given by Spitzer (1982). There is, however, a basic flaw in the model. Like the logarithmic transformation, (5) can only be applied to positive values, but unlike the logarithm the transformed variable is restricted as a result. By (5) we have for all y_i, and hence for $\mathbf{y}_i$

$$y_i^{(\lambda)} > -\frac{1}{\lambda} \qquad \text{if } \lambda > 0$$

and

$$y_i^{(\lambda)} < -\frac{1}{\lambda} \qquad \text{if } \lambda < 0$$

and this is strictly inconsistent with the Normal distribution of the disturbance in (7) or (11). The defect of the model turns up when we try to establish its regularity, as in exercise 8.2, and it should presumably be remedied by truncating the Normal distribution of the disturbance (Poirier 1978). Models that involve such truncation are discussed in Section 11.1, and we do not pursue this complication in the present context.

Questions and exercises

8.1 Consider the elasticity of y in respect of x in the relation

$$y^{(\lambda)} = \alpha + \beta x^{(\lambda)}$$

and show that it is invariant under changes in the units of measurement of x and y. Examine its behavior for $\lambda = 1$ and for $\lambda \to 0$.

8.2 Derive the score vector corresponding to the loglikelihood (14) and verify whether the elements have zero expectation if we ignore the truncation of ϵ.

8.3 (Continuation.) Can the scoring method still validly be used to obtain estimates if we ignore the truncation of the disturbances?

8.4 (Continuation.) Can the hypotheses $\lambda = 1$ or $\lambda = 0$ readily be tested by a Lagrange Multiplier test?

CHAPTER 9

Time series data and dynamic models

According to Judge et al., "economic data are generated by economic relations that are dynamic, stochastic and simultaneous" (1980: 623). They are probably thinking of the macroeconomic aggregates as given in the National Accounts for consecutive years or quarters. Such data are indeed the mainstay of traditional econometrics. A major source of concern is that successive observations cannot readily be assumed to be independent, so that the order in which they have arisen must be respected. This is characteristic of a *time series,* which is an ordered sequence $\{z_t\}$ with z random or nonrandom, vector or scalar, and with t denoting successive periods or equidistant points in time. The series may in principle range from $t = -\infty$ to $t = \infty$; sample observations are labeled by the index $t = 1, 2, \ldots, T$ instead of $i = 1, 2, \ldots, n$.

Since their order is given, we may submit the elements of a time series without ambiguity to the *lag operator* L defined by

$$L(z_t) = z_{t-1}$$

and to related operators, such as the *first difference operator* $\Delta = (I - L)$.[38] Repeated application of these operators is indicated by raising L (or Δ) to integer powers, and this leads to the definition of power series in L or *lag polynomials* like

$$\phi(L) = \sum_{j=0}^{n} \beta_j L^j$$

It has indeed proved possible to develop an algebra of this operator that closely resembles the ordinary algebra of real-valued variables (Dhrymes 1971: Chapter 2).

The reason why we are reluctant to assume too quickly that macroeconomic aggregates of successive periods are independent is the belief that they are ultimately determined by an intricate system of structural relationships, with cause preceding effect, and with the effect often spread over several periods, the entire structure being jolted along by spontaneously generated random shocks (Hendry and Richard 1983;

[38] The identity operator L^0 is denoted by I.

Sims 1980). Thus Hendry and Richard characterize an economy as "an inherently dynamic, stochastic, multidimensional, interdependent, nonlinear and evolving entity of considerable complexity, the overall functioning of which is only partly understood" (1983: 111). The systematic structure of this *data-generating process* is ultimately determined by the behavior of individual economic agents in conditions of uncertainty. But for the innovation represented by random shocks that come from outside, this view of the world is not essentially different from the grandiose universal deterministic model briefly unveiled by Laplace (1814: 3): As cause inexorably precedes its certain effect, and the laws governing these processes can be known, some vast and superior intelligence might one day be capable of seeing it all and predicting the entire future.[39] But whereas Laplace at once dismisses this model as an impracticable absurdity, and then turns to probability statements to cloak our fundamental ignorance, Hendry and Richard reduce the economic model to manageable proportions by the magic of aggregation; although the data-generating process involves a myriad of individual agents, their econometric model is a fairly simple regression equation for the transactions demand for money (1983: 111). The passage from the one to the other requires aggregation, simplification, isolation of a subset of relevant variables, and substantive assumptions that permit conditioning on exogenous variables, as has been briefly described in Section 4.4. Dynamic elements are likely to persist in the final result, where they are reflected by the presence of variables from earlier periods, lagged with respect to the current y_t, in the density function of that y_t.

A regression equation is thus rendered dynamic by the presence of lagged exogenous variables, by lagged endogenous variables, or by serial correlation of the disturbances. In addition to the aggregate effect of the shocks that hit the true structural system, the disturbances also represent various imperfections, omissions, and approximations, as explained in Section 6.1. In the present case, however, the distinction between the systematic part and the random disturbances is somewhat blurred, since the dynamics may at times be shifted at will from the one to the other: A particular lag structure of the one may be equivalent to a stochastic process of the other. There is often a choice of conceptually different models with similar if not identical properties, stretching from statistical time series models to subtle considerations of adaptive behavior. In these circumstances the specification of the model is of greater

[39] This Newtonian view of the universe has of course been thoroughly upset by modern physics.

concern than the correct application of Maximum Likelihood theory. The literature reflects this state of affairs.

The subject is much too vast for a single chapter; it deserves a textbook of its own. Several excellent texts have indeed been written (Dhrymes 1971; Harvey 1981). We here deal only with a few selected illustrative examples, without going deeply into the theory.

9.1 General remarks

We adopt the usual tacit assumption that the observations form part of a perennial time series from the infinite past to the distant future, $-\infty \cdots t \cdots +\infty$. We also assume that we can partition off weakly exogenous variables x_t (if any), so that the observed x_t can be treated as if they were given constants, even though in fact they also belong to an infinite time series. As we have seen in Section 4.4 this resolves the conceptual problem of how to envisage the generation of additional observations for $T \to \infty$. At the same time, however, the passage to infinity for t imposes certain constraints on the model parameters. It is generally regarded as unnatural that any variable varies beyond all bounds as $t \to \infty$, and such behavior is moreover definitely undesirable when we wish to establish asymptotic properties of the estimators and of other sample statistics. This leads to assumptions about the exogenous variables and to restrictions of the parameters that exclude explosive behavior and ensure stability or stationarity of the disturbance and of the endogenous variable.

A dynamic model relates the current endogenous y_t to current exogenous x_t, lagged values of both categories, and current disturbances v_t. Successive disturbances may be dependent, but we suppose that this can be taken care of by entering lagged values of y_t and x_t into the density of v_t. Altogether we may then express the *conditional* density of y_t, given its past realizations $y_{t-1}, \ldots$, as a function of x_t, $\tilde{L}(y_t)$ and $\tilde{L}(x_t)$, with $\tilde{L}(\ )$ denoting one or more lagged values. This gives

$$f(y_t|\tilde{L}(y_t)) = P_{y_t}(w_t, \theta^\circ, x_t, \tilde{L}(y_t), \tilde{L}(x_t)) \tag{1}$$

The density, and hence the likelihood, of the entire sample can be constructed by recursion from these conditional densities, as in

$$L(y, \theta, x) = f(y_t|\tilde{L}(y_t))\, f(y_{t-1}|\tilde{L}(y_{t-1})) \cdots \tag{2}$$

When we successively substitute the right-hand side of (1) into this expression we shall, however, sooner or later run into trouble. Each term includes a tail of earlier values of x and y, and as we proceed backward in time through the right-hand side of (2) we must at some stage come across lagged variables that have not been observed since they precede the sample period. This raises the problem of *initial conditions* or *starting values*. It can be solved (a) by regarding the sample once more as conditional on the first few observations, (b) by assigning conventional values to the nearest unknown pre-sample lagged variables, or (c) by estimating these unknowns as additional parameters. But the importance of the initial conditions (and of their treatment) diminishes with increasing sample size, and in the limit they do not affect the asymptotic properties of the (other) estimates at all.

Having decided in this matter we may write down the likelihood function (2) and maximize it in respect of the parameters θ. These are ML estimates, or at least estimates obtained by the Maximum Likelihood principle, but it does not follow that they have the attractive asymptotic properties sketched in Chapter 2. The derivation of these properties – consistency, asymptotic Normality, and efficiency – relies heavily on convergence theorems for sums of independent variates, and in the present case it is by no means certain that the loglikelihood function (and the score vector and information matrix) can be written in this form, even though the stochastic process under consideration is ultimately driven along by independent Normal shocks. In these circumstances one may establish asymptotic properties of the estimators for a particular case from first principles, as Dhrymes did (1971: 77–97), or try to determine the conditions for general consistency (or asymptotic Normality and efficiency) of estimators based on stochastically dependent observations. The latter course has been followed by Heijmans and Magnus (1983a,b). It must be admitted that the issue is also often altogether ignored.

9.2 Dynamic regression equations

Without much loss of generality we consider the common dynamic regression equation that is linear in scalar x and y and has Normal disturbances, as in the general model

$$\psi(L)y_t = \alpha + \phi(L)x_t + v_t \tag{3a}$$

$$\rho(L)v_t = \epsilon_t, \qquad v_t = \rho(L)^{-1}\epsilon_t \tag{3b}$$

$$\epsilon_t \text{ independent} \sim N(0, \sigma^2) \tag{3c}$$

The expressions $\psi(L)$, $\phi(L)$, and $\rho(L)$ are *lag polynomials*

$$\psi(L) = \sum_{j=0}^{m} \gamma_j L^j, \; \gamma_0 = 1 \tag{4a}$$

$$\phi(L) = \sum_{j=0}^{n} \beta_j L^j \tag{4b}$$

$$\rho(L) = \sum_{j=0}^{k} \rho_j L^j, \; \rho_0 = 1 \tag{4c}$$

The restriction on the first term of ψ is a harmless normalization, which permits us to rewrite (3a) as

$$y_t = \alpha - \sum_{j=1}^{m} \gamma_j L^j(y_t) + \phi(L)x_t + v_t \tag{5}$$

which looks like a standard linear regression. The values of the β_j and γ_j must meet certain constraints in the interest of stationarity, as must the ρ_j, and with sizeable n or m further restrictions may be in order to reduce the number of parameters of the model. Such patterns may be suggested by the nature of the delays they describe, or they may represent technical devices for a flexible yet parsimonious parametrization of the lag structure. We refer to the surveys of Griliches (1967) and of Judge et al. (1980: 631). Under certain technical conditions we may also rewrite (3a) as

$$y_t = \psi^{-1}(L)\alpha + \frac{\phi(L)}{\psi(L)}x_t + \psi(L)^{-1}v_t \tag{6}$$

The quotient of the lag polynomials defines a *rational lag structure*; Jorgenson has shown that with values of m and n of, say, two or three this gives a reasonable approximation to almost any *infinite distributed lag* of the x with the help of only a handful of parameters γ_j and β_j (1966).

In (3b) we have also introduced a lag polynomial that relates the disturbance v_t to the familiar IID $N(0, \sigma^2)$ variates ϵ_t, in the time series context known as *white noise*. The restriction on the first coefficient serves to normalize the variances and covariances of v_t with respect to σ^2. This lag polynomial represents an *autoregressive process;* for $k = 1$ we have the well-known first-order case

$$(I - \rho L)v_t = \epsilon_t \qquad v_t = \rho v_{t-1} + \epsilon_t \tag{7}$$

or

$$v_t = \epsilon_t + \rho\epsilon_{t-1} + \rho^2\epsilon_{t-2} + \cdots \tag{8}$$

The v_t are therefore again Normal with expectation zero and with variance and covariances

$$Ev_t^2 = \frac{\sigma^2}{1-\rho^2}, \qquad Ev_tv_{t-s} = \frac{\sigma^2}{1-\rho^2}\rho^s \tag{9}$$

Similar (but more complicated) expressions can be found for higher order autoregressive processes. As a result the distribution of a sequence of T disturbances υ_t can be derived; for this $(T \times 1)$ vector υ we find

$$\upsilon \sim N(0, W) \tag{10}$$

where the covariance matrix W is fully determined by σ^2 and by the ρ_j of (4c). The first few rows and columns need special attention since they refer to initial values.

We now return to (5), and consider the $T - S$ values of y_t for $t = S + 1, S + 2, \ldots, T$ with density determined by the first S sample observations, at given parameters, and arrange them in a vector $\boldsymbol{y}$; S depends on m and n of (4). The corresponding vector of $T - S$ disturbances is υ^*, and as in (10)

$$\upsilon^* \sim N(0, W^*) \tag{11}$$

By (5), the Jacobian matrix

$$\left[\frac{\partial \upsilon_t}{\partial y_s}\right] \tag{12}$$

is lower triangular with unity on the main diagonal, so that its determinant is 1. The loglikelihood corresponding to this model can therefore be written down as

$$\log L(\theta) = -\tfrac{1}{2} \log |W^*| + \tfrac{1}{2}\, u^T W^{*-1} u \tag{13}$$

with

$$u = u(\alpha, \beta_j, \gamma_j) \tag{14}$$

the *residuals* from (5), and

$$W^* = W^*(\sigma^2, \rho_j) \tag{15}$$

Although (13) cannot be concentrated in respect of the covariance parameters like earlier loglikelihood functions (just try), it may of course still be maximized in respect of the parameters, and this will yield ML estimates of α, σ^2, and of the β_j, γ_j, and ρ_j. But even though the stochastic process is driven by white noise, it is not in general possible to rewrite (13) in such a way that the loglikelihood and its derivatives appear as sums of stochastically independent terms.

Questions and exercises

9.1 Write (5) in full for $m = 2$, $n = 1$, and verify that the matrix (12) is lower triangular and has a unit diagonal.

9.2 Verify that the variance of v_t as given by (8) is bounded for $t \to \infty$ only if $|\rho| < 1$. What about its fourth moment?

9.3 From (3a) and (3b) we have

$$\rho(L)\,\psi(L)y_t = \rho(L)\,\alpha + \rho(L)\,\phi(L)\,x_t + \epsilon_t$$

with ϵ_t white noise, as always. Rewrite this in full for $m = 2$, $n = 1$, $k = 1$, solve it for y_t as in (5) and examine the loglikelihood function as in (13). Can the loglikelihood be rewritten as a sum of T or $T - 1$ independent terms? Can the scores?

9.3 An infinite distributed lag

Fairly simple considerations about the formation of expectations or about adaptive behavior soon lead to the expression

$$\beta(x_t + \lambda x_{t-1} + \lambda^2 x_{t-2} + \cdots), \quad 0 < \lambda < 1$$

for the current effect of infinitely many lagged values of an exogenous variable (Friedman 1957; Koyck 1954). This is the *geometric distributed lag* structure. The term in brackets can be expressed as the inverse of a simple lag polynomial, since

$$(I - \lambda L)^{-1} = I + \lambda L + \lambda^2 L^2 + \cdots \tag{16}$$

We use this in a simple equation with a single regressor variable

$$y_t = \alpha + \frac{\beta}{I - \lambda L}\,x_t + \epsilon_t \tag{17}$$

As the disturbances consist of white noise, the dynamic element resides exclusively in the exogenous variable. Even so this simple model serves to illustrate some earlier points, in particular the initial conditions issue.

Upon multiplication of both sides by $(I - \lambda L)$ (17) yields a regression equation like (5), namely

$$y_t = \alpha' + \lambda y_{t-1} + \beta x_t + v_t \tag{18a}$$

with

$$v_t = \epsilon_t - \lambda\epsilon_{t-1} \tag{18b}$$

and

$$\alpha' = \alpha(1 - \lambda L) \tag{18c}$$

Estimation by the maximization of a loglikelihood function like (13) is complicated by the fact that the parameter λ enters both in the residuals u_t and in the covariance matrix W. This course is therefore neither analytically nor computationally convenient, and we prefer to return to the original expression (17) as a basis for estimation. Both (17) and (18) are of course fully equivalent reformulations of the same model.

At first sight (17) resembles a generalized (nonlinear) regression equation like (6.33), say

$$y_t = \phi(x(t), \alpha, \beta, \lambda) + \epsilon_t \tag{19}$$

As the disturbances are independent, we can now go at once to the standard concentrated loglikelihood function (6.40)

$$\log L_c = C_c - \frac{T}{2} \log \sum_{t=1}^{T} e_t^2 \tag{20a}$$

with

$$e_t = y_t - \phi(x(t), \alpha, \beta, \lambda) \tag{20b}$$

There is however a complication in that $x(t)$ stands for the infinite sequence

$$x(t) = x_t, x_{t-1}, x_{t-2}, \cdots$$

and that we cannot for given parameter values derive the $\phi(x(t), \alpha, \beta, \lambda)$ fully from the sample observations. To bring this out we partition the infinite sum involved in each of these T terms into three parts, as in

$$\left.\begin{aligned} \phi(x(t), \alpha, \lambda, \beta) &= \alpha + \beta \sum_{j=0}^{\infty} \lambda^j x_{t-j} \\ &= \alpha + \beta \sum_{j=0}^{t-2} \lambda^j x_{t-j} \\ &\quad + \beta \lambda^{t-1} x_1 \\ &\quad + \beta \lambda^t \sum_{j=0}^{\infty} \lambda^j x_{-j} \end{aligned}\right\} \tag{21}$$

The last term cannot be determined for given λ and β since the x_{-j} precede the first observed value. This is the initial conditions problem. We briefly indicate two solutions.

The first approach has been discussed at some length by Dhrymes (1971: 98–101). We rewrite the last term of (21) as

$$\beta\lambda^t x^*, \qquad x^* = \sum_{j=0}^{\infty} \lambda^j x_{-j} \tag{22}$$

and then treat x^* as an additional unknown parameter. This is estimated along with α, λ, and β by maximizing (20) with

$$\phi(x(t), \alpha, \lambda, \beta) = \alpha + \beta \sum_{j=0}^{t-1} \lambda^j x_{t-j} + \beta\lambda^t x^* \tag{23}$$

This differs in two respects from a linear regression equation with parameter constraints: The extent of the summation in the second term varies with t, in other words the number of regressor variables involved varies with t, and moreover the coefficients of these x_{t-1} and of x^* also vary with t. Since $0 < \lambda < 1$, the "weight" of x^* in ϕ declines exponentially with increasing t; conversely, successive observations at ever-larger t contribute less and less information about x^*. This may explain why the estimator of x^* does not converge for $T \to \infty$, so that it is an ML estimator that is not consistent (Dhrymes 1971: 101).

An alternative solution to the estimation of (19) from (20) is to take the *two* last terms of (21) together, and so to substitute

$$y_1 = \alpha + \beta \sum_{j=0}^{\infty} \lambda^j x_{1-j} \tag{24}$$

By (17) this is equivalent to assigning a zero value to ϵ_t; it may also be interpreted as treating the observed sample as conditional upon y_1, which enters into the likelihood as a known constant. If we adopt (24), the loglikelihood is of the form of (20a), but it has $(T-1)$ terms only, as in

$$\log L_c = C_c' - \frac{T-1}{2} \log \sum_{t=2}^{T} e_t^2 \tag{25a}$$

$$e_t = y_t - \phi(x(t), \alpha, \lambda, \beta, y_1) \tag{25b}$$

$$\begin{aligned} \phi(x(t), \alpha, \beta, \lambda, y_1) &= \alpha + \beta \sum_{j=0}^{t-2} \lambda^j x_{t-j} + \beta \lambda^{t-1} (y_1 - \alpha) \\ &= \alpha(1 - \beta\lambda^{t-1}) + \beta \sum_{j=0}^{t-2} \lambda^j x_{t-1} + \beta \lambda^{t-1} y_1 \end{aligned} \tag{25c}$$

The last expression, obtained by substitution of (24) into (21), is particularly messy, and the result of this approach is in the present case as intractable as (23), if not more so.

In practice the estimation of β and λ in models of this type seldom proceeds by strict ML methods, and instrumental variable approaches to (18) (where disturbances and regressors are not independent) prevail (Dhrymes 1971: 110–26).

9.4 Autoregressive disturbances

In this section we consider a model where the dynamics are confined to the disturbance term, as in

$$y_t = \phi(x_t, \beta) + v_t$$

$$\rho(L) v_t = \epsilon_t$$

Without much loss of generality we replace ϕ by a simple linear function, and restrict $\rho(L)$ to the first-order autoregressive process of (7), or

$$y_t = \alpha + \beta x_t + v_t \tag{26a}$$

$$v_t = \rho v_{t-1} + \epsilon_t \tag{26b}$$

Interest in this model dates from the late 1940s. It was realized that with time series data the disturbances are rarely serially independent. First-order autocorrelation is an obvious alternative, and it appears as such in Durbin and Watson's test of independence. The choice between the two models is important, for with autoregressive disturbances OLS gives very inefficient estimates of β and biased estimates of its covariance matrix.

For the model (26) we write the loglikelihood of the full $(T \times 1)$ vector y along the lines of (13) as

$$\log L = C - \tfrac{1}{2} \log |W| - \tfrac{1}{2} u^T W^{-1} u \tag{27a}$$

with u a $T \times 1$ vector with elements

$$u_t(\alpha, \beta) = y_t - \alpha - \beta x_t \tag{27b}$$

and

$$W(\rho, \sigma^2) = \frac{\sigma^2}{1-\rho^2} \begin{bmatrix} 1 & \rho & \rho^2 & & \cdots \\ \rho & 1 & \rho & & \cdots \\ & \cdots & & & \cdots \\ & \cdots & & \rho^2 & \rho & 1 \end{bmatrix} \tag{27c}$$

This $T \times T$ matrix follows from (9), and its inverse is

$$W^{-1} = \frac{1}{\sigma^2} \begin{bmatrix} 1 & -\rho & & & \cdots & \\ -\rho & (1+\rho^2) & -\rho & & \cdots & \\ & \cdots & & & \cdots & \\ & \cdots & & 0 & -\rho & 1 \end{bmatrix} \tag{28}$$

which can be decomposed as

$$W^{-1} = \frac{1}{\sigma^2} R^T R, \; R = \begin{bmatrix} \sqrt{1-\rho^2} & 0 & 0 & & \cdots & \\ -\rho & 1 & 0 & & \cdots & \\ & \cdots & & & \cdots & \\ & \cdots & & 0 & -\rho & 1 \end{bmatrix} \tag{29}$$

(Theil 1971: 252).

For the standard GLS or Cochrane–Orcutt method of estimation we rewrite (26), as in exercise 9.3, as

$$y_t = (1-\rho)\alpha + \rho y_{t-1} + \beta x_t - \beta \rho x_{t-1} + \epsilon_t \tag{30}$$

and minimize the corresponding residual sum of squares over $(T-1)$

observations,

$$\text{RSS}_{T-1}(\alpha, \beta, \rho)$$

This is usually accomplished by alternating between OLS estimates of α and β for given ρ from

$$(y_t - \rho y_{t-1}) = (1 - \rho)\alpha + \beta(x_t - \rho x_{t-1}) \tag{31}$$

on the one hand (this yields RSS_{T-1}), and estimates of ρ for given α and β from the residuals

$$u_t = y_t - \alpha - \beta x_t$$

on the other hand. Inspection will show that, by (31),

$$\text{RSS}_{T-1} = \frac{1}{\sigma^2} u^T R_*^T R_* u \tag{32}$$

where u is a $(T \times 1)$ vector, as in (27), but R_* is a $\big((T-1) \times T\big)$ matrix, namely, R of (29) without its first row (Cochrane and Orcutt 1949).

In this approach we lose the first observation and treat the sample in effect as conditional upon the first disturbance. It may be thought that we must necessarily do so in order to cope with the initial conditions, but this is not so; we can perfectly well include the first observation in the likelihood with its marginal density

$$v_1 \sim N\left(0, \frac{\sigma^2}{1-\rho^2}\right)$$

This is a step toward the proper ML estimation by maximizing the full likelihood (27) over all T observations, as advocated by Beach and MacKinnon (1978). By (29) and (32), (27a) yields

$$\log L = C - \frac{T}{2}\log \sigma^2 + \frac{1}{2}\log(1-\rho^2) - \frac{1}{2\sigma^2}\left(u_1^2(1-\rho^2) + \text{RSS}_{T-1}\right) \tag{33}$$

This can be concentrated in respect of σ^2 as in

$$\log L_c = C_c + \frac{1}{2}\log(1-\rho^2) - \frac{T}{2}\log\left(u_1^2(1-\rho^2) + \text{RSS}_{T-1}\right) \tag{34}$$

Maximizing this function differs in two respects from minimizing RSS_{T-1}: It includes the first residual term, and it contains a term in log $(1-\rho^2)$, which ensures that the stability condition $|\rho| < 1$ is respected by $\hat{\rho}$. This term comes from the Jacobian of the transformation from v to ϵ, which is usually overlooked in GLS procedures, even when these are based on the full RSS

$$\mathrm{RSS}_T = u^T W^{-1} u = u^T R^T R u$$
$$= u_1^2(1-\rho^2) + \mathrm{RSS}_{T-1} \tag{35}$$

If we consider the first-order conditions for a maximum of (34), and set the score vector equal to zero, the partial derivatives in respect of the regression coefficients (α, β) lead of course to this GLS prescription, as is readily seen from (34); the difficulty lies in the first-order condition for ρ. Beach and MacKinnon give an elegant solution which leads to a fast iterative algorithm (1978: 53).

The same authors also report Monte Carlo experiments, with sample sizes of 20 and 50, that show that ML estimation is superior to the Cochrane–Orcutt procedure in terms of bias and of mean square error. While the major improvement is in the estimation of α, which is usually of little interest, the estimates of β and to a lesser extent of ρ are also better by ML. This result may restore our confidence in the small sample performance of the method.

9.5 Lagged dependent variables

We now turn to special cases of (3) where the dynamics reside in the dependent variable itself. This is the *pure autoregressive model*

$$\psi(L)y_t = \alpha + \epsilon_t, \qquad \gamma_0 = 1$$

or

$$y_t = \alpha - \gamma_1 y_{t-1} \cdots - \gamma_m y_{t-m} + \epsilon_t \tag{36}$$

and the *mixed autoregressive case,* which contains exogenous regressor variables as well, as in

$$y_t = \alpha + \beta x_t - \gamma_1 y_{t-1} \cdots - \gamma_m y_{t-m} + \epsilon_t \tag{37}$$

Conceptually it makes no difference whether there are several exogenous regressors or a (finite) number of lagged exogenous variables. Since ϵ_t is white noise the loglikelihood is the same as in the standard linear regression model, but for some adjustment of the range of summation. If we accept the first m values of y_t as conditioning constants, ML estimation is equivalent to OLS adjustment to the last $T - m$ observations of y_t. Even with white noise disturbances, however, it is not at all easy to establish that these ML estimators have the desired asymptotic properties. For (36) this has been done by Mann and Wald in one of the earliest applications of Maximum Likelihood theory to an econometric equation; they also treat the case that y_t is a vector (Mann and Wald 1943). The mixed case (37) was dealt with by Anderson and Rubin (1950) and by Koopmans, Rubin, and Leipnik (1950). These analyses are far beyond the level of this book, and the interested reader is advised to turn to Anderson (1958: 183–211).

Once we accept the convenient but conceptually uneasy conditioning treatment of the initial values, ML estimation of linear regressions involving lagged dependent variables, exogenous regressors, and white noise disturbances can be accomplished by OLS. This is a very effective general result, since all models like (3)

$$\psi(L)y_t = \alpha + \phi(L)x_t + \rho(L)^{-1}\epsilon_t$$

can be written in this form, provided the lag polynomials are of finite order. All we have to do is to multiply both sides by $\rho(L)$ to obtain

$$\rho(L)\,\psi(L)y_t = \rho(L)\alpha + \rho(L)\,\phi(L)x_t + \epsilon_t \tag{38}$$

and to solve this for y_t – by (4a) and (4c) both $\rho(L)$ and $\phi(L)$ have unit coefficients for the current value, and so has their product. We thus obtain an ordinary regression equation with lagged dependent and lagged exogenous variables, but with restrictions among the parameters that reflect its origin. If we are confident that the underlying specification is correct we should impose these restrictions on the estimators in the interest of efficiency.

In actual fact the analyst is usually not so sure of his model, and he may have to search for the simplest acceptable specification. By the general method of Section 3.2 one should start from an unrestricted and somewhat overparametrized regression equation like (37), including generous numbers of lags for all variables involved. One way of simplifying this is to test mechanically for the significance of the last coefficients of the lag polynomials, thus reducing their order. Another simplifying assumption is that the lag structures of y_t and of all the exogenous variables $x_t, z_t, \ldots$ have a *common factor*, which may then be attributed to disturbance dynamics. The polynomial $\rho(L)$ is such a common factor in (38). It is not difficult to derive the Wald statistic of Section 3.5 for the hypothesis that a simple equation like

$$y_t = \alpha' + \beta_1 x_t + \beta_2 x_{t-1} + \gamma y_{t-1} + \epsilon_t \tag{39}$$

represents (30), or that it satisfies

$$y_t = (1 - \rho)\alpha + \beta(1 - \rho L)x_t + \rho y_{t-1} + \epsilon_t$$

that is, in terms of (39),

$$H_0: \beta_2 + \beta_1 \gamma = 0$$

For this simple case we refer to Harvey (1981: 281–5). The general case with several exogenous variables and higher order common polynomial factors quickly becomes much more difficult; it has been treated by Sargan (1980).

Questions and exercises

9.4 If the disturbance of (17) follows an autoregressive process like (7), and $\rho = \lambda$, ML estimation of (18) is equivalent to OLS. Verify this. Is it a case of a common factor of Section 9.5? Is $\rho = \lambda$ a likely assumption?

9.5 Suppose y_1 is estimated by maximizing $\log L_c$ of (25) in respect of its value. Show that the estimate is less and less sensitive to new observations as the sample size increases.

9.6 Derive the information matrix of $(\alpha, \beta, \sigma^2, \rho)$ of (26) by examining (33) (Beach and MacKinnon 1978: 57).

CHAPTER 10

Discrete choice models

The three remaining chapters of this book are concerned with *probability models.* Just like regression models – indeed like *any* econometric model – these models determine the probability density function of the dependent variable; the difference lies in the role of the random variation. In regression models this is cursorily treated by the introduction of the disturbance, which is a nuisance variable characterized by nuisance parameters; to eliminate it, and let y take its expected value, is the ideal, or at any rate the standard, case for interpretation and discussion. The interest of the analysis lies precisely in this expected value, which is the "systematic component" of the model, and much ingenuity is spent on its design. In probability models, in contrast, the random variation is the essential phenomenon, and in the construction of the model it is the probability mechanism rather than the systematic component that is elaborated. Probability models are designed to describe individual variation, and they have no immediate bearing on aggregate data. Since they usually account fully for the observed variation there is no need to allow explicitly for neglected factors or other imperfections.

These general characteristics will be demonstrated in the sequel. Like the regression model, most probability models have their origin in biology and in medical research. Numerous studies of transport choice, of the demand for durables, and of occupational choice reflect a lively interest in their application to microeconomic data. This is of course part of the wider revival of microeconomic studies that has been called forth by the vast improvement in computing facilities. The process is by no means completed, and further probability models are likely to be elaborated before long.

The present chapter deals with discrete choice models, by now a standard part of econometrics, and the next chapter with related extensions, combinations, and variants. A much wider review of this field can be found in Amemiya's survey and in Maddala's recent textbook (Amemiya 1981; Maddala 1983). The emphasis is here on the application of likelihood theory. The final chapter gives a sketchy introduction to the empirical analysis of stochastic processes, which is still something of a novelty in econometrics.

10.1 The discrete choice model and its likelihood

The discrete choice model is a static probability model which describes the outcome (not the process) of a choice among S *alternatives*, such as the housing status of households, the profession of individuals, or the location of firms. We thus consider an exhaustive set of mutually exclusive possibilities or disjunct *states* $s = 1, 2, \ldots, S$, we observe the actual state of $i = 1, 2, \ldots, n$ observations, and we describe this dependent variable by a vector of S elements y_i, defined as follows:

"If observation i is in state s, $y_{is} = 1$ and $y_{ir} = 0$, $r \neq s$" (1)

The vector y_i is of course the realization of a random vector $\mathbf{y}_i$ that has a multinomial distribution characterized by the $(S \times 1)$ vector of probabilities

$$p_i - [p_{is}]$$

so that

$$E\mathbf{y}_i = p_i \tag{2}$$

This is a conditional distribution and the p_i are conditional probabilities, determined as a vector function of k regressor variables x_i and of l parameters β, as in

$$p_i = p(x_i, \beta) \tag{3}$$

This is a very general formulation. The regressor vector x_i usually contains characteristics of the individual (or of the household or firm) that vary from one observation to the other, but it may also include other variables that have the same value for all i. This applies to the unit constant or intercept variable, always present in these models, but also to particular characteristics of the alternatives like the travel time of various modes of transport. Naturally the addition of such *alternative-specific* variables to the *observation-specific* variables calls for special safeguards in the further specification of the model, as we shall see below.

The symbol p in (3) denotes any vector function that generates proper probabilities for all feasible x and for all β in the parameter space. It must therefore identically satisfy

$$p_s(x, \beta) \geqq 0 \qquad \forall s \tag{4}$$

and

$$\sum_{s=1}^{S} p_s(x, \beta) = 1 \tag{5}$$

In practice (4) is an inequality, for we exclude functions that permit any p_s to attain the values 0 or 1: We shall see that these values are awkward. Both conditions affect the choice of p and of its parametrization.

The condition (5) is matched by the property of the sample observations

$$\sum_{s=1}^{S} y_{is} = 1 \qquad \forall i \tag{6}$$

It follows that we may limit the dependent variable as well as the model to $S - 1$ states only, without impairing the description of the observations and without losing information. This can be illustrated for the common binary model of a single attribute like cigarette smoking or automobile ownership. Although there are two states, a single (0, 1) dependent variable is sufficient for a complete description of the data; it would be pompous to insist on a (2×1) vector y_i for reasons of symmetry, as the second element would be the complement of the first. For the simple dichotomy of a single attribute we shall therefore use a single (0, 1) dependent dummy variable D_i, defined as

$D_i = 1$ if individual i has the attribute

$D_i = 0$ otherwise

The model is likewise specified in scalar form as

$$P(\boldsymbol{D}_i = 1) = p(x_i, \beta) \tag{7a}$$

$$P(\boldsymbol{D}_i = 0) = 1 - p(x_i, \beta) \tag{7b}$$

The symbol y_i will however continue to denote a full and somewhat redundant $(S \times 1)$ vector variable.

In the sequel we consider two specific probability models. The *probit* model offers a close analogy to the classic regression model for the dichotomous case, while the *logit* model can more easily be extended to more than two states. First, however, we examine the general likelihood theory for any static probability model a little further.

We take it for granted that the observations have been obtained by a sample survey, as is usually the case. The individual observations then satisfy the important assumption of stochastic independence of Section 2.7, and asymptotic arguments can be justified along the lines of Section 4.5. We also assume that the x_i are exogenous, that is, that the joint density of $(\boldsymbol{x}_i, \boldsymbol{y}_i)$ can be so partitioned that the x_i may be treated as conditioning constants.

Because of the independence of the observations the *regularity property* of Section 2.3 carries over to the entire sample if it holds for a single observation. It is easy to see that it does. Since $\mathbf{y}_i$ has a discrete distribution, the integral in (2.3) must be replaced by summation, and the issue is whether

$$\left(\sum_{s=1}^{S} p_s(x_i, \beta)\right)' = \sum_{s=1}^{S} p_s'(x_i, \beta)$$

under differentiation in respect of (elements of) β. Since this always holds for finite S, any static probability model is regular of the first and higher order.

The independence property also leads to a simple loglikelihood function

$$\log L(\beta) = \sum_i y_i^T\{\log p(x_i, \beta)\} = \sum_i \sum_s y_{is} \log p_s(x_i, \beta) \tag{8}$$

In the second expression, $\{\log p(x_i, \beta)\}$ denotes a row vector with the logarithms of the S probabilities as its elements. In the absence of obvious nuisance parameters there is little point in concentrating this loglikelihood. We at once find

$$q_h = \sum_i \sum_s \frac{y_{is}}{p_{is}} \frac{\partial p_s(x_i, \beta)}{\partial \beta_h} \tag{9}$$

for a typical element of the score vector q; here p_{is} is an abbreviation of $p_s(x_i, \beta)$, and the two expressions are interchangeable.[40] For the Hessian matrix Q we have

$$Q_{hm} = \sum_i \sum_s \frac{y_{is}}{p_{is}} \frac{\partial^2 p_{is}}{\partial \beta_h \, \partial \beta_m} - \sum_i \sum_s \frac{y_{is}}{p_{is}^2} \frac{\partial p_{is}}{\partial \beta_h} \frac{\partial p_{is}}{\partial \beta_m} \tag{10}$$

In order to obtain the information matrix H we must reverse the sign and take the expectation over the random $\mathbf{y}_{is}$. We make use of

$$E\mathbf{y}_{is} = p_s$$

from (2), and then find that the first term vanishes because of (5), and that the second is simplified, so that

$$H_{hm} = -E\mathbf{Q}_{hm} = \sum_i \sum_s \frac{1}{p_{is}} \frac{\partial p_{is}}{\partial \beta_h} \frac{\partial p_{is}}{\partial \beta_m} \tag{11}$$

The inverse serves of course as the (asymptotic) covariance matrix of the estimates,

$$\hat{V}\hat{\boldsymbol{\beta}} = H(\hat{\beta})^{-1} \tag{12}$$

[40] Vector notation is not very helpful in the derivations that follow.

So much for the standard functions. Clearly we run into trouble with the loglikelihood (8) should any state that happens to occur have zero probability at some β, for with $y_{is} = 1$ and $p_{is} = 0$ for any (i, s), $\log L$ is not defined. If on the other hand some p_{is} equals 1, the likelihood is not affected, but complications arise over the differentiation of p_{is} in respect of β, and over the continuity of the derivative as a function of β. Both cases are in practice avoided since we exclude models that allow the p_s to take either extreme value. Note that $\log L$ is always negative as the p_{is} are genuine probabilities and lie between 0 and 1.

Reverting to matrix notation we can rewrite (11) as

$$H = \sum_i A_i^T \bar{p}_i^{-1} A_i \tag{13}$$

where

$$A_i = \left[\frac{\partial p_{ij}}{\partial \beta_h}\right]$$

is the $(S \times l)$ matrix of derivatives of (the elements of) p_i with respect to (the elements of) β, and $\bar{p}_i$ is a diagonal matrix that contains the elements of p_i on its main diagonal.[41] It is easy to see that each ith term of (13) is a positive semi-definite matrix, provided $l \geqq S$; hence H is positive semi-definite. If we disregard the possibility that H is singular we have a positive definite information matrix for any feasible parameter vector β. As the sample is usually fairly large, this will also hold approximately for $-Q$, so that the Hessian will almost certainly be negative definite over the entire parameter space.[42]

This result suggests that β should be estimated by one of the iterative quadratic approximation methods of Section 5.6. If we use the scoring method that employs the information matrix, we now know that by equation (5.26) the parameter vector will always be adjusted in a feasible direction, leading to an increase in likelihood, whatever the point of evaluation. This means that the process will always move in the right direction from any starting point we may adopt, although the choice is of course still important for the number of iterations until convergence. Insofar as we are confident that the Hessian is negative definite over the parameter space, the iterative process will converge to a unique global maximum according to the argument of Section 5.10.

The present notation (which we shall continue to employ) has been determined by the introduction of the dependent vector variable y_i of

[41] The same notation was earlier used in Section 6.5.

[42] McFadden has listed the conditions for the Hessian of the logit model to be everywhere negative definite (McFadden 1974: 119; see also Section 10.5, below).

(1). A widely used alternative is to dispense with an explicit dependent variable altogether and to record the observed states by *index sets*:

$$\text{“}i \in A_s \text{ if observation } i \text{ is in state } s\text{”} \tag{14}$$

The loglikelihood function (8) is then written as

$$\log L(\beta) = \sum_s \sum_{A_s} \log p_s(x_i, \beta) \tag{15}$$

In the dichotomous model (7) we may denote the index sets simply as "0" and "1," and write the loglikelihood as

$$\log L(\beta) = \sum_0 \log(1 - p(x_i, \beta)) + \sum_1 \log p(x_i, \beta) \tag{16}$$

This notation extends of course immediately to the score vector (9) and to the Hessian (10). If the observations are arranged by states, it can be helpful in organizing the computations. If we wish to take expectations, however, as in deriving the information matrix, we must allow for the random allocation of observations to sets, and in this connection the former notation is more convenient.

10.2 Grouped data

Although the model describes the state of a single individual entity, the data often consist of frequencies among groups of observations with a common value of the regressor variable. This necessarily happens if we have a sample of several hundreds of households, say, and consider the number of persons as the only regressor variable. A similar format may hold for household income, which is often reported by a limited number of income classes only, either through the design of the questionnaire or as the result of data processing. In these cases it is customary (and probably harmless) to disregard within-class income variation, and to assign a single conventional income level to all observations in the same class.

The regressor variables now take only a limited number J of different values x_j, and at each value we have n_j observations in all and n_{js} with state s,

$$\sum_s n_{js} = n_j, \qquad \sum_j n_j = n$$

We treat each set of n_j observations as the result of independent repeated trials with identical regressor values; the frequencies $\boldsymbol{n}_{js}$ are the random variables, and they have a multinomial distribution with

$$E\boldsymbol{n}_{js} = n_j p_{js}$$

where of course

$$p_{js} = p_s(x_j, \beta) \tag{17}$$

It is not difficult to adapt the standard formulas to this case. The loglikelihood (8) is replaced by

$$\log L(\beta) = C + \sum_j \sum_s n_{js} \log p_s(x_j, \beta) \tag{18}$$

where C is the sum of (the logarithms of) J combinatorial constants of the multinomial distribution. By (9), a typical element of the score vector now reads

$$q_h = \sum_j \sum_s \frac{n_{js}}{p_{js}} \frac{\partial p_s(x_j, \beta)}{\partial \beta_h} \tag{19}$$

while for the information matrix (11) we find

$$H_{hm} = \sum_j \sum_s \frac{n_j}{p_{js}} \frac{\partial p_s(x_j, \beta)}{\partial \beta_h} \frac{\partial p_s(x_j, \beta)}{\partial \beta_m} \tag{20}$$

The group frequency data may at times permit operations that cannot be performed on individual data. We may, for example, equate the observed relative frequencies

$$f_{js} = n_{js}/n_j$$

to the corresponding model probabilities, as in

$$f_{js} \approx p_s(x_j^T \beta) \tag{21}$$

In several cases we can find an inverse of the vector function p of (3), say p^{-1}, which can be applied to the vector of relative frequencies f_j and then yields a simple linear relation. When we extend both sides of (21) to form a vector, and transform them in this manner, we find

$$p^{-1}(f_j) \approx x_j^T \beta \tag{22}$$

with the left-hand side a vector of transformed frequencies. This again holds only approximately. It does of course carry the irresistible suggestion that β should be estimated by OLS, and although there is no statistical justification for this technique it can be quite helpful for finding starting values of β for an iterative ML scheme. The reason why this does not work for individual data is that the specification of p never allows zero or unit values, so that the inverse of such relative frequencies does not exist; with individual data we have no other relative frequencies than 0 or 1.

Another technique that is restricted to grouped data is the *minimum chi-square method of estimation.* For each j we have a frequency distribution of n_j observations over S cells, and for some estimate $\tilde{\beta}$ of β we may calculate the classical chi-square statistic defined as

$$\sum_s \frac{(n_{js} - \tilde{n}_{js})^2}{\tilde{n}_{js}} \tag{23a}$$

with

$$\tilde{n}_{js} = n_j p_s(x_j, \tilde{\beta}) \tag{23b}$$

Summation over all J groups yields

$$\chi^2(\tilde{\beta}) = \sum_j \sum_s \frac{(n_{js} - \tilde{n}_{js})^2}{\tilde{n}_{js}} \tag{24}$$

The traditional role of this statistic is to test the goodness of fit of the model, with $\hat{\beta}$ substituted for $\tilde{\beta}$; we shall discuss this in the next section. The chi-square quantity (24) may however also be used as a criterion function for the estimator that minimizes it. This minimum chi-square estimator is not identical to the ML estimator of β, although it has the same asymptotic properties (Rao 1955). The spirited defense of the minimum chi-square method by Berkson stresses its superiority over ML in small samples, but the issue is controversial (Berkson 1980).

10.3 Tests of simplifying assumptions and of goodness of fit

The tests of simplifying assumptions of Chapter 3 apply to the present class of models as a matter of course, and they provide counterparts for most of the standard tests of regression analysis. An obvious example is the t-test for the significant departure from zero (or from any other given value) of a single regression coefficient. This is matched by the asymptotic t-ratio for a single element of β, constructed from $\hat{\beta}$ and its asymptotic covariance matrix, which is (asymptotically) standard Normal; its square corresponds to the Wald statistic of Section 3.5, which is asymptotically distributed as chi-square with one degree of freedom.

The equivalent of the F-test of the significance of an entire regression equation is not so immediately apparent, since the present models have no disturbances and hence no residuals and no residual sums of squares. We may however construct a Likelihood Ratio test to check whether the p_{is} are indeed affected by the variation of the x_i from one observation to another, which is the issue under review. The standard of comparison is the case of a constant or base-line probability vector $\bar{p}$ for all observations. This is a restrictive or simplified case that is nested within the specification that is being tested, provided the latter allows for a constant among the regressors with S intercept coefficients; in that case the simplifying assumption is that all the other $l - S + 1$ parameters are zero.[43] This is a straightforward analogue to the F-test, where we also consider the sample mean as the standard of reference. It is easy to see that the ML estimate of the restricted model will always yield

$$\bar{p} = \frac{1}{n} \sum_i y_i$$

or constant probabilities equal to the relative frequencies in the sample. With an obvious notation of n_s for the overall sample frequencies we have

$$\bar{p}_s = n_s / n \tag{25}$$

This amounts of course to the fitting of $S - 1$ parameters. The likelihood ratio statistic (3.22) is then

$$2 \sum_i \sum_s y_{is} \log(p_s(x_i, \hat{\beta}) / \bar{p}_s) \tag{26}$$

and according to Section 3.4 this is asymptotically chi-square distributed with $l - S + 1$ degrees of freedom. For grouped data the test statistic is of course

$$2 \sum_j \sum_s n_{js} \log(p_s(x_j, \hat{\beta}) / \bar{p}_s)$$

and this has the same distribution.

The tests of Chapter 3 can naturally be adapted to other simplifying restrictions, but we do not pursue the subject further. Instead we turn to *tests of goodness of fit.* These early specification tests bear on the null hypothesis that the observations agree with the model, or that the model adequately describes the observations. This can be tested because probability models completely specify the form of the distribution of the observations. There is no counterpart for regression models. While R^2 is sometimes quoted as if it provides a validation, this is an error: It is merely a transformation of F, and can only test the same null hypothesis.

The traditional goodness of fit test is Pearson's chi-square test for the agreement of a frequency distribution with a probability distribution; see, for example, Mood et al. (1974: 442–8). Within each jth class of

[43] The somewhat contrived wording is necessary to cover models with several alternative-specific regressor variables that have the same value for all i.

grouped data the quantity

$$\sum_s \frac{(n_{js} - \hat{n}_{js})^2}{\hat{n}_{js}}$$

with

$$\hat{n}_{js} = n_j p_s(x_j, \hat{\beta})$$

is chi-square distributed under the null hypothesis of agreement, provided none of the $\hat{n}_{js}$ is smaller than a minimum number of 5 or so. Because of the independence of these terms their sum

$$\sum_j \sum_s \frac{(n_{js} - \hat{n}_{js})^2}{\hat{n}_{js}} \tag{27}$$

is chi-square distributed, too. The number of degrees of freedom is $J \times (S-1) - l$.

Another goodness of fit test can be constructed from a likelihood ratio. We regard the fitted model as a restricted variant of a *saturated* model, with $J \times (S-1)$ parameters, that is capable of a perfect fit in the sense that the predicted probabilities for each cell are equal to the observed frequencies (Bishop, Fienberg, and Holland 1975: 125–6). With a little ingenuity we can always invent such a general model within which the fitted model is nested. As before we denote relative frequencies as

$$f_{js} = n_{js}/n_j$$

The Likelihood Ratio test statistic is then

$$2 \sum_j \sum_s n_{js} \log(f_{js} / p_s(x_j, \hat{\beta})) \tag{28}$$

and this is once more asymptotically chi-square distributed with $J \times (S-1) - l$ degrees of freedom.

For grouped data we may thus distinguish three values of $\log L$ with $S-1$, l, and $J \times (S-1)$ fitted parameters respectively. Omitting the common combinatorial constant these are, in ascending order,

$$\text{(base-line)} \quad \sum_j \sum_s n_{js} \log \bar{p}_s = \sum_s n_s \log n_s - n \log n \tag{29a}$$

$$\text{(model)} \quad \sum_j \sum_s n_{js} \log p_s(x_j, \hat{\beta}) \tag{29b}$$

$$\text{(saturated model)} \quad \sum_j \sum_s n_{js} \log f_{js} = \sum_j \sum_s n_{js} \log n_{js} - \sum_j n_j \log n_j \tag{29c}$$

A comparison of the first two quantities leads to the likelihood ratio (26), which tests whether the model contributes significantly to an explanation of the observed frequencies, and a comparison of the last two quantities leads to the likelihood ratio (28), which tests for the agreement between the model and the observed frequencies. The overall likelihood ratio based on a comparison of (29c) and (29a) indicates whether the classification of the data into groups according to the value of the regressor variables is at all relevant to the discrete choice under review, regardless of the model specification.

Both goodness of fit test statistics (27) and (28) have the same asymptotic distribution, but they are not identical and they may well differ in finite samples. Both tests apply to grouped data.[44] We can therefore relate the test statistics to the relative agreement of cell frequencies and probabilities. This is immediately apparent in the likelihood ratio (28)

$$\sum_j \sum_s n_{js} \log(f_{js}/\hat{p}_{js})^2$$

while the chi-square (27) can be rewritten as

$$\sum_j \sum_s n_j \frac{(f_{js} - \hat{p}_{js})^2}{\hat{p}_{js}}$$

If the level of the discrepancies between frequencies and probabilities were constant, both test statistics would increase linearly with the overall sample size n. According to the law of large numbers, however, their increase will be kept in check: As the f_{js} and $\hat{p}_{js}$ converge to the same true probabilities, their ratio converges to one and their difference to zero. Even so, in practice sample sizes of two or three thousand may well produce highly significant test statistics while the actual agreement between the f_{js} and $\hat{p}_{js}$ looks reasonable enough. Many experienced analysts hold that the test is too strict, since it prescribes rejection of what looks like an acceptable result. With large samples, significant values of the test statistic are rarely taken seriously.

Questions and exercises

10.1 Verify from (9) that $E\boldsymbol{q} = 0$.

10.2 What is the combinatorial term C in (18)?

10.3 Consider the case of a single attribute, as in (7), and of grouped data, and assume that there is only a single parameter so that β is scalar. Obtain the variance of the estimate from (20).

[44] The chi-square test is explicitly restricted to data with a minimum number of observations in each cell.

10.4 Suppose the probabilities p_s of (4) do not depend on x but only on a single parameter α_s each, say $p_s(\alpha_s)$. Verify that the predicted probabilities $\hat{p}_s = p_s(\alpha_s)$ coincide with the overall sample frequencies.

10.5 We have $S = 4, J = 10$, and $l = 6$. The three loglikelihoods of (29) are

(base-line) 2800
(fitted model) 2700
(saturated model) 2650

What do you conclude from these values?

10.4 The probit model

The *probit* model was devised in the 1920s to describe the discrete or *quantal* response of living organisms to stimuli that are continuous variables. The model has its origin in biology and medicine, and the stock example of its application is bio-assay, where experimental dosages of a pesticide provide the stimulus and the death of an insect is the response. The effect of household income on car ownership can be described in exactly the same terms.

In the simple case of a single scalar stimulus variable x, a certain tolerance level or threshold value $\tilde{x}$ is attributed to each individual, and it is assumed that these values have a Normal (μ, σ_*^2) distribution over individuals. The observations constitute a random sample from this distribution. If the ith individual is exposed to a stimulus x_i, the probability of the appropriate response is

$$P(\boldsymbol{D}_i = 1) = P(\tilde{\boldsymbol{x}}_i < x_i) \tag{30a}$$

$$\tilde{\boldsymbol{x}}_i \sim N(\mu, \sigma_*^2) \tag{30b}$$

Upon introducing the notation $\Phi(.)$ for the standard Normal distribution function we have

$$\overline{P}_i = P(\boldsymbol{D}_i = 1) = \Phi\left(\frac{x_i - \mu}{\sigma_*}\right) \tag{31}$$

The function $\Phi(.)$ is defined as

$$\Phi(w) = \int_{-\infty}^{w} \frac{1}{\sqrt{2\pi}} \exp(-\tfrac{1}{2}\, t^2)\, dt \tag{32}$$

We denote its derivative, the standard Normal density, as

$$Z(w) = \frac{1}{\sqrt{2\pi}} \exp(-\tfrac{1}{2}\, w^2) \tag{33}$$

Note that the density corresponding to (31) is

$$\frac{1}{\sigma_*} Z\left(\frac{x_i - \mu}{\sigma_*}\right) \tag{34}$$

This is the probit model. By (31), the probability of a positive response increases with x along the familiar sigmoid Normal distribution function. The parameter σ_*, which reflects the dispersion of the threshold values, or the heterogeneity of the population under review, determines the slope of this curve.

An extensive review of this model and its variants in the context of biological applications has been given by Finney (1971). The model in its present form is easily adapted to economic relationships, and this was done in the early 1950s; Farrell used probit Engel curves for the ownership of automobiles of different vintage, and Adam fitted probit demand curves for the purchase of a single item like a cigarette lighter, with the reciprocal of the price being the stimulus (Adam 1958; Farrell 1954). The stimulus variable in such models is usually the logarithm of income or of price. Many other economic examples of probit analysis can be found in the excellent monograph on the lognormal distribution by Aitchison and Brown (1957).

The probit equation (31) can of course be reparametrized as

$$\bar{P}_i = \Phi(\alpha_0 + \alpha_1 x_i) \tag{35a}$$

with

$$\alpha_0 = -\mu/\sigma_*, \qquad \alpha_1 = 1/\sigma_*$$

Since we consider a dichotomous model like (7), with a single attribute and only two states, this is supplemented by

$$\bar{Q}_i = P(\boldsymbol{D}_i = 0) = 1 - \bar{P}_i = \Phi(-\alpha_0 - \alpha_1 x_i) \tag{35b}$$

because of the symmetry around zero of the standard Normal distribution. This formulation comes very close to the derivation of the model from a classical regression equation for a latent variable $\boldsymbol{y}_i^*$, which sets off the observed response $\boldsymbol{D}_i$ when it exceeds a given limit. This limit can be set at zero without loss of generality, so that we have

$$\boldsymbol{y}_i^* = x_i^T \beta_* + \boldsymbol{\epsilon}_i \tag{36a}$$

$$\boldsymbol{\epsilon}_i \text{ independent} \sim N(0, \sigma^2) \tag{36b}$$

$$\boldsymbol{D}_i = 1 \text{ iff } \boldsymbol{y}_i^* > 0 \tag{36c}$$

As a result

$$\bar{P}_i = P(y_i^* > 0) = P(\epsilon_i > -x_i^T \beta_*) = P(\epsilon_i < x_i^T \beta_*)$$

that is

$$\bar{P}_i = \Phi\left(\frac{x_i^T \beta_*}{\sigma}\right) = \Phi(x_i^T \beta) \tag{37}$$

Note that only $\beta = \beta_* / \sigma$ is identified; the original parameters (β_*, σ^2) are not.

Exactly the same expression is obtained from an underlying *random utility model*. We assume that the individual attributes a utility measure u_s to each alternative, and that this is determined by classical regression equations, as in

$$u_{0i} = x_i^T \gamma_0 + \epsilon_{0i} \tag{38a}$$

$$u_{1i} = x_i^T \gamma_1 + \epsilon_{1i} \tag{38b}$$

The pairs of disturbances are the usual independent $N(0, \Omega)$ variates, and they represent the effect of neglected variables and of other imperfections as well as of individual tastes. The alternative with the highest utility is adopted, and in the binary model this leads at once to equation (37) with

$$\beta_* = \gamma_1 - \gamma_0$$

and σ determined by the elements of Ω. Clearly we cannot retrieve the parameters of the underlying model (38) from the identified elements of (37), and it is therefore immaterial whether we impose independence on the two utilities by a diagonal Ω or not. But this holds only in the simple bivariate case.

The generalization of the probit model to more than two alternatives is difficult but full of interest. Conceptually the random utility model (38) is of course readily extended to any number of options, but to find the probability that a choice is adopted we must derive an expression for the probability that one out of S joint Normal variates exceeds all others. Hausman and Wise have shown how this can be done, at least for moderate S, and they give an illustration for $S = 3$ (1978). The major difference with the bivariate model discussed above is that for $S > 2$ elements of Ω do turn up in the estimated model, that they are themselves identified, and that the outcome is substantially affected by the restrictive assumption of utility independence, or diagonal Ω. There is no need to impose this restriction, and utility independence is a testable assumption. As we shall see, the freedom in this matter is a distinct advantage of the multivariate probit model over the rival multinomial logit. Its major disadvantage is that the derivations and the computations are onerous. This may account for the fact that the model has not yet been widely adopted, in spite of the exemplary work of Hausman and Wise and of the book by Daganzo, another ardent advocate of the model (1979).

We return to the simpler dichotomous model and discuss its estimation. By (37) and (35) the model to be estimated is

$$\bar{P}_i = \Phi(x_i^T\beta) \tag{39a}$$

$$\bar{Q}_i = \Phi(-x_i^T\beta) \tag{39b}$$

The estimation of β is straightforward and follows at once from the equations of Sections 10.1 and 10.2. For the loglikelihood of (8) or (18) we need values of $\Phi(.)$, once taken from printed tables but nowadays obtained from standard subroutines found in most software catalogues. The score vector (9) or (19) and the information matrix (11) or (20) make use of the derivatives

$$\frac{\partial \bar{P}_i}{\partial \beta_h} = x_{ih} Z(x_i^T\beta)$$

By (33) these are easily calculated.

For grouped data we may consider the equivalent of (22)

$$\Phi^{-1}(f_j) \approx x_j^T\beta \tag{40}$$

The expression on the left hand side is the inverse of the standard Normal distribution function, or *probit of* f_j, which can be read off from the familiar tables of Φ when they are entered with the fraction f_j; it is this function that gives the model its name. At one time special tabulations were provided (Fisher and Yates 1957: 64–8). Quite good initial estimates of β are obtained by OLS regression of probit (f_j) on x_j. In the case of a single regressor, estimates of α_0 and α_1 of (35) are even more simply obtained by plotting the f_j against x_j on probability paper which turns the sigmoid function $\Phi(.)$ into a straight line. Aitchison and Brown have shown that this yields quite reliable results (1957: 48–50).

10.5 The logit model

In the simple case of a binary model with a single regressor the *logit model* is

$$\bar{P}_i = P(\boldsymbol{D}_i = 1) = \frac{1}{1 + \exp(\alpha_0 + \alpha_1 x_i)} \tag{41a}$$

$$\bar{Q}_i = P(\boldsymbol{D}_i = 0) = 1 - \bar{P}_i$$
$$= \frac{\exp(\alpha_0 + \alpha_1 x_i)}{1 + \exp(\alpha_0 + \alpha_1 x_i)}$$
$$= \frac{1}{1 + \exp(-\alpha_0 - \alpha_1 x_i)} \tag{41b}$$

This is the direct counterpart of the probit model of (35), although α_0 and α_1 of course stand for different parameters (α_1 is of opposite sign in the two models). The probability $\bar{P}_i$ again follows an *S*-shaped curve as x_i increases, and it behaves indeed very much like a probit probability; with appropriate adjustment of the coefficients, the two curves (35) and (41) virtually coincide over a large part of their range, as has been known for some time (Aitchison and Brown 1957: 74; Amemiya 1981: 1487; Winsor 1932). Unless we attach an exaggerated importance to the extreme tail probabilities, the empirical fit seldom provides grounds for preferring one model over the other.

The logit model has a curious history. When we replace x_i in (41) by time t we have the *logistic growth curve*

$$P(t) = \frac{1}{1 + \exp(\alpha_0 + \alpha_1 t)} \tag{42}$$

This satisfies the differential equation

$$\frac{\partial P(t)}{\partial t} = -\alpha_1 P(t)(1 - P(t)) \tag{43}$$

With negative α_1, (42) is thus an obvious modification of the exponential growth curve in the presence of an upper limit or saturation level, here set equal to unity by appropriate scaling. The logistic was first put forward in this light as a model of population growth in 1845 by Verhulst, who taught mathematics to Belgian artillerymen, and who was himself a pupil of the great statistician Quetelet (Miner 1933). The function was next rediscovered independently in the same role by Pearl and Reed (1920). Familiarity with the logistic curve passed from these medical men to Berkson, who extended its use from population growth to (other) autocatalytic processes, and then proceeded to adopt it as an alternative for the probit model in bio-assay; he coined the name *logit*, and argued strongly that it represented the superior model (Berkson 1944, 1951). From this, the model spread around 1960 to economic applications, and in particular to the analysis of the choice of a mode of transport, or *modal split*.

This static logit model is far removed from the considerations that led to the logistic growth curve. Its justification as a discrete choice model came only afterward, after it had been in use for some time and after its generalization had been completed. The extension to a larger number of regressor variables is as straightforward as before, and we once again simply replace $\alpha_0 + \alpha_1 x_i$ by $x_i^T \beta$. The generalization to more than two alternatives is technically much easier than in the probit case: We may indeed derive the multinomial logit mechanically from rather primitive first principles. When we wish to attach conditional probabilities to S alternatives as a function of a $(k \times 1)$ regressor vector x_i, an obvious course is to consider

$$x_i^T \gamma_s$$

as the determinant of the probability of state s, to write

$$\exp(x_i^T \gamma_s)$$

since probabilities must be nonnegative, and finally

$$p_{is} = \frac{\exp(x_i^T \gamma_s)}{\Sigma_r \exp(x_i^T \gamma_r)} \tag{44}$$

since probabilities must sum to unity. This is the symmetrical representation of the logit model, with $S \times k$ parameters in the vectors γ_s; but it will be appreciated that these are not identified, as we may multiply the denominator and the numerator of (44) by any term like

$$\exp(x_i^T \eta)$$

without affecting the probabilities at all. We must therefore standardize, and we do so by taking the first alternative $s = 1$ as the standard of comparison, putting

$$\beta_s = \gamma_s - \gamma_1 \tag{45}$$

so that $\beta_1 = 0$. Instead of (44) we then obtain

$$p_{i1} = \frac{1}{1 + \Sigma_{r=2}^{S} \exp(x_i^T \beta_r)} \tag{46a}$$

$$p_{is} = \frac{\exp(x_i^T \beta_s)}{1 + \Sigma_{r=2}^{S} \exp(x_i^T \beta_r)} \quad \text{for } s \neq 1 \tag{46b}$$

Note the range of summation in the denominator; there are only $(S-1) \times k$ identifiable independent parameters. This is the multinomial logit model as first put forward by Theil (1969). The simple model of (41) is the special case of $S = 2$.

In the above formulation the regressor variables x_i vary over individuals but not over alternatives, as their coefficients β_s do. In the case of transport choice with walking, driving, taking a taxi, and so on as alternative modes, the x_i exclusively represent characteristics of the individual who decides and, perhaps, of the trip he is contemplating. The model can however be generalized by allowing for alternative-specific regressor variables such as the speed or the cost of a transport mode. This may again be done in two ways, since these variables may take the same value for all observations i, or they may not. If the observations refer to individuals who are considering the same trip, the speed and cost of each mode are the same for all i; but if distances vary this is no longer so. Along with observation-specific regressors like x_i we must thus also admit two types of alternative-specific regressors like x_s or x_{si}. All three types of regressor may occur in isolation or in combination in the logit model, and since they can all be subsumed in a single vector x_{is} the general logit model formulation is

$$p_{is} = \frac{\exp(x_{is}^T \beta_s)}{\Sigma_{r=1}^S \exp(x_{ir}^T \beta_r)} \tag{47}$$

Some or all of the elements of the x_{is} may be identical for all s, or for all i, or both (like the intercept unit dummy); such equalities impose restrictions on (elements of) the β_s.[45] Regressor variables with the same value for all alternatives call for standardization of their coefficients, as we have seen in the passage from (44) to (46); but since we cannot standardize away all coefficients, it follows that these must vary with s, as they do in (46). We may however very well impose a single common parameter for regressors that do vary across alternatives, like speed and cost; the underlying idea is that the one is equally attractive, and the other equally repellent, whatever the vehicle. If all regressor variables are of this type and moreover vary with i as well as with s we may write, say,

$$p_{is} = \frac{\exp(\alpha_s + x_{is}^T \beta)}{\Sigma_{r=1}^S \exp(\alpha_r + x_{ir}^T \beta)} \tag{48}$$

The intercepts that we have added must be standardized by putting $\alpha_1 = 0$; note that they represent the only alternative-specific effect in the model. Some purists would object to their presence on the grounds that the alternatives are completely characterized by the (other) regressor variables that reflect their properties.

So much for the various forms of the operational logit model as employed in current practice. Several rival theoretical derivations have

[45] There is no point in introducing parameters β_{si} in (47) in the interest of still great generality, as we would be hard put to estimate n vectors from n observations.

been put forward, as the model can be related to such diverse fields as discriminant analysis and axiomatic choice theory (Amemiya 1981; Maddala 1983). In economic applications, the justification most fertile in interpretation is a random utility argument similar to that of the (multinomial) probit specification. Like so many results in connection with the logit model this is due to McFadden, who has effectively developed the model to its full extent by his tireless exploration of its possibilities. Instead of (38) it is now assumed that the utilities $\boldsymbol{u}_{si}$ attached to the states $s = 1, 2, \ldots, S$ are independent random variables that have type I extreme value distributions (Johnson and Kotz 1970: I, 272–89).[46] This means that they have the distribution function

$$P(\boldsymbol{u}_{si} < w) = F_{si}(w) = \exp(-\exp(-\lambda_{si} - w)) \tag{49}$$

Each utility thus has a distribution of its own with a single parameter λ_{si}, and this is in turn related to the regressor variables by the specifications

$$\lambda_{si} = -x_i^T \gamma_s \tag{50a}$$

or

$$\lambda_{si} = -x_{is}^T \beta_s \tag{50b}$$

Upon assuming once more that the alternative with the highest utility is in fact adopted, these specifications lead to (44) and to (47) respectively for the probability that state s obtains. We do not give the derivation but refer the reader to Domencich and McFadden (1975: 63–5).

This random utility interpretation raises the status of the logit model from a convenient sigmoid transformation, easily adapted for the multinomial case, to the statistical expression of a structural model of discrete choice (Manski 1981). This is not only a matter of respectability (with slight ideological overtones) but it does contribute to our insight into the working of the model and to the interpretation of the results.

A major drawback of the model is the assumption of stochastic independence of the random utilities, which reflects the property of the operational model that the odds ratio p_{is}/p_{ir} for a given pair (s, r) is independent of the number and the nature of all third alternatives that are simultaneously considered. The general formulation (47), for instance, yields

$$\frac{p_{is}}{p_{ir}} = \frac{\exp(x_{is}^T \beta_s)}{\exp(x_{ir}^T \beta_r)} \tag{51}$$

Similar expressions hold for the other logit models we have considered.

[46] This distribution (49) is at times referred to as a Weibull or a Gumbel distribution.

Clearly the odds ratio is invariant under additions to or deletions from the wider set of alternatives to which s and r belong, as none of the other elements of this set occur in (51). This property is known as the *independence of irrelevant alternatives* (IIA), and is best demonstrated by McFadden's famous example of the red and blue buses. Consider the ratio (51) with s denoting private car use and r public transport or, specifically, a red bus. Imagine now the introduction of a new bus line that provides an identical service by blue buses. The ratio (51) remains the same. This is an unpalatable result, since in fact the probability of traveling by red bus will be reduced by the new alternative. The paradoxical result is related to the stochastic independence of the random utilities $\boldsymbol{u}_{si}$ of (49), which contradicts the reasonable expectation that the utilities of red and blue buses should be closely correlated over individuals. But the IIA property is of course inherent in any operational model that leads to (51), regardless of the underlying utility theory (Hausman and Wise 1978). This limitation of logit models is removed if the alternatives are no longer treated symmetrically, but arranged in ordered sets and subsets. In the example just given the choice between private and public transport then precedes the conditional choice between red and blue buses once public transport has been selected. This leads to the *nested logit* model, where (51) no longer obtains. For the algebra of the model and an algorithm for its estimation we refer to McFadden (1978, 1982). McFadden also shows that the model can be related to a random utility model where the utilities have an extreme-value distribution but are not independent.

For the straightforward ML estimation of the simpler logit model by the formulas of Section 10.1 we need the derivatives

$$\frac{\partial p_{is}}{\partial \beta_h}$$

For these derivatives it does make a difference whether the scalar element β_h belongs to the vector β_s that has the same state index as p_{is}, or to one of the other vectors β_r. From (47) we find

$$\text{if } \beta_h \in \beta_s, \qquad \frac{\partial p_{is}}{\partial \beta_h} = x_{is}(h) p_{is}(1 - p_{is}) \tag{52a}$$

$$\text{if } \beta_h \in \beta_r,\ r \neq s, \qquad \frac{\partial p_{is}}{\partial \beta_h} = -x_{ir}(h) p_{is} p_{ir} \tag{52b}$$

We use $x_{is}(h)$ for the element of the vector x_{is} to which β_h applies; this is *not* necessarily the hth element of that vector. These derivatives can next be substituted in (9) for the score vector and in (11) for the information matrix.

For special forms of the general model (47) we can sometimes obtain quite simple expressions for the scores and the information matrix by means of tedious but straightforward algebraic manipulation. We illustrate this for (46), which is a special case of (47) with $x_{is} = x_i$ for all s and with $\beta_1 = 0$. The complete parameter vector β thus consists of $S - 1$ segments of length k, which are the β_s for $s = 2, 3, \ldots, S$. For the score vector we consider a typical element as given in (9), or

$$q_h = \sum_i \sum_s \frac{y_{is}}{p_{is}} \frac{\partial p_{is}}{\partial \beta_h}$$

If β_h belongs to the segment β_r of β we find from substitution of (52)

$$\begin{aligned} q_h &= \sum_i \frac{y_{ir}}{p_{ir}} x_i(h) p_{ir}(1 - p_{ir}) - \sum_i \sum_{s \neq r} \frac{y_{is}}{p_{is}} x_i(h) p_{is} p_{ir} \\ &= \sum_i y_{ir} x_i(h)(1 - p_{ir}) - \sum_i \sum_{s \neq r} y_{is} x_i(h) p_{ir} \\ &= \sum_i y_{ir} x_i(h) - \sum_i p_{ir} x_i(h) \end{aligned}$$

where we make use of (6). The final result is

$$\beta_h \in \beta_r, \qquad q_h = \sum_i (y_{ir} - p_{ir}) x_i(h) \tag{53}$$

or for the entire rth segment of q

$$q_{(r)} = \sum_i (y_{ir} - p_{ir}) x_i \tag{54}$$

which is a $(k \times 1)$ vector, as it should be. Note that an expression like

$$\sum_i y_{ir} x_i(h)$$

is a sum over all n observations, which includes only selected items for which $y_{ir} = 1$.

In the present case the information matrix is best obtained by differentiating q, not by substituting (52) into (11) which requires laborious simplification. For the second derivative in respect of β_h and β_m we must again distinguish the two cases that β_m belongs to the same segment β_r as β_h, or that it belongs to an alien subvector β_s. From (53) and (52) we find the typical elements of the Hessian as

$$\beta_h, \beta_m \in \beta_r, \qquad Q_{hm} = - \sum_i x_i(h) x_i(m) p_{ir}(1 - p_{ir}) \tag{55a}$$

$$\beta_h \in \beta_r,\ \beta_m \in \beta_s, \qquad Q_{hm} = \sum_i x_i(h)x_i(m)p_{ir}p_{is} \tag{55b}$$
$$r \neq s$$

Since this Hessian contains no stochastic elements the information matrix is at once obtained by reversing signs. If we go for matrix notation, as in (54), the complete information matrix H can be partitioned in $S-1$ submatrices of order k, and these are

$$\text{for } r = s, \qquad H_{(rr)} = \sum_i p_{ir}(1 - p_{ir})x_i x_i^T \tag{56a}$$

$$\text{for } r \neq s, \qquad H_{(rs)} = \sum_i p_{ir}p_{is}x_i x_i^T \tag{56b}$$

Schmidt and Strauss give the same result in a different notation (1975a: 485).

The formulas can of course be further simplified if we have only two alternatives, or only a single regressor, or grouped data, but we leave these exercises to the reader. We do however present a procedure along the lines of (21) and (22) that permits regression estimation, at least in certain cases. The inverse of the logit probability function is the log of the odds ratio, and if we transform the observed group frequencies as well as the probabilities of the general model (47) in this manner we find

$$\log(f_{js}/f_{jr}) \approx x_{is}^T\beta_s - x_{ir}^T\beta_r \tag{57}$$

In the special case of (46) $x_{is} = x_i$ and $\beta_1 = 0$, so that

$$\text{for } s = 2, 3, \ldots, S \qquad \log(f_{js}/f_{j1}) \approx x_i^T\beta_s \tag{58}$$

For (48) we find

$$\text{for all } r \neq s \ \log(f_{js}/f_{jr}) \approx (\alpha_s - \alpha_r) + (x_{is} - x_{ir})^T\beta \tag{59}$$

Both equations permit the estimation of the parameters by OLS.

Questions and exercises

10.6 Equate the values of the probit function (31) and of the logit function (46a) to one another at the point $p = .5$ and at the point of inflexion, and derive the relations between the parameters.

10.7 Assume that equation (31) describes the probability of car ownership, with x the log of income. What is the income elasticity of car ownership? At what ownership level is the elasticity at a maximum?

10.8 Consider equation (47) with $x_{is} = x_s$ for all i. Verify that the parameter vector β_s is not identified if $k > 1$.

10.9 If x_i contains an intercept dummy, the average predicted probability of any state equals the overall sample relative frequency. Verify this from equation (54).

CHAPTER 11

Hybrid and mixed dependent variables

This chapter deals with various mixtures and combinations of discrete and continuous dependent variables within a single likelihood function. The case for pooling different information in this way arises when the range of a continuous variable is limited, or when discrete and continuous variables interact in the economic model or in the observational process. Such issues have gained in interest since modern computing facilities first permitted the analysis of large samples of individual microeconomic data; they have prompted a set of novel models and techniques that is still growing. Maddala's recent book gives an excellent survey of this fertile but rugged area (Maddala 1983). We here restrict the discussion to a few selected models only, and we rely even more than before on the literature. Our main purpose is to show how easy it is to think of a new model, and how quickly unexpected difficulties arise in the sequel.

The models under review have at most two dependent variables. The continuous dependent variable always follows from a classical linear regression equation with independent $N(0, \sigma^2)$ disturbances, though the actual observations can be somewhat distorted. The discrete variable may be generated by the same process or not; it depends in either case on a latent classical continuous regression variable passing a zero threshold. It is thus a probit variable with the derivation of (10.36). We disregard logit models for the discrete variable, although they do turn up in the literature; there seems to be little point in using logits in conjunction with Normal disturbances for the continuous variable. Technically, however, this presents no particular difficulties, for Lee has recently shown how the case can be handled by a transformation of the logit (Lee 1983: 508).

11.1 Tobin's model

A family budget survey yields detailed data on income and expenditure of individual households, and a quite ordinary Engel curve model for

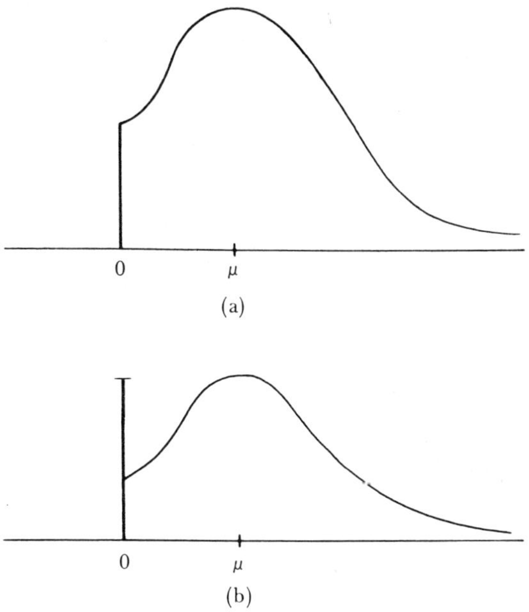

Figure 5. Truncated and censored Normal densities: (a) a truncated Normal density; (b) a censored Normal density.

such data would read

$$y_i = \alpha + \beta x_i + \epsilon_i \qquad (1a)$$

$$\epsilon_i \text{ independent} \sim N(0, \sigma^2) \qquad (1b)$$

with y expenditure on a particular commodity, x, say, the logarithm of disposable income, and i an index denoting single households. Yet this model is incorrect: The distribution of ϵ_i implies that y_i can attain all real values, while in fact expenditure is nonnegative.[47] If y is food expenditure, and if we have monthly data, the zero bound is so remote that the issue can safely be ignored. But if y is a luxury expenditure that is beyond the means of numerous households, zero observations will occur, and their incidence will moreover vary systematically with the income level x. A full model should account for this phenomenon, and

[47] This applies to a great many economic variables: most prices and quantities are necessarily nonnegative. The inconsistency with the model (1) disappears if y is the logarithm of such a variable. In other cases, the log transformation may restrict a variable to positive values while this is not factually correct. For the insidious nonzero bound implied by the Box–Cox transformation see Section 8.2.

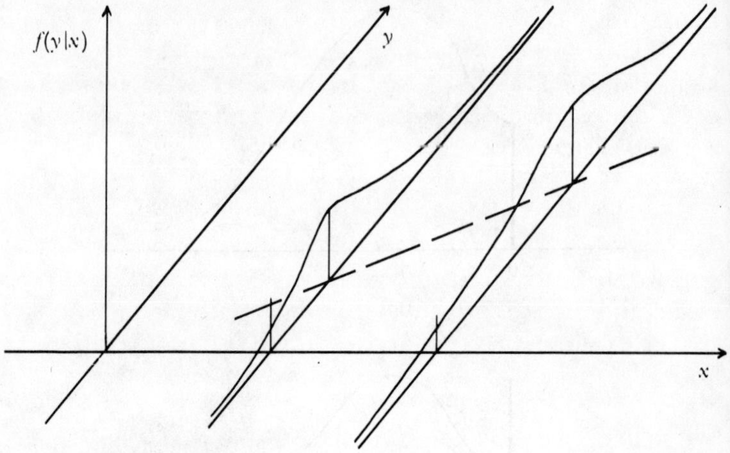

Figure 6. Tobin's model.

this has been done in Tobin's model, also known as the *tobit* model, because of its affinity with probits (Tobin 1958).

The main idea of this model is that would-be negative values of $\mathbf{y}_i$ according to (1a) are in fact bunched together at the zero bound. The conditional density of $\mathbf{y}_i$ at given x_i is a *censored* Normal density function; considered in isolation, the nonzero y_i for $\mathbf{y}_i > 0$ have an incomplete or *truncated* Normal density, but in the present case they are supplemented by zero values that indicate the number or frequency (but not the position) of observations beyond the point of truncation.[48] The two cases, which are easily confused, are illustrated in Figure 5, while Figure 6 gives an artist's impression of the overall model.

The model is conceptually simple, but its formal representation and the ensuing algebra are not. We write

$$\left.\begin{aligned} \mathbf{y}_i^* &= x_i^T\beta + \boldsymbol{\epsilon}_i \\ \mathbf{y}_i &= \mathbf{y}_i^* \text{ if } \boldsymbol{\epsilon}_i > -x_i^T\beta \\ \mathbf{y}_i &= 0 \text{ otherwise, that is if } \boldsymbol{\epsilon}_i \leqq -x_i^T\beta \end{aligned}\right\} \tag{2}$$

The $\boldsymbol{\epsilon}_i$ are, as always, independent $N(0, \sigma^2)$ variates. As a result we have

$$\begin{aligned} P(\mathbf{y}_i \neq 0) = F_i &= P(\boldsymbol{\epsilon}_i > -x_i^T\beta) = P(\boldsymbol{\epsilon}_i < x_i^T\beta) \\ &= \Phi(x_i^T\beta/\sigma) \end{aligned} \tag{3a}$$

As in Section 10.4, Φ denotes the standard Normal distribution func-

[48] For the distinction between censoring and truncation see Aitchison and Brown (1957: 87–8).

tion and Z its density function. If we only distinguish between zero and nonzero values of y_i, their incidence will thus follow the probit model of (10.37). In contrast to that model, however, the alternative to zero is not a single discrete value like unity but a whole range, bounded at one side only. The conditional density of the nonzero y_i is the truncated Normal density of Figure 5a, that is

$$p(y_i) = \frac{1}{\sigma} \cdot \frac{Z\{(y_i - x_i^T\beta)/\sigma\}}{F_i}, \qquad y_i > 0 \tag{3b}$$

If we were to set up some sort of regression model for the nonzero observations alone, equation (3b) would define a subtle nonlinear relation of the mean of the nonzero y_i to x_i, say

$$E(y_i | y_i > 0) = \mu_y(x_i) \tag{4}$$

We shall derive this expression since it plays a role in various further extensions of the model. Without loss of generality we examine the case of a truncated Normal variate with zero mean

$$\mu_\epsilon = E(\epsilon | \epsilon > c) \qquad \text{with } \epsilon \sim N(0, \sigma^2)$$

Using the same expression for the truncated density as in (3b) we have

$$\mu_\epsilon = \frac{1}{F} \int_c^\infty \frac{1}{\sigma\sqrt{2\pi}}\, t \exp\left(-\frac{t^2}{2\sigma^2}\right) dt$$

with

$$F = P(\epsilon > c) = 1 - \Phi(c/\sigma) = \Phi(-c/\sigma)$$

Straightforward analysis now gives

$$\begin{aligned}
\mu_\epsilon &= \frac{1}{F} \frac{\sigma}{\sqrt{2\pi}} \int_\infty^c -\frac{t}{\sigma^2} \exp\left(-\frac{t^2}{2\sigma^2}\right) dt \\
&= \frac{\sigma}{F} \left\{ \frac{1}{\sqrt{2\pi}} \exp\left(-\frac{t^2}{2\sigma^2}\right) \Big|_\infty^c \right\} \\
&= \frac{\sigma}{F} Z\left(\frac{c}{\sigma}\right) = \sigma V\left(\frac{c}{\sigma}\right)
\end{aligned} \tag{5}$$

We shall be using $V(u)$ for the *hazard function* of a standard Normal variate, defined as

$$V(u) = \frac{Z(u)}{1 - \Phi(u)} \tag{6}$$

The reciprocal $1/V(u)$ is known as *Mills's ratio*, so named after the author of an early tabulation of this variable; it has been the object of many numerical approximations (Johnson and Kotz 1970: II, 277–83; Mills 1926). It follows from (5) that the mean of the nonzero observations $y_i > 0$ of (4) is given by

$$\mu_y(x_i) - \sigma V\left(-\frac{x_i^T\beta}{\sigma}\right) = \sigma\frac{Z(x_i^T\beta/\sigma)}{\Phi(x_i^T\beta/\sigma)} \tag{7}$$

$V(.)$ also turns up in various other places in connection with truncated Normal variates. If higher moments are required they can be obtained by a similar development as above of the moment-generating function; the result is given by Johnson and Kotz (1970: I, 81–3).

We return to Tobin's model, and complete the preliminaries by defining a dummy dependent variable $\boldsymbol{D}_i$

$$\boldsymbol{D}_i = 0 \quad \text{if } \boldsymbol{y}_i = 0, \qquad \boldsymbol{D}_i = 1 \quad \text{if } \boldsymbol{y}_i \neq 0 \tag{8}$$

This is of course a random variable like $\boldsymbol{y}_i$ with a simple Bernoulli density

$$P(\boldsymbol{D}_i = 0) = 1 - F_i, \qquad P(\boldsymbol{D}_i = 1) = F_i \tag{9}$$

We have $E\boldsymbol{D}_i = F_i$, and the expectation of products like $\boldsymbol{D}_i\boldsymbol{y}_i$ and $\boldsymbol{D}_i\boldsymbol{y}_i^2$ is readily derived from (8) in conjunction with the moments of a truncated Normal variate.

In the loglikelihood function we combine the evidence on the frequency of zero values with the information of the nonzero observations, adding the zero frequency to the truncated density (3b) to obtain the censored distribution of Figure 5b

$$\left.\begin{aligned} &P(\boldsymbol{y}_i = 0) = 1 - F_i \\ &y_i \neq 0 : P(y_i) = \frac{1}{\sigma} Z((y_i - x_i^T\beta)/\sigma) \end{aligned}\right\} \tag{10}$$

As in Section 10.1 we may choose between two equivalent notations for the same function, namely,

$$\log L = C + \sum_0 \log(1 - F_i) - \sum_1 \log\sigma - \frac{1}{2\sigma^2}\sum_1 (y_i - x_i^T\beta)^2 \tag{11a}$$

or

$$\log L = C + \sum_i ((1 - D_i)\log(1 - F_i) - D_i \log\sigma - D_i(y_i - x_i^T\beta)^2/2\sigma^2) \tag{11b}$$

The first formula, with its obvious index set notation, is convenient for the computational design; the second allows us to concentrate on a single term when we wish to take expectations. Note that terms from a discrete and from a continuous density are combined in this loglikelihood without further ado.

Changing the parameters to

$$h = 1/\sigma, \qquad \alpha = \beta/\sigma \tag{12}$$

simplifies matters in several respects. The loglikelihood function (11a) now reads

$$\log L = C + \sum_0 \log(1 - F_i) + \sum_1 \log h - \frac{1}{2} \sum_1 (hy_i - x_i^T\alpha)^2 \tag{13}$$

with scores

$$\left(\frac{\partial \log L}{\partial \alpha}\right)^T = -\sum_0 \frac{Z(x_i^T\alpha)}{1 - \Phi(x_i^T\alpha)} x_i + \sum_1 (hy_i - x_i^T\alpha)x_i \tag{14a}$$

$$\frac{\partial \log L}{\partial h} = \sum_1 \left(\frac{1}{h} - (hy_i - x_i^T\alpha)y_i\right) \tag{14b}$$

Upon equating the latter derivative to zero we obtain at once

$$\hat{\sigma}^2(\beta) = \frac{1}{N_1} \sum_1 (y_i - x_i^T\beta)y_i$$

which is used in several algorithms. This might serve to concentrate the loglikelihood function, but little is gained in the process.

Even with this reparametrization the further algebra of scores, Hessian and information matrix can be quite laborious, as is shown by the valiant survey of Maddala (1983: 149–59). We here only list some results. With the help of expressions like (6) the scores are found to have zero expectation, which confirms that the model is regular. Estimation is greatly helped by the knowledge that the Hessian of the loglikelihood (13) is everywhere negative (semi-)definite; this extends of course to (11), and it implies that when a maximum of log L is found it is unique (Olsen 1978b). The information matrix of (11) has been established at an early date by Amemiya (1973).

11.2 Heckman's model

Tobin's model for a limited dependent variable can be generalized to the case where the probit model, which determines whether y_i is observed at all, is distinct and separate but not independent of the relation that governs the density of the observed values. Labor may be withheld by persons who dislike the wage rate they are being offered, households may buy a home and thus withdraw from the rental housing market. Let the dependent variable be the wage rate and the rent respectively. The first example demonstrates that we cannot always identify the missing observations with zero values, and the second shows that they are not always missing because their putative value falls short of some lower bound. In either case the decision to abstain does not necessarily depend on the purported value of $\boldsymbol{y}_i$, and it may well be governed by a relation of its own. Tobin's model may even be too simple for the Engel curve example that we used to introduce it: The consumer's decision to eat caviar may not be prompted by the same considerations that determine the amount that will be eaten.

We specify two linear regression equations to describe this state of affairs

$$\boldsymbol{y}_{1i} = x_{1i}^T\beta + \boldsymbol{\epsilon}_{1i} \tag{15a}$$

$$\boldsymbol{y}_{2i}^* = x_{2i}^T\gamma + \boldsymbol{\epsilon}_{2i} \tag{15b}$$

Note that the regressor vectors x_{1i} and x_{2i} are not identical, although they will usually have some elements in common. The disturbances have a joint Normal distribution; in self-evident notation

$$\boldsymbol{\epsilon}_i \text{ independent} \sim N(0, \Omega) \tag{15c}$$

$$\Omega = \begin{bmatrix} \sigma_1^2 & \rho\sigma_1\sigma_2 \\ \rho\sigma_1\sigma_2 & \sigma_2^2 \end{bmatrix} \tag{15d}$$

The first equation (15a) is the main object of the analysis: We wish to estimate its parameter vector β. The other equation (15b) is an auxiliary regression equation that merely serves to derive a probit model for the market participation of the ith individual, that is for observation of $\boldsymbol{y}_{1i}$. The variable $\boldsymbol{y}_{2i}^*$ may indeed be latent, that is unobserved, since we need it only to define

$$\begin{aligned} \boldsymbol{D}_i &= 1 \quad \text{if } \boldsymbol{y}_{2i}^* > 0 \\ \boldsymbol{D}_i &= 0 \quad \text{if } \boldsymbol{y}_{2i}^* \leqq 0 \end{aligned} \tag{16}$$

The random dummy variate that is thus generated determines whether $\boldsymbol{y}_{1i}$ is observed, as we assume

$$\begin{aligned} &\boldsymbol{y}_{1i} \quad \text{observed if } \boldsymbol{D}_i = 1 \\ &\boldsymbol{y}_{1i} \quad \text{not observed if } \boldsymbol{D}_i = 0 \end{aligned} \tag{17}$$

As in (10.36), (15a) and (17) lead to a probit model for the incidence of observations of y_{1i} of the form (10.37)

$$P(D_i = 1) = F_{2i}(\gamma, \sigma_2) = \Phi(x_{2i}^T \gamma / \sigma_2) \tag{18}$$

It remains to be seen whether γ and σ_2 cannot be separately indentified, as in Section 10.4, or whether we may here take advantage of additional information. We can also derive the conditional density of the observed y_{1i}, as in (3b), although this is of a more complicated form. Writing

$$p(\epsilon_1, \epsilon_2)$$

for the bivariate Normal density function of the two disturbances we define a marginal density function

$$\tilde{Z}(y_{1i} - x_{1i}^T \beta) = \int_{-x_{2i}^T \gamma}^{\infty} p(\epsilon_1, \epsilon_2)\, d\epsilon_2$$

or, to bring out what parameters are involved,

$$\tilde{Z}_i(\beta, \gamma, \sigma_1, \sigma_2, \rho) \tag{19}$$

The conditional density of observed y_{1i} is then, as in (3b)

$$p(y_i) = \frac{\tilde{Z}_i(\beta, \gamma, \sigma_1, \sigma_2, \rho)}{F_i(\gamma, \sigma_2)} \tag{20}$$

Although Heckman himself is careful to acknowledge the precedence of others we shall name this Heckman's model (1974, 1976). If we have a censored sample, that is, if we can identify the observations without y_{1i} and know their x_{1i}, x_{2i}, the loglikelihood has the same structure as in Tobin's case. This is not surprising since we are once more adding together information about the same parameters from the observed y_{1i} and from the observed extent of nonobservation or nonparticipation. In the index set notation of (11a), with 0 now standing for the absence of y_{1i} and 1 for its presence, we find

$$\log L = C + \sum_0 \log(1 - F_{2i}(\gamma, \sigma_2)) + \sum_1 \log \tilde{Z}_i(\beta, \gamma, \sigma_1, \sigma_2, \rho) \tag{21}$$

The first term does not contain β, but it still strengthens β's estimation since it contributes to the information about γ and σ_2 that also occur in the second term.

As in the case of Tobin's model we may work out the expected value of the observed y_i from their truncated distribution with density (20). This leads to

$$\mu_{y_i}(x_{1i}, x_{2i}) = x_{1i}^T \beta + \rho(\sigma_1/\sigma_2) V(-x_{2i}^T \gamma / \sigma_2) \tag{22}$$

where $V(.)$ is again the reciprocal of Mills's ratio as defined by (6).

Heckman has proposed a simple two-step estimation method in the spirit of Section 5.7, which is based on a single iteration between (18) and (22). In the first step γ/σ_2 is estimated from the probit relation (18), and the result is used to construct the variable

$$V_i = V(-x_{2i}^T\gamma/\sigma_2)$$

This can be used in a Generalized Least Squares estimation of (22) (Heckman 1976, 1979). The method has recently been amended so as to permit a logit instead of a probit formulation of the probability model (18) for $\boldsymbol{D}_i$ (Lee 1983).

The analysis of models of this type is continuing, and further developments in their estimation may be expected. The original application was to the labor market and the housing market, with the observation of $\boldsymbol{y}_{1i}$ contingent on market participation (Heckman 1974; King 1980; Rosen 1978). Clearly, however, the same model also applies when observations of $\boldsymbol{y}_{1i}$ are censored by the sampling scheme. Whenever the probability that a unit is included in the observed sample is directly or indirectly affected by the same random disturbances as the dependent variable, we must allow for this form of endogenous sample selection. This is accomplished by specifying the auxiliary relation (15b) so that it represents the operation of the sample censoring mechanism.

11.3 Truncated samples

Endogenous sample selection may distort the density of the observed dependent variable relatively to the population from which the sample is taken, and it may govern the composition of the sample by the imposition of a bound of the type discussed above. If this is the case and we have endogenous sample selection only and no market participation effect, the value of the dependent variable will usually determine whether the individual unit is observed at all. It is no longer a matter of missing values of $\boldsymbol{y}_{1i}$, but of missing the observation i altogether; the observed sample is truncated, not just censored.

A common and straightforward case is that the observation i is conditional upon $\boldsymbol{y}_i$ exceeding some lower bound. This occurs when $\boldsymbol{y}$ is income and the sample is drawn from income tax returns, when $\boldsymbol{y}$ is the duration of unemployment and the sample is drawn from the unemployment register, or when $\boldsymbol{y}$ is a mode of transport and a sample is drawn by interviewing bus passengers. If we are dealing with a regression model, and the lower bound is zero, the observed sample corresponds to the nonzero elements in Tobin's model. They therefore have the density function (3b) or, with (3a),

$$p(y_i) = \frac{1}{\sigma} \frac{Z((y_i - x_i^T\beta)/\sigma)}{\Phi(x_i^T\beta/\sigma)}$$

The loglikelihood therefore reads

$$\log L = C - n \log \sigma + \sum_i \log Z_i - \sum_i \log \Phi_i \tag{23a}$$

with

$$Z_i = Z((y_i - x_i^T\beta)/\sigma) \tag{23b}$$

$$\Phi_i = \Phi(x_i^T\beta/\sigma) \tag{23c}$$

In more complex cases the last term of (23a) may also include some specific sample selection parameters γ. A truncated sample offers of course much less evidence about these than a censored sample, but their presence does not materially alter the situation. As we have already argued in Section 4.5, the additional term can only be safely ignored if it no longer contains β, that is, if the sample selection is no longer endogenous.

The same general argument of Section 4.5 does of course apply to other models than the linear regression equation, with loglikelihoods similar to (23a). We do not pursue the matter further; it is just a question of working out the details of specific models.

11.4 Attempts at simultaneity

If there is a connection between union membership and the wage level this can be attributed to two causal relations of opposite direction: Strong unions may impose higher wages, but it can also be argued that high wages attract union membership. In the same vein high mobility calls forth automobile ownership, and automobile ownership adds to mobility. Such examples of interdependence immediately bring to mind the familiar economic model of simultaneous equations with jointly dependent variables. One of these dependent variables is now an attribute of individual observations, but at first sight this is not a major obstacle.

Let D_i denote automobile ownership or union membership, and y_{1i} annual travel or earnings of individual i. The model is then

$$y_{1i} = x_i^T\beta_1 + \alpha D_i + \epsilon_{1i} \tag{24a}$$

$$y_{2i}^* = x_i^T\beta_2 + \gamma y_{1i} + \epsilon_{2i} \tag{24b}$$

$$D_i = 1 \qquad \text{if } y_{2i}^* > 0 \tag{24c}$$

This is the direct analogue of the standard simultaneous model

$$y_{1i} = x_i^T\beta_1 + \alpha y_{2i} + \epsilon_{1i} \tag{25a}$$

$$y_{2i} = x_i^T\beta_2 + \gamma y_{1i} + \epsilon_{2i} \tag{25b}$$

where an observed continuous variable replaces the latent variable and the corresponding dummy. We assume that all coefficients of *this* model are identified; since x_i contains all the exogenous variables of the model, this is a matter of having appropriate zero elements in β_1 and β_2. Interest centers of course on the parameters α and γ; the substantive issue is which of the two joint relations is predominant, that is, how the values of α and γ compare, or whether one of them is perhaps zero. They may also be of opposite sign, as the interdependence between the two dependent variables need not be self-reinforcing (as it is in the examples given above).

None of these questions can however be studied, for α and γ must satisfy the fundamental restriction

$$\alpha\gamma = 0 \tag{26}$$

To see this, substitute (24a) into (24b), as in

$$y_{2i}^* = x_i^T(\beta_2 + \gamma\beta_1) + \gamma\alpha D_i + (\epsilon_{2i} + \gamma\epsilon_{1i}) \tag{27}$$

In contrast to the standard case we cannot solve this equation to obtain the reduced form expression for y_{2i}^*. Instead we must conclude that the density of y_{2i}^*, and hence the probability of $D_i = 1$, cannot logically depend on the occurrence of that event. Hence (26) must hold. It follows at once that either α or γ (or both) must be zero, so that the simultaneous model (24) is recursive. It also follows that it is fruitless to speculate about the relative size, sign, or significance of α and γ, as there can be no question of separate estimates of these parameters. This considerably diminishes the interest of the model.

This odd and surprising condition (26) is the counterpart of a similar restriction that arises in simultaneous equation models for two dummy variables. At given regressor variables the outcome of such a model is fully described by the probabilities of a 2×2 contingency table for (D_{1i}, D_{2i}). It will be clear that this involves at most three distinct values (since the probabilities sum to one) and that this imposes a symmetry restriction on the parameters of the model. A demonstration in the context of two simultaneous logit equations has been given by Schmidt and Strauss (1975b).

The whole field of simultaneous equation systems with some or all discrete variables is indeed beset by pitfalls and restrictions that are easily overlooked. A model like (24), but with a logit instead of a probit formulation, was applied by Schmidt and Strauss to the union–wage issue without recognition of the condition (26); the presence of a corresponding restraint was pointed out later by Olsen, and Lee demonstrated that the model could not be distinguished from a recursive model involving the same variables (Lee 1979; Olsen 1978a; Schmidt and Strauss 1976). Maddala devotes a whole chapter to this particular example (Maddala 1983: Chapter 11).

For a further review of the ramifications of this problem we refer to the literature. Maddala surveys the various types of simultaneous equation systems, and both Heckman and Schmidt have given a systematic review of the restrictions that arise (Heckman 1978; Maddala 1983: Chapter 7; Schmidt 1981). The likelihood function of models like (24), with the constraint (26) taken into account, can be found in Heckman's article (1978: 941, Appendix).

CHAPTER 12

Simple random process models

A simple but powerful model of the spacing of events in time is found in the work of Erlang, who, at the turn of the century, considered the distribution of incoming calls at a telephone exchange.[49] Such events are independent of one another. We assume that the probability of a single occurrence during a brief time interval is proportional to its duration but otherwise constant, or

$$P(\text{one event in interval } t, t + dt) = \lambda\, dt, \lambda > 0 \tag{1}$$

The parameter λ is known as the *intensity* of the process under review. If the interval is brief enough – we shall presently make it tend to zero – multiple events have a negligible probability. Now consider the count of events from time zero up to time t, say $(\boldsymbol{k}, t)$. This is a discrete random variable with range 0, 1, 2, ... By (1), the discrete density function $f(k, t)$ must satisfy

$$f(k, t + dt) = f(k - 1, t)\, \lambda\, dt + f(k, t)(1 - \lambda\, dt) \tag{2}$$

This leads to the differential equations

$$\frac{df(k, t)}{dt} = -\lambda(f(k, t) - f(k - 1, t)) \tag{3}$$

for all $k = 0, 1, 2, \ldots$, with the side condition

$$f(k, t) = 0 \qquad \text{for } k < 0 \tag{4}$$

These are easily solved, first for $k = 0$ and then for other k by recursion, and we obtain

$$f(k, t) = \frac{(\lambda t)^k}{k!} \exp(-\lambda t) \tag{5}$$

This expression yields two distributions. In the first place we may set the length of the finite time period t at 1, and consider the number of events during a standard period of unit duration, as determined by the

[49] The works of this Danish telephone engineer are not easily accessible; the reader may try to get hold of the volume by Brockmeyer, Holstrøm, and Jensen (1948).

definition of λ, which has dimension number$/t$. The result is of course the *Poisson* density function

$$f_k(k) = \frac{\lambda^k}{k!} \exp(-\lambda) \tag{6}$$

In the second place we may set $k = 0$, and regard (5) as the probability that no event has occurred up to time t. For the random *waiting time* $\boldsymbol{t}$ until the first event this implies

$$P(\boldsymbol{t} > t) = f(0, t) = \exp(-\lambda t) \tag{7}$$

or

$$P(\boldsymbol{t} < t) = F_t(t) = 1 - \exp(-\lambda t) \tag{8}$$

Hence the waiting time $\boldsymbol{t}$ has an *exponential distribution* with density function

$$f_t(t) = \lambda \exp(-\lambda t) \tag{9}$$

It follows that we have

$$\frac{f_t(t)}{1 - F_t(t)} = \lambda \tag{10}$$

The left-hand side is known as the *hazard rate,* and for an exponential distribution this is a constant, equal to the intensity of the original process.

Both distributions are of course entirely governed by the same underlying process and by its single parameter λ, which determines their means and variances (as well as higher moments and other characteristics). So much for the statistical model. In econometrics, the parameter λ is in turn related to regressor variables believed to affect the process for the observations concerned.

12.1 Poisson regression

In the Poisson regression model, k_i is the observed number of accidents at a particular installation in a given month, or the number of patents taken by a certain firm in a particular year. This is a random variable governed by (6) with parameter λ_i, which is believed to vary with observable characteristics x_i of the installation and the month, or of the firm and the year. In order to ensure that all λ_i are positive the relation is specified as

$$\lambda_i = \exp(x_i^T \beta) \tag{11}$$

For a sample of independent observations we find the loglikelihood as

$$\log L(\beta) = \sum_i k_i \log \lambda_i(\beta) - \sum_i \log k_i! - \sum_i \lambda_i(\beta) \tag{12}$$

The score vector is

$$q = \sum_i (k_i - \lambda_i(\beta))x_i \tag{13}$$

and the Hessian

$$Q = -\sum_i \lambda_i(\beta)x_i x_i^T \tag{14}$$

It is not difficult to establish that the model is regular. Determination of the MLE $\hat{\beta}$ by a quadratic scheme of Section 5.6 leads to an iterative algorithm that closely resembles Generalized Least Squares, or weighted linear regression, with "weights" $\lambda_i(\beta)$ that are adjusted in each round.

Poisson regression is not a common econometric model, as is demonstrated in the lean review by Maddala (1983: 51–4). A recent example is the analysis of numbers of patents by means of a modification of the model by Hausman, Hall, and Griliches (1984).

12.2 Models of duration

While the basic model we have sketched above permits repeated events, the exponential distribution (8) can also apply to the random time of waiting for an event that effectively terminates the experiment by changing the state of the subject. Examples are the destruction of an object, the death of an organism, the recovery of a patient, and the hiring or firing of a worker; these events put an end to periods of existence, life, illness, employment or unemployment – all of random duration. The basic considerations in respect of such a terminal event naturally refer to the probability of its first occurrence or its incidence among the population at risk. Let the random preceding spell $\boldsymbol{t}$ have a distribution function

$$P(\boldsymbol{t} < t) = G(t) \tag{15a}$$

with density

$$g(t) = \frac{dG(t)}{dt} \tag{15b}$$

The probability of first occurrence of the terminal event at time t is then

$$\frac{g(t)}{1 - G(t)}$$

or the *hazard rate*. Small wonder that this concept has originally arisen in studies of mortality and survival.

When we assume a constant hazard rate, we obtain an exponential distribution of the preceding interval or spell, as (10) suggests; but this is a restrictive assumption and a special case.[50] A much more general specification is to define the hazard rate as a function of regressor variables for the *i*th observation as well as of the time t that has elapsed since the start of the interval at time zero. We then have

$$\lambda(x_i, t) = \frac{g_i(t)}{1 - G_i(t)} \qquad (16)$$

as the basic equation that determines $G_i(t)$ and $g_i(t)$, subject to the further specification of the function $\lambda(x_i, t)$. The general solution of this differential equation is

$$G_i(t) = 1 - \exp\left(-\int_0^t \lambda(x_i, s)\, ds\right) \qquad (17)$$

Since $G_i(t)$ is a distribution function, it must increase monotonically with t from 0 to 1; as we have noted before, $\lambda(x_i, t)$ must be nonnegative, and moreover care must be taken that the integral in (17) diverges. Apart from this, the specification of $\lambda(x_i, t)$ can be any compromise between realism and convenience. If the hazard rate is thought to be strongly affected by outside conditions that vary over time, dated variables may be included among the x_i; different x_i will then hold over successive stretches of time, and the integral in (17) must accordingly be evaluated by pieces. In the simpler case of constant x_i an analytical solution of (17) may be possible, depending on the form of $\lambda(x_i, t)$ and in particular on its dependence on t.

The essential assumption of the class of *proportional hazard* specifications is that the hazard function is separable as in

$$\lambda(x_i, t) = \lambda_1(x_i, \theta_1)\, \lambda_2(t, \theta_2) \qquad (18)$$

The hazards of different individuals or cases i now stand in a fixed proportion to one another over their entire time path. The model was devised by Cox for analyzing the course of illness under various treatments. In this case the main interest lies in θ_1, without regard to the form of λ_2 or the value of θ_2, and Cox suggested a method of estimation that fits and exploits these conditions (Cox 1972). In economic applications we are however equally interested in $\lambda_2(t, \theta_2)$, which determines whether the hazard goes up or down as the spell lengthens. If t is the

[50] This is not a theoretical case. When fatal accidents are the main cause of death, as with small fish and prey birds, the length of life has an exponential distribution.

interval between infrequent purchases such as the replacement of major durables, the hazard should increase, but if t is a spell of unemployment conflicting considerations apply: Prolonged unemployment may render a person unfit for work or it may lead to a greater readiness to accept any job offer. By a judicious specification of $\lambda_2(t, \theta_2)$ the issue may be decided on empirical grounds.

The main econometric application of the proportional hazard model (and of other hazard models) is indeed the analysis of the duration of spells of unemployment (Lancaster 1979; Lancaster and Nickell 1980; Nickell 1979). As an example of the further specification of the functions λ_1 and λ_2 we quote from Lancaster's first publication (1979). He assumes

$$\lambda_1(x_i, \theta_1) = \exp(x_i^T \beta) \tag{19}$$

which is a convenient choice that respects the nonnegativity constraint. The vector x_i consists of a constant, the individual's age, the *replacement ratio* or the ratio of unemployment income to the last wage, and the local unemployment percentage. The time dependence function is specified as

$$\lambda_2(t, \theta_2) = \alpha t^{(\alpha-1)}, \quad \alpha > 0 \tag{20}$$

which allows for increasing or decreasing hazard rates with $\alpha > 1$ or $\alpha < 1$. For $\alpha = 1$ this specification reduces to the unit constant, which implies an exponential distribution of each t_i.[51]

With these particular specifications it is not hard to express the distribution function (17) and hence the density function of t as analytical functions of x_i and of the parameters β and α, say $G(t, x_i, \theta)$ and $g(t, x_i, \theta)$. In the normal course of events we would indeed do so, and then go on to consider the implications for the loglikelihood function and its derivatives. But in the case of unemployment spells questions of data collection and selection predominate, and the passage from the density function to the likelihood is not immediate. We return to this problem in Section 12.4.

12.3 Additional heterogeneity

Both models of the present chapter prescribe identical distributions of the random variate under review for all cases that have identical values of the regressor variables. In this respect they do not differ from any

[51] As a matter of fact Lancaster finds that there is significant time dependence of the hazard rate with $\alpha < 1$.

other econometric model; we have, after all, identified such a model with a conditional density function in Chapter 2, and this holds for all models we have reviewed. In the case of the Poisson model and the duration models of this chapter, however, it is persistently suggested that the random variation that these models permit is in some sense insufficient, and that further explicit provision must be made for additional variation between cases or individuals with identical regressor variable values. The reason for this suggestion is perhaps that the present models, unlike the others, do not contain a separate disturbance term that explicitly catches the effects of neglected variables. Against this it may be argued that neglected effects are precisely reflected by the random variation that these models do permit; but it must be conceded that this variation is restricted, as both the Poisson and the exponential distribution are entirely determined by a single parameter. The additional nuisance variance or covariance parameters σ^2 or Ω of Additive Normal Disturbance models are absent.[52] Allowing for individual variation or *heterogeneity* of the underlying process introduces at least one additional parameter in the present univariate models, but this is not the variance of a Normal disturbance: The form of the heterogeneity is dictated by convenience.

In the case of the Poisson model, heterogeneity is introduced through the time-honored device of superimposing random variation of the intensity parameter λ of (6) on the model. If the values of λ in successive observations are themselves independent and identically distributed random variables with a Gamma distribution, the variate $\boldsymbol{k}$ has a Negative Binomial distribution (Greenwood and Yule 1920). This has two parameters as against one in the Poisson case, and its variance is larger than in the Poisson model where it equals the mean. This useful result has been adapted to a Negative Binomial regression replacing the Poisson regression by Hausman et al. (1984). We refer for details to their work.

For the duration models the natural course is to add a multiplicative disturbance term onto the hazard function (16), defining the hazard rate of the ith individual now as

$$\lambda_i = \lambda(x_i, t)v_i \tag{21}$$

[52] Up to a point this also holds for the probit and logit models of Chapter 10, which determine the probabilities of binomial or multinomial distributions. The underlying models contain variates with a variance, but this is a figment of interpretation: It does not enter as a separate parameter in the likelihood, as is illustrated by (10.37). Attempts to introduce additional heterogeneity lead to artefacts or to redundancy. With grouped data one may, however, allow for additional variance between classes; see Amemiya and Nold (1975).

where v_i is a nonnegative random variable with unit expectation. Conditional upon the realization of this variate for the ith individual, the duration distribution function of (17) now reads

$$G(t, x_i, \theta, v_i) = 1 - \exp\left(-\int_0^t v_i \lambda(x_i, \theta, s)\, ds\right) \tag{22}$$

The value of v_i is however unobservable, and the object of empirical analysis is G conditional upon x_i alone. To obtain this we must take the expected value of (22) over the distribution of v_i, or, assuming that all v_i have the same density $f(v)$,

$$G(t, x_i, \theta) = \int_0^\infty G(t, x_i, \theta, v) f(v)\, dv \tag{23}$$

Taking Lancaster's proportional hazard model once more as an example it turns out that this integral can be solved if the v_i have a Gamma distribution with unit mean and one additional parameter. We refer to the original article for details (Lancaster 1979).

At first sight the presence of an unobservable individual factor in the hazard rate of leaving unemployment appears to be almost indistinguishable from a decline of the hazard rate with increasing duration, as for instance modeled in (20) with $\alpha < 1$. If spells of unemployment that are already long tend to persist even longer, this may be caused by a declining chance of re-employment, or it may reveal that the individual is (and always has been) difficult to place. At first sight the two interpretations are observationally equivalent, and it has been thought that they are unidentified (Lancaster and Nickell 1980: 145–7). Quite recent analyses have, however, shown that this is not the case (Elbers and Ridder 1982; Heckman and Singer 1984).

12.4 Some duration model likelihoods

We have hinted above that inference about duration models may be hampered by the nature of the data, particularly in the case of spells of unemployment. We begin by recapitulating. For a given hazard function with or without a random heterogeneity element the distribution function

$$G(t, x_i, \theta) \tag{24}$$

is in principle determined by (17) or (23), and the density

$$g(t, x_i, \theta) \tag{25}$$

follows by differentiation. No matter whether these are neat analytical functions or messy expressions that can only be evaluated by numerical integration or the like, once these expressions have been established it is tempting to write the loglikelihood of the observed durations in the familiar form

$$\log L(\theta) = \sum_i \log g(t_i, x_i, \theta) \tag{26}$$

If durations are known by class intervals only, or if observation ceases before the last spell has run its course, the likelihood must of course be adjusted. In the course of a survey we may record the length of unemployment of the sample individuals at a first interview, and then follow their fates. Some will be re-employed but others will be still unemployed at the end of the field work. Some spells t_j are thus known only to exceed a known duration τ_j, and we have truncation at an upper bound that varies between individuals. These incomplete spells have probability

$$P(t_i < \tau_i) = 1 - G(\tau_i, x_i, \theta) \tag{27}$$

As in Section 11.1, we obtain a loglikelihood that closely resembles (11.11), namely,

$$\log L(\theta) = \sum_f \log g(t_i, x_i, \theta) + \sum_u \log(1 - G(\tau_i, x_i, \theta)) \tag{28}$$

where f and u designate full and uncompleted spells, respectively.

It is doubtful, however, whether these loglikelihood functions apply. The expressions (25) and (27) do correctly represent the conditional distribution of the unemployment duration of individual i (conditional, that is, on his characteristics x_i), but this does not warrant that the loglikelihood (26) or (27) is in order. The data usually constitute a genuine sample, and we must face the issue of Section 4.5 whether the joint density of $(\boldsymbol{x}_i, t_i)$ factors into the conditional density under review and a marginal density of $\boldsymbol{x}_i$ that is fixed or at least independent of θ. The case of a given and fixed marginal distribution would correspond to nonrandom x_i, as in an experiment where selected individuals with given characteristics are fired from their present jobs and we observe how long they take to find other employment. This is of course not practicable. The feebler case of independence obtains when we follow the subsequent history of a random sample from the influx of unemployed at a certain moment, or when we look for people who become unemployed in a random sample from the entire working population. The latter procedure is a very roundabout way of collecting data about unemployment, and either survey must be continued for a considerable time or the durations will be truncated at an early point. The usual procedure is therefore to select individuals who are already unemployed and to record the time already elapsed. The density of the sample observations, and hence the likelihood, must then be constructed with great care; it does not in general permit of factorization in the conditional densities (25) or (27) on the one hand and an unrelated marginal density of the $\boldsymbol{x}_i$ on the other. On closer analysis duration data, moreover, turn out to be particularly sensitive to certain types of the selection bias involved.

We illustrate this point by the example of sampling from the unemployment register. This is one of the cases treated at greater length in the careful analysis of Ridder (1984). A sample is drawn from the population of unemployed at calender time zero, and the duration p of each individual's unemployment up to now is recorded. To simplify matters we assume that observation then continues until all sample spells of unemployment are terminated, so that no uncompleted spells occur. We also assume random sampling, so that instead of the sample we may directly consider the population of unemployed at time zero.

First consider the origins of the (sub-)population of unemployed. It consists of individuals who have become unemployed at time $-p$, and who are still unemployed at time zero. Its composition therefore depends on three factors. The first is $h(x, \zeta)$, the frequency distribution of the characteristics x among the entire working population. The second is $q(-s, x, \eta)$ which represents the chance of becoming unemployed at some date $-s$ prior to the time zero of drawing the sample. The third is the conditional density $g(t, x, \theta)$ of the duration of (25). The joint density of $\boldsymbol{p}$, $\boldsymbol{t}$, and $\boldsymbol{x}$ among the unemployed at time zero is therefore

$$f(p, t, x, \theta, \zeta, \eta) = \frac{q(-p, x, \eta)h(x, \zeta)g(t, x, \theta)}{C(\eta, \zeta, \theta)}, \quad t \geqq p \tag{29}$$

As observation is contingent upon the condition $t > p$ for unemployment to last until time zero, the distribution is truncated and C is the constant required to make its integral equal to 1. This is the probability for a member of the working population to be unemployed at time zero, or

$$C(\eta, \zeta, \theta) = \int_s \int_w q(-s, x, \eta)h(w, \zeta)(1 - G(s, w, \theta))\, ds\, dw \tag{30}$$

The marginal density of $\boldsymbol{x}$ in the sample is now obtained from (29) by integration over all p and over all $t > p$, or

$$f(x, \theta, \zeta, \eta) = \frac{\int_s q(-s, x, \eta)\, h(x, \zeta)(1 - G(s, x, \theta))\, ds}{C(\eta, \zeta, \theta)} \tag{31}$$

This is clearly a function of θ. The sample observations on the $\boldsymbol{x}$ are thus informative about these parameters of the conditional density (25), which are the object of interest. To condition on the x_i and to use the conventional likelihood functions like (26) is thus at best an inefficient method of estimation.

It may be felt that the above approach is unnecessarily complex and laborious, and that it is idle to strive for generality when so little is usually known about the functions q and h. Even then the present treatment does however lead to interesting results. As an example we consider the conditional density of the *observed* duration $\boldsymbol{t}$, conditional upon x, in a much simplified setting where the entry rate or inflow of unemployed for any given x is constant over time, or

$$q(-p, x, \eta)h(x, \zeta) = \alpha \tag{32}$$

The conditional density of pairs $(\boldsymbol{p}, \boldsymbol{t})$ is found as the quotient of (29) and (30), or, with the present simplification,

$$f(p, t; x) = \frac{\alpha g(t, x, \theta)}{\int_s \alpha(1 - G(s, x, \theta))\, ds}, \; t \geqq p \tag{33}$$

The α will of course cancel out, but its presence serves as a reminder of the random $\boldsymbol{p}$ with constant density. For the conditional density of $\boldsymbol{t}$ alone we must thus integrate (33) over $p < t$, and this finally yields

$$f(t; x) = \frac{t\, g(t, x, \theta)}{\int_s (1 - G(s, x, \theta))\, ds}, \; t \geqq 0 \tag{34}$$

As the denominator equals $E\,\boldsymbol{t}$, this is a proper density which integrates to one.

Upon comparing (34) to (25) we see that the conditional density of *observed* spells of unemployment differs from the conditional density of any spell by a factor t, or in proportion to the length of the spell itself. This reflects that in the present sampling scheme longer spells have a proportionally larger chance of including the time zero at which the sample is drawn than do briefer spells; hence longer spells are overrepresented in the sample. The phenomenon is known as the waiting time paradox (Feller 1957: II, 10).

For further cases of the effects of particular sampling schemes we refer to Ridder's study, from which the present example was drawn (1984).

References

Adam, D. 1958. *Les Réactions du Consommateur devant les Prix.* Paris: SEDES.

Aitchison, J., and J.A.C. Brown. 1957. *The Lognormal Distribution.* Cambridge: Cambridge University Press.

Aitken, A.C. 1935. "On Least Squares and linear combinations of observations," *Proceedings of the Royal Society of Edinburgh* 55: 42–8.

Amemiya, T. 1973. "Regression analysis when the dependent variable is truncated Normal," *Econometrica* 41: 997–1016.

— 1981. "Qualitative response models: a survey," *Journal of Economic Literature* 19: 1483–1536.

Amemiya, T., and F. Nold. 1975. "A modified logit model," *Review of Economics and Statistics* 57: 255–6.

Anderson, T.W. 1958. *The Statistical Analysis of Time Series.* New York: Wiley.

Anderson, T.W., and H. Rubin. 1950. "The asymptotic properties of estimates of the parameters of a single equation in a complete system of stochastic equations," *Annals of Mathematical Statistics* 21: 570–82.

Aoki, M. 1971. *Introduction to Optimization Techniques.* New York: Macmillan.

Arrow, K.J., H.B. Chenery, B.S. Minhas, and R.M. Solow. 1961. "Capital–labor substitution and economic efficiency," *Review of Economics and Statistics* 43: 225–50.

Bard, Y. 1974. *Nonlinear Parameter Estimation.* New York: Academic Press.

Barnett, W.A. 1976. "Maximum Likelihood and iterated Aitken estimation of nonlinear systems of equations," *Journal of the American Statistical Association* 71: 354–60.

Barten, A.P. 1964. "Consumer demand functions under conditions of almost additive preferences," *Econometrica* 32: 1–38.

— 1969. "Maximum Likelihood estimation of a complete system of demand equations," *European Economic Review* 1: 7–73.

— 1977. "The systems of consumer demand functions approach: a review," *Econometrica* 45: 23–51.

Beach, C.M., and J.G. Mackinnon. 1978. "A Maximum Likelihood procedure for regressions with autocorrelated errors," *Econometrica* 46: 51–8.

Belsley, D.A., E. Kuh, and R.E. Welsch. 1980. *Regression Diagnostics.* New York: Wiley.

Berkson, J. 1944. "Application of the logistic function to bio-assay," *Journal of the American Statistical Association* 39: 357–65.

— 1951. "Why I prefer logits to probits," *Biometrics* 7: 327–39.

— 1980. "Minimum Chi-square, not Maximum Likelihood!" (with discussion), *Annals of Mathematical Statistics* 8: 457–87.

Berndt, E.R., and L.R. Christensen. 1973. "The translog function and the substitution of equipment, structures, and labor in U.S. manufacturing 1929–68," *Journal of Econometrics* 1: 81–114.

Berndt, E.R., B.H. Hall, R.E. Hall, and J.A. Hausman. 1974. "Estimation and inference in non-linear structural models," *Annals of Economic and Social Measurement* 3: 653–65.

Bishop, Y.M.M., S.E. Fienberg, and P.W. Holland. 1975. *Discrete Multivariate Analysis.* Cambridge: M.I.T. Press.

Bodkin, R.G., and L.R. Klein. 1967. "Nonlinear estimation of aggregate production functions," *Review of Economics and Statistics* 49: 28–44.

Box, G.E.P., and D.R. Cox. 1964. "An analysis of transformations," *Journal of the Royal Statistical Society Series B* 26: 211–43.

Box, G.E.P., and G.C. Tiao. 1973. *Bayesian Inference in Statistical Analysis.* Reading: Addison-Wesley.

Boylan, T.A., and I.G. O'Muircheartaigh. 1981. "The functional form of the U.K. demand for money," *Applied Statistics* 30: 296–9.

Breusch, T.S. 1979. "Conflict among criteria for testing hypotheses: extensions and comments," *Econometrica* 47: 203–7.

Brockmeyer, E., H.L. Holstrøm, and A. Jensen. 1948. *The Life and Work of A.K. Erlang.* Copenhagen: Copenhagen Telephone Company.

Brown, B.W. 1981. "Sample size requirements in Full Information Maximum Likelihood estimation," *International Economic Review* 22: 443–59.

Brown, J.A.C., H.S. Houthakker, and S.J. Prais. 1953. "Electronic computation in economic statistics," *Journal of the American Statistical Association* 48: 414–28.

Cochrane, D., and G.H. Orcutt. 1949. "Application of Least Squares regression to relationships containing autocorrelated error terms," *Journal of the American Statistical Association* 44: 32–61.

Cox, D.R. 1972. "Regression models and life tables," *Journal of the Royal Statistical Society Series B* 34: 187–202.

Cox, D.R., and D.V. Hinkley. 1974. *Theoretical Statistics.* London: Chapman & Hall.

Cramér, H. 1946. *Mathematical Methods of Statistics.* Princeton: Princeton University Press.

Daganzo, C. 1979. *Multinomial Probit.* New York: Academic Press.

Deaton, A.S. 1974. "The analysis of consumer demand in the United Kingdom, 1900–1970," *Econometrica* 42: 341–67.

— 1976. "NLFIML user's guide," Mimeograph. University of Bristol.

— 1978. "Specification and testing in applied demand analysis," *Economic Journal* 88: 524–36.

Deaton, A.S., and J. Muellbauer. 1980a. *Economics and Consumer Behavior.* Cambridge: Cambridge University Press.

— 1980b. "An almost ideal demand system," *American Economic Review* 70: 312–26.

DeGroot, M.H. 1975. *Probability and Statistics.* Reading: Addison-Wesley.

Dhrymes, P.J. 1971. *Distributed Lags.* San Francisco: Holden-Day.

Diewert, W.E. 1974. "Applications of duality theory," in M.D. Intriligator and D.A. Kendrick (eds.), *Frontiers of Quantitative Economics, vol. II.* Amsterdam: North Holland.

Domencich, T.A., and D. McFadden. 1975. *Urban Travel Demand: A Behavioral Analysis.* Amsterdam: North Holland.

Edwards, A.W.F. 1972. *Likelihood.* Cambridge: Cambridge University Press.

Elbers, C., and G. Ridder. 1982. "True and spurious duration dependence: the identifiability of the proportional hazard model," *Review of Economic Studies* 49: 403–10.

Engle, R.F., D.F. Hendry, and J.F. Richard, 1983. "Exogeneity," *Econometrica* 51: 277–304.

Farrell, M.J. 1954. "The demand for motor-cars in the United States," *Journal of the Royal Statistical Society Series A* 117: 171–200.

Feller, W. 1957. *An Introduction to Probability Theory and Its Applications.* 2 vols. 2d edition. New York: Wiley.

Finney, D. 1971. *Probit Analysis.* 3d edition. Cambridge: Cambridge University Press.

Fisher, F.M. 1966. *The Identification Problem in Econometrics.* New York: McGraw-Hill.

Fisher, R.A. 1921. "On the mathematical foundations of theoretical statistics," *Philosophical Transactions of the Royal Society of London Series A* 222: 309–68.

— 1925. "Theory of statistical estimation," *Proceedings of the Cambridge Philosophical Society* 22: 700–25.

Fisher, R.A., and F. Yates. 1957. *Statistical Tables for Biological, Agricultural and Medical Research.* 3d edition. Edinburgh: Oliver and Boyd.

Fletcher, R. 1980. *Practical Methods of Optimization.* 2 vols. Chichester: Wiley.

Friedman, M. 1957. *A Theory of the Consumption Function.* Princeton: Princeton University Press.

Gantmacher, F.R. 1959. *The Theory of Matrices.* 2 vols. New York: Chelsea.

Gnedenko, V. 1962. *The Theory of Probability.* New York: Chelsea.

Goldberger, A.S. 1964. *Econometric Theory.* New York: Wiley.

— 1968. "The interpretation and estimation of Cobb–Douglas functions," *Econometrica* 36: 464–72.

Greenwood, M., and G.U. Yule. 1920. "An inquiry into the nature of frequency distributions of multiple happenings," *Journal of the Royal Statistical Society* 83: 255–79.

Griliches, Z. 1967. "Distributed lags: a survey," *Econometrica* 35: 16–49.

Haavelmo, T. 1943. "The statistical implications of a system of simultaneous equations," *Econometrica* 11: 1–12.

— 1944. "The probability approach in econometrics," *Econometrica* 12: 1–115.

Hadley, G. 1961. *Linear Algebra.* Reading: Addison-Wesley.

Hall, B.M. 1981. *MAXLIK Version 2.1 User's Guide.* Stanford: TSP International.

Harvey, A.C. 1981. *The Econometric Analysis of Time Series.* Deddington: Philip Allan.

Hausman, J.A., and D.A. Wise. 1978. "A conditional probit model for qualitative choice," *Econometrica* 46: 403–26.

Hausman, J., B. Hall, and Z. Griliches. 1984. "Econometric models for count data with an application to patents," *Econometrica* 52: 909–38.

Heckman, J.J. 1974. "Shadow prices, market wages and labor supply," *Econometrica* 42: 679–94.

— 1976. "The common structure of statistical models of truncation, sample selection and limited dependent variables and a simple estimator for such models," *Annals of Economic and Social Measurement* 5: 475–92.

— 1978. "Dummy endogenous variables in a simultaneous equation system," *Econometrica* 46: 931–59.

— 1979. "Sample selection bias as a specification error," *Econometrica* 47: 153–61.

Heckman, J., and B. Singer. 1984. "A method for minimizing the impact of distributional assumptions in econometric models for duration data," *Econometrica* 52: 271–320.

Heijmans, R.D.H., and J.R. Magnus. 1983a. "Consistency of Maximum Likelihood estimators when observations are dependent," Faculty of Actuarial Science and Econometrics, University of Amsterdam.

— 1983b. "On the asymptotic efficiency of the Maximum Likelihood estimator with dependent observations," Faculty of Actuarial Science and Econometrics, University of Amsterdam.

Hendry, D.F., and J.F. Richard. 1983. "The econometric analysis of economic time series," *International Statistical Review* 51: 111–63.

Hogan, W.P. 1958. "Technical progress and production functions," *Review of Economics and Statistics* 40: 407–11.

Hood, Wm.C., and T.C. Koopmans (eds.) 1953. *Studies in Econometric Method.* New York: Wiley.

Hotelling, H. 1940. "The selection of variates for use in prediction," *Annals of Mathematical Statistics* 11: 271–83.

Jennrich, R.I. 1969. "Asymptotic properties of non-linear least squares estimators," *The Annals of Mathematical Statistics* 40: 633–43.

Johnson, N.L., and S. Kotz. 1970. *Distributions in Statistics: Continuous Univariate Distributions.* 2 vols. New York: Wiley.

Jorgenson, D.W. 1966. "Rational distributed lag functions," *Econometrica* 34: 135–49.

Judge, G.G., W.E. Griffiths, R.C. Hill, and T.C. Lee. 1980. *The Theory and Practice of Econometrics.* New York: Wiley.

Kendall, M.G., and A. Stuart. 1963. *The Advanced Theory of Statistics.* 3 vols. 2d edition. London: Griffin.

King, M.A. 1980. "An econometric model of tenure choice and demand for housing as a joint decision," *Journal of Public Economics* 14: 137–59.

Kliman, M.L., and E.H. Oksanen. 1973. "The Keynesian demand-for-money function," *Journal of Money, Credit and Banking* 5: 215–20.

Konstas, P., and M. Khouja. 1969. "The Keynesian demand-for-money function," *Journal of Money, Credit and Banking* 1: 765–77.

Koopmans, T.C. (ed). 1950. *Statistical Inference in Dynamic Economic Models.* New York: Wiley.

Koopmans, T.C., and W.C. Hood. 1953. "The estimation of simultaneous linear economic relationships," in W.C. Hood and T.C. Koopmans (eds.), *Studies in Econometric Method.* New York: Wiley.

Koopmans, T.C., H. Rubin, and R.B. Leipnik. 1950. "Measuring the equation systems of dynamic economics," in T.C. Koopmans (ed.), *Statistical Inference in Dynamic Economic Models.* New York: Wiley.

Koyck, L.M. 1954. *Distributed Lags and Investment Analysis.* Amsterdam: North Holland.

Lancaster, A. 1979. "Econometric methods for the duration of unemployment," *Econometrica* 47: 939–56.

Lancaster, A., and S. Nickell. 1980. "The analysis of re-employment possibilities for the unemployed," *Journal of the Royal Statistical Society Series A* 143: 141–65.

Laplace, P.S. de. 1814. *Essai Philosophique sur les Probabilités.* Paris: Courcier.

Le Cam, L. 1953. "On some asymptotic properties of Maximum Likelihood estimates and related Bayes's estimates," *University of California Publications in Statistics* 1: 277–330.

Lee, L.F. 1979. "Mixed logit and fully recursive logit models," *Economics Letters* 4: 151–5.

— 1983. "Generalized econometric models with selectivity," *Econometrica* 51: 507–12.

McFadden, D. 1974. "Conditional logit analysis of qualitative choice behavior," in P. Zarembka (ed.) *Frontiers of Econometrics.* New York: Academic Press.

— 1978. "Modelling the choice of residential location," in A. Karlquist et al. (eds.), *Spatial Interaction Theory and Residential Location.* Amsterdam: North Holland.

— 1982. "Econometric models of probabilistic choice," in C. Manski and D. McFadden (eds.), *Structural Analysis of Discrete Data.* Cambridge: M.I.T.

Madansky, A. 1976. *Foundations of Econometrics.* Amsterdam: North Holland.

Maddala, G.S. 1983. *Limited-dependent and Qualitative Variables in Econometrics.* Cambridge: Cambridge University Press.

Magnus, J.R. 1978. "Maximum Likelihood estimation of the GLS model with unknown parameters in the disturbance covariance matrix," *Journal of Econometrics* 7: 281–312, with corrigenda 10: 261.

— 1979. "Substitution between energy and non-energy inputs in the Netherlands 1950–1976," *International Economic Review* 20: 465–84.

Magnus, J.R., and H. Neudecker. 1980. "The elimination matrix: some lemmas and applications," *SIAM Journal on Algebraic and Discrete Methods* 1: 422–49.

Malinvaud, E. 1964. *Méthodes Statistiques de l'Econometrie.* Paris: Dunod.

— 1970. "The consistency of nonlinear regression," *The Annals of Mathematical Statistics* 41: 956–69.

Mann, H.B., and A. Wald. 1943. "On the statistical treatment of linear stochastic difference equations," *Econometrica,* 11: 173–220.

Manski, C.F. 1981. "Structural models for discrete data: the analysis of discrete data," in S. Leinhardt (ed.), *Sociological Methodology.* San Francisco: Jossey-Bass.

Marquardt, D.W. 1963. "An algorithm for least squares estimation of nonlinear parameters," *Journal of the Society of Industrial Applied Mathematics* 11: 431–41.

Mills, J.P. 1926. "Table of the ratio: area to bounding ordinate, for any portion of Normal curve," *Biometrika,* 18: 395–400.

Mills, T.C. 1978. "The functional form of the U.K. demand for money," *Applied Statistics* 27: 52–7.

Miner, J.R. 1933. "Pierre-François Verhulst, the discoverer of the logistic curve," *Human Biology* 5: 673–89.

Mizon, G.E., and D.F. Hendry. 1980. "An empirical application and Monte Carlo analysis of tests of dynamic specification," *Review of Economic Studies* 57: 21–45.

Mood, A.M., F.A. Graybill, and D.C. Boes. 1974. *Introduction to the Theory of Statistics.* 3d edition. New York: McGraw-Hill.

Nickell, S. 1979. "Estimating the probability of leaving unemployment," *Econometrica* 47: 1249–66.

Oberhofer, W., and J. Kmenta. 1974. "A general procedure for obtaining Maximum Likelihood estimates in generalized regression models," *Econometrica* 42: 579–90.

Olsen, R.J. 1978a. "Comment on 'The effect of unions on earnings and earnings on unions: a mixed logit approach,'" *International Economic Review* 19: 259–61.

— 1978b. "Note on the uniqueness of the Maximum Likelihood estimator of the Tobit model," *Econometrica* 46: 1211–15.

Parke, W.R. 1982. "An algorithm for FIML and 3SLS estimation of large nonlinear models," *Econometrica* 50: 81–95.

Pearl, R., and L.J. Reed. 1920. "On the rate of growth of the population of the United States since 1790 and its mathematical representation," *Proceedings of the National Academy of Sciences* 6: 275–88.

Pesaran, M.H. 1974. "On the general problem of model selection," *Review of Economic Studies* 41: 153–71.

Phillips, P.C.B., and M.R. Wickens. 1978. *Exercises in Econometrics.* Deddington, England: Philip Allan.

Poirier, D.J. 1978. "The use of Box–Cox transformations in limited dependent variable models," *Journal of the American Statistical Association* 73: 284–7.

Powell, M.J.D. 1964. "An efficient method for finding the minimum of a function of several variables without calculating derivatives," *Computer Journal* 7: 155–62.

Prais, S.J., and H.S. Houthakker. 1955. *The Analysis of Family Budgets*. Cambridge: Cambridge University Press.

Pregibon, D. 1981. "Logistic regression diagnostics," *The Annals of Statistics* 9: 705–24.

Rao, C.R. 1948. "Large sample tests of statistical hypotheses concerning several parameters with applications to problems of estimation," *Proceedings of the Cambridge Philosophical Society* 44: 50–7.

— 1955. "Theory of the method of estimation by minimum chi-square," *Bulletin de l'Institut International de Statistique* 35: 25–32.

— 1973. *Linear Statistical Inference and Its Applications*. 2nd edition. New York: Wiley.

Rao, P. 1974. "Specification bias in seemingly unrelated regressions," in W. Sellekaerts (ed.), *Econometrics and Economic Theory, Essays in Honour of Jan Tinbergen*. London: Macmillan.

Ridder, G. 1982. "GRMAX: een algemeen Maximum Likelihood programma," (in Dutch), Faculty of Actuarial Science and Econometrics, University of Amsterdam.

— 1984. "The distribution of single-spell duration data," in G.R. Neumann and N.C. Westergård-Nielsen (eds.), *Studies in Labor Market Dynamics*. Berlin: Springer.

Ringstad, V. 1974. "Some empirical evidence on the decreasing scale elasticity," *Econometrica* 42: 87–101.

Rosen, H.S. 1979. "Housing decisions and the U.S. income tax," *Journal of Public Economics*. 11: 1–23.

Rothenberg, T.J. 1971. "Identification in parametric models," *Econometrica* 39: 577–91.

Sargan, J.D. 1980. "Some tests of dynamic specification for a single equation," *Econometrica* 48: 879–97.

Schlesselman, J. 1971. "Power families: a note on the Box and Cox transformation," *Journal of the Royal Statistical Society Series B* 33: 307–11.

Schmidt, P. 1981. "Constraints on the parameters in simultaneous tobit and probit models," in C.F. Manski and D. McFadden (eds.), *Structural Analysis of Discrete Data with Econometric Applications*. Cambridge: M.I.T. Press.

Schmidt, P., and R.P. Strauss. 1975a. "The prediction of occupation using multiple logit models," *International Economic Review* 16: 471–86.

— 1975b. "Estimation of models with jointly dependent qualitative variables: a simultaneous logit approach," *Econometrica* 43: 745–755.

— 1976. "The effect of unions on earnings and earnings on unions: a mixed logit approach," *International Economic Review* 17: 204–12.

Seal, H.L. 1967. "The historical development of the Gauss linear model," *Biometrika* 54: 1–24.

Silvey, S.D. 1959. "The Lagrange multiplier test," *Annals of Mathematical Statistics* 30: 389–407.

— 1970. *Statistical Inference*. London: Chapman & Hall.

Sims, C.A. 1980. "Macroeconomics and reality," *Econometrica* 48: 1–48.
Spitzer, J.J. 1976. "The demand for money, the liquidity trap, and functional forms," *International Economic Review* 17: 220–7.
— 1982. "A primer on Box–Cox estimation," *Review of Economics and Statistics* 64: 307–12.
Theil, H. 1969. "A multinomial extension of the linear logit model," *International Economic Review* 10: 251–9.
— 1971. *Principles of Econometrics.* New York: Wiley.
Tinbergen, J. 1939. *Statistical Testing of Business Cycle Theories.* 2 vols. Geneva: League of Nations.
Tobin, J. 1958. "Estimation of relationships for limited dependent variables," *Econometrica* 26: 24–36.
U.S. Department of Commerce, Bureau of the Census. 1966. *Long-Term Economic Growth 1860–1965.* Washington: U.S. Government Printing Office.
— Bureau of Economic Analysis. 1978. *Business Statistics.* Washington: U.S. Government Printing Office.
University of Western Ontario Computing Centre. 1978. *Time Series Processor User's Manual.* 3d edition. London, Ontario: University of Western Ontario.
van der Waerden, B.L. 1957. *Mathematische Statistik.* Heidelberg: Springer.
Wald, A. 1943. "Tests of statistical hypotheses concerning several parameters when the number of observations is large," *Transactions of the American Mathematical Society* 54: 426–82.
— 1949. "Note on the consistency of the maximum likelihood estimate," *Annals of Mathematical Statistics* 20: 595–601.
Wallis, K.F. 1973. *Topics in Applied Econometrics.* London: Gray-Mills.
Walsh, G.R. 1975. *Methods of Optimization.* London: Wiley.
Westin, R.B. 1974. "Predictions from binary choice models," *Journal of Econometrics* 2: 1–16.
White, K.J. 1972. "Estimation of the liquidity trap with a generalized functional form," *Econometrica* 40: 193–200.
Wilks, S.S. 1962. *Mathematical Statistics.* New York: Wiley.
Winsor, C.P. 1932. "A comparison of certain symmetrical growth curves," *Journal of the Washington Academy of Sciences,* 22: 73–84.
Wymer, C.R. 1978. *RESIMUL Manual.* Washington: International Monetary Fund.
Zarembka, P. 1968. "Functional form in the demand for money," *Journal of the American Statistical Association* 63: 502–11.
Zehna, P.W. 1966. "Invariance of Maximum Likelihood estimation," *Annals of Mathematical Statistics* 37: 744.
Zellner, A. 1962. "An efficient method of estimating seemingly unrelated regressions, and tests for aggregation bias," *Journal of the American Statistical Association* 57: 348–68.
— 1971. *An Introduction to Bayesian Inference in Econometrics.* New York: Wiley.

Author index

Subject index